Charlie Connelly is a bestselling travel writer, award–winning broadcaster and the auth   previous books. His last book *Attention All Shipping:*   *und the Shipping Forecast* was a Radio 4 Book of the .ie   cast experience includes the *Holiday* program   *vellers' Tree*. Charlie is a former rock 'n' ro   ortuary assistant and, somehow, marked   man   nped below.   pl. *Works of Lenin*. In addition he is the   .il   Acc. No   la .d for a breakaway Lithuanian republic, has   he press after being falsely accused of ir   Rockall and been challenged to a fight by   by accident. He lives in London with his beloved Charlton Athletic.

Also by Charlie Connelly

Stamping Grounds: Liechtenstein's Quest
for the World Cup

Attention All Shipping: A Journey Round
the Shipping Forecast

IN SEARCH OF

A Journey to Find the
Man Beneath the Jumpsuit

Charlie Connelly

Little, Brown

LITTLE, BROWN

First published in Great Britain in 2007 by Little, Brown

Copyright © Charlie Connelly 2007

The moral right of the author has been asserted.

A CIP catalogue record for this book is
available from the British Library.

ISBN 978-0-316-73055-6

Typeset in Bembo by M Rules
Printed and bound in Great Britain by
Clays Ltd, St Ives plc

Little, Brown
An imprint of
Little, Brown Book Group
Brettenham House
Lancaster Place
London WC2E 7EN

A Member of the Hachette Livre Group of Companies

www.littlebrown.co.uk

*For Anita: an inspiration and
Elvis Presley's biggest fan*

Contents

Lonmay, Scotland

It's early lunchtime in the Star Café, a London institution just off Oxford Street. There's only one other customer apart from Bap and me, so the wood-panelled old dining room is a shiny sea of red-and-white-checked plastic tablecloths. It's been a while since we last met – Bap's a little greyer around the temples these days – but the wry smile and lightning-quick Belfast wit are still in place just like they used to be. A music channel is playing on the television in the corner: Elvis is singing 'Lawdy Miss Clawdy' as part of NBC's *'68 Comeback Special*. The sun streams through the window and picks out particles floating in the air. Bap looks up at the screen and says, 'Takes you back to the halcyon days, doesn't it?'

Sunday lunchtimes were always the best. It was the summer of 1996 at Filthy MacNasty's, at the time pretty much the coolest pub in London. Shane MacGowan was a regular customer, while the likes of Johnny Depp and Kate Moss were frequent patrons, which wasn't bad for a backstreet Irish boozer in Islington. I was barely scraping a living hollering cover versions in pubs and flailing on a cheap acoustic guitar: twenty quid in your hand and four pints of Guinness for a couple of hours of rough, unrefined country, rock and Irish covers. And Elvis, of course. There was always Elvis.

Bap had a regular Sunday spot at Filthy's. I'd known him for years ever since he was the front man of Energy Orchard, arguably the best rock 'n' roll band ever to come out of Belfast. Bap and the band had moved to London; young kids with no money but a bucketful of dreams crossing the Irish Sea for the bright lights. A major record label, five albums, a couple of minor hits and an endless raft of stories of life on the road later, Bap went solo, and became a singer-songwriter of such talent that even Van Morrison writes songs with him. He recorded an album in Nashville and when we met was just back from a tour of the US with Mark Knopfler. A music business veteran, and the archetypal musician's musician – Pete Doherty regards him as a personal guru and they've been known to perform low-key gigs together – Bap used somehow to put up with my basic guitar playing and dreadful attempts at singing and even allow me to share the corner stage of a pub with him.

The Filthy's Sunday lunchtime sessions became legendary. A small group of us, led by Bap, would roll up with our instruments, set up a rudimentary PA and launch into an afternoon of raucous, ragged rock 'n' roll that would sometimes last well into the evening. We'd all made different musical journeys to come together for those sessions, journeys in some cases spanning thousands of miles and several years, but when the songs took off with a momentum of their own, it felt somehow right that our travels ended together in the back bar of a London Irish pub over three chords and a few creamy pints. For both Bap, a highly successful professional musician who'd travelled the world with his songs, and me, a ham-fisted strummer and hollerer for whom this represented the peak of his musical career, they were terrific days.

Back in the Star Café a decade later, Bap and I looked up at Elvis, in black leather jumpsuit, impossibly handsome, and completely lost in the passion of the music, and reflected on what a big part he'd played in those times. A significant number of the songs we did were Elvis ones. Somehow, whenever I played an Elvis song with Bap, or even on my own in a pub or bar, the place would immediately come alive. Not, I hasten to add, as a result of my performance – more in spite of it, in fact. But eyes would light up, heads turn, and glances of mutual recognition would be exchanged between otherwise barely interested punters whenever we launched into an Elvis number. There was, we reflected, definitely something about Elvis.

I've always been a bit of an Elvis fan. Not an obsessive one, but thanks to my parents, who had the presence of mind to have me the very week 'The Wonder of You' went to number one, and, more specifically, their four-cassette *Reader's Digest* collection of his greatest hits, some of the earliest music I ever heard was performed by Elvis Presley. Given that the only other items in their music library that I can recall were by James Last and Boney M, I had in hindsight a fairly lucky escape (although I still say the latter's *Nightflight To Venus* album is criminally underrated).

There are some worryingly obsessed people out there but, thank goodness, I'm not one of them. For example, on an Elvis internet newsgroup to which I subscribe there have been recent posts by someone who has painstakingly catalogued which jumpsuit Elvis wore at each of his concerts in the 1970s. My favourite, however, is the post from the person who went through every concert recording he could find listening to Elvis's traditional opener 'See See Rider', and compiling a definitive list of whether the King prefixed the eponymous first line with a 'Yeah', a 'Well', a 'Whoa', an 'Oh' or nothing at all. From analysing the results of his survey, he felt able to deduce exactly what kind of mood Elvis was in at each gig. Whether similar assumptions could be made from his choice of jumpsuit we never found out, as the discussion degenerated almost immediately into the kind of viciously spiteful mudslinging that only the internet can induce, with particular reference to the alleged sexual proclivities of certain correspondents' mothers.

I am also nowhere near as obsessed as Frankie 'Buttons' Horrocks, an American woman who first saw Elvis in *Blue Hawaii* in 1966 and immediately gave the rest of her life to him, to such an extent in fact that when her husband filed for divorce, 'excessive devotion to Elvis Presley' was one of the reasons he cited. When Elvis died, grief-stricken Frankie upped sticks and moved to Memphis to be near him, leaving her son to get through his final year at school on his own.

So, thankfully, my affection for Elvis Presley remains strictly under control. I don't own every recording he ever made. I don't have an encyclopedic knowledge of Elvis trivia. I've seen only a few of his films so can't recite great chunks of *Tickle Me*, nor tell you every location used in the filming of *Clambake*. However, I am aware that there was and is something remarkable about this Memphis truck driver who shook his hips and flailed his guitar in such a way that the entire world took notice and changed for ever. And for me, an appreciation of the power Elvis holds over the world began on the very day he died.

As Tuesday, 16 August 1977 dawned my impending seventh birthday was uppermost in my mind. It was the summer holidays, and without school to distract me I could concentrate seriously on presents. It's likely that the recently released *Star Wars* was also occupying my attention, but I can't remember specifically. If I'd been aware that Brotherhood of Man's 'Angelo', three minutes of mawkishness, was the biggest selling single that week, I don't remember it. Nor do I recall that England had just walloped the Aussies by an innings and 85 runs at Headingley to clinch the Ashes. Just around the corner from our house in Lewisham that weekend more than 200 people had been arrested and 54 police officers injured during riots at a National Front march. I don't remember that either.

What I do remember about that day, though, is sitting on the carpet dismembering my Action Man while my mum ploughed through a big basket of ironing. The early evening news came on the television and announced that Elvis Presley had died. I'm sure this wasn't the first announcement, but it was the first I'd heard and I can remember it with complete clarity. I recall that they kept mentioning how he'd been known as 'Elvis the Pelvis'. I didn't know what a pelvis was, but it sounded funny. I also knew that the death of Elvis Presley was a major event, enough for that news broadcast to stick in my memory for life. Why? Why did the announcement of the death of an American pop star, of whom I had little or no prior knowledge, lodge in my six-year-old mind with the significance of the passing of a close relative (my grandfather had died the previous year and I remember as much if not more about Elvis's passing as I do his)?

As I grew older I began to play my parents' tapes, which came in a shiny presentation box and included a pink booklet printed on cheap paper that gave a brief account of Elvis's life. I remember how I'd push the first cassette into the player, close the lid and press the 'play' button, hear the slight change in the hiss through the speakers as the run-in tape gave way to the real stuff and then the thrilling, reverb-layered, barely controlled energy of the unaccompanied opening line of 'Heartbreak Hotel' filling the room. I remember the lazy, almost sleazy descending bass line, the searing guitar breaks and above all the power of Elvis's voice, as if the rhythm of the song was the only thing restraining the passion and tension in him from bursting forth with a satanic howl. I was spellbound and, in truth, a little unnerved.

Years passed, and I grew into a wincingly pretentious teenager. While schoolmates were listening to Madonna, Alexander O'Neal and Whitney Houston, the needle of my record player was running along the grooves of Hüsker Dü, Bogshed and Stump. If it was noisy, obscure and you couldn't make out the words, it was fairly safe to assume I'd at some point handed over hard currency for it with an eager smile. I wore a big black coat and a stupid little woolly hat. I carried in my pockets books of poetry and philosophy (of which I understood not a word), purely so girls might mistakenly think I was deep and interesting. I looked like, acted like, and unquestionably was, a complete twat. I scoffed at Elvis, who came to symbolise everything that was wrong with music, popular culture and indeed the world. The *Reader's Digest* collection was never played in anger again. How on earth could anyone listen to that stuff? Couldn't they see it was worthless? I mean, hadn't they heard The Jesus and Mary Chain's *Psychocandy*, for heaven's sake?

Fortunately such Elvis antipathy, along with the coat and the hat, didn't last long and eventually I started to buy my own Elvis records, the early Sun recordings in particular. For me these had a raw energy that even out of the context of the mid-1950s when they were made retained the excitement and freshness with which they were crafted. It was rock 'n' roll in its purest form, stripped down and simple, where the feel and power of the song was more important than accomplished musicianship. With the powerful slap of Bill Black's bass, the pioneering chops of Scotty Moore on guitar and Elvis's frantic rhythm guitar underpinning that extraordinary voice, even all those years after

Sam Phillips rolled the tapes the songs sounded as new-minted as the day the three youngsters walked in through the door of 706 Union Avenue in Memphis carrying battered instrument cases. And that was just the start. In the ensuing two decades Elvis Presley would become the biggest star the world had ever seen. The music would lose its energetic innocence, but Elvis would still throw his heart and soul into every song, even nausea-inducing slabs of goo like 'Old Shep'.

Paradoxically, Elvis has become a bigger deal since his death. In 2005, for example, he earned more than £25 million in royalties, which isn't bad considering he'd been dead for nearly thirty years. There are other icons who died young, from Marilyn Monroe to Kurt Cobain, but none has had the remarkable burgeoning posthumous career that Elvis has. He is everywhere. Not a day goes by without a reference to him in the press somewhere in the world, such as recently the woman in Australia who shot her husband for playing 'Burning Love' over and over again, or the Derbyshire tree that's grown into the shape of Elvis's profile. I particularly enjoyed the case of the Lincolnshire local government cashier jailed for embezzling half a million pounds from car park fees in order to fund her obsession with collecting Elvis memorabilia. He crops up in the most unlikely places – not long ago I came across a *Times Literary Supplement* reference to Elvis in a review of a book about the ivory-billed woodpecker, for goodness' sake.

So huge is the post-mortem Elvis that he's also frequently seen as a quasi-religious figure. Indeed, I have often been guilty of having a bit of fun with Bible bashers on my doorstep by arguing in all po-faced seriousness that the gospels are clearly nothing more than a prediction of the coming of Elvis. But others take it more seriously, pointing out that the family of Gladys, Vernon and Elvis form a kind of holy trinity. Vernon once said that when he stepped out on to the porch of the two-room shack in Tupelo, Mississippi, minutes after Elvis was born, he noticed a strange blue light in the night sky that appeared to bathe just the house containing the infant. In semitic languages, 'El' means supreme god, and 'vis' means power. As John Strausbaugh points out in his book, *E – Reflections on the Birth of the Elvis Faith*, it took a good couple of hundred years after Christ for Christianity to become anything more than a minor cult. Elvis has been dead for three decades and already he's revered with pseudo-religious devotion by his followers around the world, a secular religion that Strausbaugh names Elvism. At least once a year there are newspaper reports of an Elvis statue weeping somewhere on the planet and there are numerous stories of a mysterious Elvis-like figure appearing and 'saving' potential suicides and people down on their luck.

Elvis was himself a deeply religious man. Gospel was by far his favourite music – the only three Grammies he ever won were for gospel albums – and when people referred to him as the King, he would wince and point out that there was only one king and that was Jesus Christ. Today, however, Elvis almost transcends religion. In fact he transcends practically every barrier you can think of, be it of class, politics, religion or geography. The former prime minister of Japan, for example, the magnificently bouffanted Junichiro Koizumi, is a massive Elvis fan (he shares the same birthday, 8 January, as his hero) and listens to the same records with the same admiration as, say, a mullet-haired couple living in a trailer park outside Kalamazoo, Michigan, or an Australian sheep farmer in his sleeveless check shirt somewhere in the outback. No other artist has such a wide following. Indeed, it's probably safe to say that no other artist has or ever will have the remarkable appeal of this man, who after all never wrote a song in his life and possessed only rudimentary skills on the guitar. In 1992, for instance, all major American news channels carried live coverage of the US postal service's announcement of its winning design in the competition to design an Elvis Presley postage stamp. That same year Bill Clinton's saxophone solo from 'Heartbreak Hotel' performed on *The Arsenio Hall Show* arguably won him the election – at the time of the broadcast he was behind in the polls. All this some fifteen years after Elvis's death.

I'd long been intrigued by the Elvis legacy and in Bap, whom I hadn't seen for years before that day in the Star Café, I had a kindred spirit.

'When I was a kid growing up in Belfast, Elvis's films were always on the telly,' he said. 'It's like he was part of the wallpaper really, part of the social fabric in Ireland somehow. When I became a professional musician I realised that Elvis is one of the few people who has pulled off being a huge commercial entity while remaining appreciated and respected by other musicians. That doesn't happen a lot. Duke Ellington and maybe Hank Williams are probably the only other ones you could name, and even they are nowhere near the scale of Elvis. I mean, Barry Manilow's a huge commercial success but I don't want to play the piano like Barry Manilow, fair play to Barry and all. With Elvis it was the whole thing: the voice, the tone, the look, the way he interpreted songs. He was a genius, a musical genius. You realise, even as a musician, that he was a great entertainer. Even the corny stuff has its merits. He was probably the most handsome man in the universe as well – if he'd had a hump on his back or something, things might have been different, but he was incredibly handsome. For me he had this multicultural look – he seemed to fit in everywhere. He could have been Native American, he could even have been Irish, from the rainforest, he could have been from anywhere in the world. He had a look about him, a universal look. And he had a voice. What a voice. If God could sing he'd probably sing like Elvis.'

When I played occasionally with Bap, he was putting together an album of songs he'd written about Elvis, having, like me, returned to the King's fold. *Lonely Street* showed off Bap's wonderful, concise songwriting to full effect, and included a number of songs written from Elvis's perspective, displaying an insight rare among even the best songwriters.

'I rediscovered Elvis around 1995 or so, not long before we used to play in Filthy's,' Bap said as two huge fry-ups were placed in front of us. 'What happened was that a friend of mine had had this five-CD Elvis set delivered to him by mistake. He gave it to me, and I just stayed at home for three days listening to it non-stop, I mean really listening to it. After that I just became obsessed with him. The impact he made will never be matched. He came along when teenagers were just becoming teenagers, and television was just becoming widespread. In commercial terms and artistic terms, he's the most amazing cultural phenomenon ever. He didn't even have to write the songs, it was the way he could interpret them. I mean, if you hear Bill Monroe's original version of 'Blue Moon of Kentucky', it's nothing like what Elvis did with it. In fact Bill Monroe, who wrote the thing, remember, ended up re-recording it Elvis's way. He went above and beyond songwriting – his creativity was in his delivery.'

Bap's first solo album was recorded in Nashville just prior to our Sunday sessions. Entirely acoustic, the album was produced by country-rock legend Steve Earle and featured some of Nashville's most respected musicians.

'When I recorded in Nashville, we stayed in the same hotel that Elvis always stayed in and I had 606, Elvis's room,' said Bap. 'It was the one he always asked for whenever he was in town. It was a pretty simple hotel, not flashy at all, other than the guitar-shaped swimming pool, and he always had this particular room, the one I had. I knew I'd got a bit obsessed with Elvis when I had a weird experience one night. I'd travelled over with a guitar player and a keyboardist and they stayed in the room with me. I'd been in the studio all day, and they'd gone out on the piss and came back in the middle of the night. I'd gone to bed and fallen asleep and they were creeping around trying not to wake me up, but I did wake up and when I saw this shape looming over me, without thinking I called out, "Elvis!". I really thought it was Elvis standing over me. That's when I knew my obsession was getting a little out of hand.'

It's this extraordinary appeal and power that interest me most about Elvis, not least because the man behind all this is such a mystery. Even those who knew him well give varying accounts of his personality and opinions, while Elvis himself rarely gave much away in interviews and remains an enigmatic figure. So enigmatic is he in fact, that he could probably be described as the enigmatic figure's enigmatic figure, if other enigmatic figures weren't too enigmatic to express an opinion.

We know so much *about* Elvis Presley and yet so little *of* him. Hundreds of books have been written: biographies, memoirs, novels, collections of short stories, academic treatises, even recipe books of his favourite dishes, but still the real Elvis, the chameleon man behind the image, stays a mystery and probably will for all time. Yet his influence continues to grow and develop, even in places you wouldn't expect it to. Record sales are increasing – he recently clocked up his one thousandth world-wide number one hit – and the number of Elvis impersonators around the world exceeds the populations of entire countries. The fact that Bap and I, two people from entirely different backgrounds who lead very different lives, both arrived back at Elvis despite some, ah, wilderness years and that we both have the same awestruck respect for a man who died three decades prior to our reunion over egg, bacon and sausage in a London café suggested to me that the Elvis phenomenon merited investigation.

There must be more people like Bap and me, I thought. What is it about Elvis that makes him so special to so many different people? As the bacon fat congealed in the ketchup on my plate, a journey began to form in my mind. A journey that would take me into the heart – and possibly some surreal hinterlands – of Elvis's world, in an attempt to discover why he remains this iconic figure to so many people of so many different backgrounds. A musical odyssey that would take me to the rawest roots of rock 'n' roll. After all, rock 'n' roll was built upon travel, and Elvis was the personification of rock 'n' roll. The music itself travelled, developing out of immigrant songs and slave spirituals; a mishmash of musics from Africa, Europe and beyond via the channels of blues, country and gospel. The musicians travelled widely. The old bluesmen were constantly on the move, stalking the dusty crossroads, hitching rides wearing cheap suits and carrying battered guitars slung over their shoulders. Robert Johnson's travels proved so inspiring that the word went round he'd sold his soul to the Devil in exchange for the gift of extraordinary musicianship with which he returned. Country pioneer Jimmie Rodgers travelled the boxcars while honing his craft, earning himself the nickname 'The Singing Brakeman'. Even Elvis covered thousands upon thousands of miles in his lifetime. In the early years in particular he, Scotty and Bill would travel immense distances in his Cadillac, guitars thrown in the back and Bill's stand-up bass strapped to the roof. For weeks on end they would literally arrive at the gig, run in, tune up, do the show, run out to the car and head off into the night to the next town on their itinerary. In his later years, after the Hollywood hiatus of the 1960s, it was a hectic touring schedule that would even contribute, some argue, to Elvis's early demise.

If rock 'n' roll grew out of and was built on journeys and travel, and if Elvis was the greatest figure it ever produced, it seemed to me that if I was to find out what made Elvis so extraordinary to this day, I would have to set off on my own journey. One that would take me to the places he knew and loved, but also to some that he'd probably never even heard of to meet people who continue to do his work and keep his name alive. These people might all be pretty different from one another, but they would all surely tell me something about this man they called the Hillbilly Cat thanks to his ability to unite the sound of the white hillbillies with that of the black blues cats and take it far beyond any musical boundaries that existed up till then.

This, though, isn't a book about Elvis himself. Others far more qualified than me have done that. Here he's more of a travelling companion than a subject in his own right, as my fascination with his elusive yet omnipresent nature led me to wonder where his spirit might be found and hence, perhaps, provide clues as to the real man behind the image. I would set off in search of Elvis, then, visiting the places he inhabited – and some he didn't, but where people continue to live by his influence and appeal. If Elvism truly is a secular religion then I would speak to its disciples in various parts of the world and learn what it is about Elvis that unites them in their devotion. At the same time I would hopefully discover why the news of his death seemed so significant to me as a six-year-old sitting in front of the BBC early evening news, a broadcast that rarely distracted me from my Dinky cars, *Star Wars* action figures or the lime-green crane that was my constant companion in my formative years.

I bade Bap farewell outside the Star Café and walked through Soho. If I wanted to go in search of Elvis, I realised that while I would have to visit Memphis, Vegas and the places most closely associated with him, I'd have to look elsewhere too, to poke around in some parts of the world where you might not expect to find Elvis. In fact my journey would start in one of the most unlikely places you could imagine.

I don't know how many hours earlier the wind had started its journey from the Arctic, but whatever fulfilling and mind-expanding experiences the odyssey south had provided they had not served to warm it up by a solitary degree. At least that's the way it felt as the chilly gusts swooped in from the North Sea, careered across a couple of farms and smacked into my shivering frame, standing at the gate of an old cemetery realising that I was in completely the wrong place. Again. I was just about to give up, climb back into the car and drive back to Aberdeen when I saw a man with a dog walking round the corner and decided to give it one last shot. I hailed him as heartily as the freezing climate would allow. 'Excuse me, mate,' I said. 'I'm looking for the old Lonmay church, the ruined one?'

'Oh aye,' he replied, turning and pointing in the direction from which I'd just come. 'Take that turning there off to the right, go past the manor house and it's a couple of hundred yards up on the right. There's not much left of it to see though, to be honest.'

He paused for a moment and weighed up the shivering figure in front of him. 'This about the Elvis thing, is it?'

It probably says a great deal about the continuing global appeal of Elvis Presley that a directional enquiry addressed to a complete stranger in a back lane in rural Aberdeenshire three decades after his death should see his name crop up almost immediately. Elvis is everywhere. There can't be many places in the world where someone stopped at random in the street couldn't sing a few bars of 'Blue Suede Shoes' or confirm that the Heartbreak Hotel is indeed situated down at the end of Lonely Street. There has never been a global cultural phenomenon to compare with Elvis, which, when you consider that he virtually never left the United States (two years' military service in Germany and three early gigs in Canada were the only ventures outside his home country), spent a decade making what are generally accepted as being some of the worst films ever produced and lived the twilight years of his short life strung out on a mixture of pills, loneliness and fried peanut butter and banana sandwiches, is a pretty remarkable achievement.

'Yes,' I replied with a slight chuckle and the hint of a shrug. 'It's about the Elvis thing.'

'Aye, we get a handful of people here for that,' he said as his dog attempted to undertake a frankly improper investigation of my groin, before heading towards the car and urinating against the front wheel. 'There's not much to see up there, but good luck anyway.'

The north-east of Scotland may seem an unlikely place to begin my search for what my new friend had vaguely yet accurately summed up as 'the Elvis thing', but there was a good reason for my determination to locate a ruined seventeenth-century church in Aberdeenshire. I climbed back into the car. I followed the directions along the bumpy lane and, sure enough, soon pulled up by a long, low wall interrupted by an iron gate, through which I could see a higgledy-piggledy collection of lopsided gravestones and an old archway and wall that were all that remained of the old parish church of Lonmay.

Pushing the gate open with a creak of rusted metal, I tramped between the stones and over the long grass to stand by the wall, in what would once have been the interior of the tiny church. I pulled my coat tighter around me in a fruitless attempt to fend off the latest gusts direct from the North Pole, and leaned against the arch for some protection from the elements. This was about as far as you could get from Graceland, it was nowhere near as much fun as Las Vegas and it was definitely chillier than Hawaii, yet it was the first place I'd sought on my journey in search of Elvis. For it was here, on this exact spot, on 27 August 1713 that Elvis Presley's great-great-great-great-great-great-grandparents were married.

The previous day I had visited the man who probably knows more than most about Elvis's Scottish roots. Stuart West, an Elvis fan who looks not unlike Vernon Presley himself, is the press officer of the Aberdeen and North-East Scotland Family History Society situated in, appropriately enough, King Street, Aberdeen. He answered the door of the grey stone building almost as soon as I'd knocked, and ushered me inside. We went downstairs to a windowless room whose shelves were packed with old documents and reference books. Everything you ever wanted to know about the Berwick 1881 census was there at your fingertips, for example. Stuart sat me at a large table, where a grey-haired man in a tweed jacket pored over some old documents, and disappeared to find the sheaf of papers he'd prepared for me.

It was a Greenock-based writer named Allan Morrison who first unearthed definitively the link between Elvis and the parish of Lonmay, some forty miles north of Aberdeen on the way to Peterhead, having traced Elvis's family tree back to Andrew

Presley, who arrived in North Carolina in 1745. Morrison discovered that Andrew's father, also Andrew, had married Elspeth Leg in Lonmay in 1713. It was this discovery that prompted me to head north and track down Stuart, who continued Morrison's research. My plan was to glean the lowdown on Elvis's ancestors and then head for the village of Lonmay itself. One of the first things I'd learn from Stuart, however, is that Lonmay village has no connection whatsoever to the Elvis story.

'Lonmay village is quite a new invention,' he explained, 'as the original village there was called Cortes. The old railway line used to stop there, and it was just a railway station that they gave the name Lonmay, after the parish. Eventually they built some new houses there, which became the village of Lonmay, but Elvis's ancestors would never have been there as it didn't exist then.'

He placed a photocopied map of the area on the table between us.

'This would have been the main village then, St Combs, right on the coast, and here,' he said, running his finger a couple of inches south-west, 'here is the site of the church where Elvis's great-great- . . . well, I forget how many greats there are off the top of my head, but this is where they were married. There is a wee bit of doubt about it, though, as there is an Andrew missing from the family tree, but the Presley family itself believed that they came from Scotland. Andrew Presley and Elspeth Leg had a son, Andrew, who was a blacksmith we think was born around 1720, but he's the one that's missing. We're pretty sure it's him that ended up in Anson County, North Carolina – the pieces all seem to fit.

'He had a son, also called Andrew, born around 1765, who had a son named Dunnan in 1805. Dunnan had a son of the same name in 1827, who in turn had a daughter Rosella Presley in 1862. Now Rosella had ten illegitimate children of whom one was Jesse D. McClowell Presley – Elvis's grandfather. So you can see the lineage is fairly straightforward from the union of Andrew and Elspeth in Lonmay's parish church.'

Back in the churchyard the wind whipped in across the fields as I pulled out the photocopy of the Lonmay parish register from August 1713 that Stuart had given me. 'Andrew Presley and Elspeth Leg,' it read in copperplate hand, 'both in this parish dignified their lawfull design of mariage; and for abstinence and performance consigned their pledges. Maried August 27th.'

I touched the big slab of wall in front of me, one that would have echoed with the marriage vows of Andrew and Elspeth nearly three hundred years earlier. Their son would go on to be one of thousands upon thousands of stories of emigration to the United States and Canada in search of a new life. The Presleys were poor. Stuart had already told me that it would be pointless looking for them here among the gravestones as they would not have been able to afford any. While there were undoubtedly Presleys beneath the ground here, there were no markers. To a poverty-stricken Presley struggling to make ends meet in Lonmay, North America would have been an attractive proposition: the promise of a better life than the drudgery and hardship of north-east Scotland, and it's likely that the young Andrew would have gone with his parents' blessing. Maybe the night before he left there would have been a farewell gathering at which old songs would have been sung, songs that Andrew may have taken with him and sung among the fields of North Carolina. Little would he have known as he toiled at his anvil that one day his great-great-great-great-great-grandson would become arguably the most famous person on the planet by singing songs from the heart just as he had done with the ditties he'd brought across the Atlantic.

I reflected again upon how the history of music is littered with journeys and arrivals, particularly the music of North America. Rock 'n' roll itself is a combination of the blues, which originated among the slaves of the South, and country music, which developed out of the musics imported with the European immigrants like Andrew Presley. Obviously it's impossible to say whether Andrew had any musical talent or inclination, but as I stood there in the old Lonmay parish churchyard where Elvis's ancestors were married I hoped the wind, which continued to assail me with icy gusts in a way I began to suspect was personal, would once have carried the songs and tunes of the early Presleys just as nearly three centuries later, the airwaves would crackle with the sound of their gifted descendant.

I jumped back into the car and headed for Lonmay village itself. Stuart was right in his assertion that there wasn't much to see there. A few modern bungalows and the Ban-Car Hotel were about it. I did enjoy a hearty lunch in the latter, however, where I was served with distinction by a young waitress called Mary (there's probably a very poor-quality joke to be found along the lines of being in 'Lonmay to tip a Mary', but I'm not going in to look for it). I was, though, disappointed to find that one of the main reasons for visiting the Ban-Car had proved groundless. I'd read about an Aberdeen kiltmaker who devised a Presley tartan soon after the Lonmay connection surfaced, and that the owner of the Ban-Car had vowed to decorate his lounge in the new colours. Alas, it appeared that he had evidently just been caught up in the heady joy of the discovery because some three years after announcing his intention the walls were still Presley-tartan free.

I turned the car around in the Ban-Car car park and headed back down the coast to Aberdeen, where I had arranged to meet the man who designed the tartan. Mike King is the proprietor of

Philip King kiltmakers, a long-established Aberdeen firm. He created the Scottish national tartan, tartans used in the film *Braveheart* and now the Presley tartan itself. His shop is a cosy, peaceful place, the walls lined with jackets, kilts and the odd sword. Mike himself is a diminutive man in his fifties, who speaks in a soft voice with just a hint of gravel.

'The tartan came about when Elvis's ancestors were traced back to Lonmay,' he told me. 'When I heard about it I went up there and had a look around, visited the churchyard, and the colours of the land and sea soon suggested a tartan to me. So I came back here, designed the pattern and registered it with the World Register of Tartans. We called it the "Presley of Lonmay" tartan rather than the Elvis tartan because obviously Elvis was well away from the area when he found his success, and the design reflects the landscape of the area where his family originated.

'I've worked in tartans for thirty-five years, so can visualise a new one fairly easily,' he continued. 'It's become like second nature to me. The thing with Lonmay, and most of this area, is that the landscape hasn't changed in hundreds of years. The fields are the same size and layout, the cotter houses may have been modernised but they're still the original design; everything you see there, even the graveyard, is just as it was in Elvis's ancestors' time. The main colour of the tartan is grey, as that's a grey area up there – the sky's usually grey, but the fields are green so that's in there too, as is the yellow of the hay. The blue's for the sea as the sea's close by and there are obviously a lot of seafaring folk in the area, and also for the nearby town of Peterhead, which is known as the "Bloo Toon". So that's where the design came from – as I walked around Lonmay I saw that pattern in my mind straight away.'

Mike produced a large roll of Presley tartan and spread some of it out on top of a glass cabinet. It's a calm design, dominated by the green and grey, with subtle stripes of blue and thin yellow lines. As I cooed over it, he offered to let me try it on.

'The kilts are made to order,' he explained, 'so I don't have one here you can try on, but we can certainly put something together.' And so commenced a rapid whirl of pinning and tucking, not to mention the unexpected public unveiling of the well-turned lower Connelly leg.

'I was an Elvis fan when I was a teenager, but I wouldn't say I was a big fan now,' said Mike through a mouthful of pins. 'I mean, don't get me wrong, I think the guy was great, and I'm really sorry about what happened to him. Some people can cope with success and some can't, but he still goes on and on even after his death. But I'm not particularly a fan these days.'

Eventually the ensemble was complete, and I stood in front of the mirror in full Presley regalia. Mike had managed to turn an uncut length of tartan into a wraparound kilt that wound up and over my shoulder. He'd even produced a special Presley sporran, with an eagle and thistle motif in gold to represent the Presleys' Scottish-American link. I wore distinctive knee-length off-white socks and black patent shoes whose laces wound up and around my shins, and Mike finally handed me a sword to complete the outfit. I looked in the mirror, feeling not unlike Mr Benn, the eponymous character from the seventies' children's television series (who, if I'd been the fez-topped shopkeeper, I would have barred from the shop on the grounds that he'd come in and try stuff on but never actually hire anything). I looked as far removed from Elvis as just about anything you could imagine. In fact I looked as far removed from anything you could imagine. I have an uncanny knack of rendering any item of clothing scruffy and ill-fitting, and had the Presleys ever had to go to war on behalf of their clan I would have been of use to the family only inasmuch as the enemy would have fallen about laughing at the very sight of me.

As dusk fell I drove back out to Lonmay for a last look at the place where the Elvis story has its most distant roots. I creaked open the gate, walked between the stones and stood once again on the spot where Andrew and Elspeth exchanged their vows. The wind had dropped and there was a quiet stillness about the place. The setting sun threw orange and purple stripes into the clouds as I leaned against the rough, thick old wall and looked west over the flat landscape. Maybe Andrew Presley had watched the sun set from here too, knowing his future lay over that same horizon at the end of a long voyage into the unknown, a journey that set the family's destiny in stone as hard and stubborn as the wall of the old church. Similarly, my journey was about to begin in earnest.

Tashkent, Uzbekistan

Uzbekistan is probably one of the last countries in the world you could name in which you'd find Elvis. Indeed, Uzbekistan is probably one of the last countries in the world you could name. One of the globe's two double-landlocked nations (the other is Liechtenstein, fact fans), Uzbekistan is a large but young state of a frankly ridiculous shape (the eastern part looks as if the cartographer knocked his inkpot over but was too embarrassed to admit it) and a human rights record as appalling as any you could find (rumours are rife of dissidents being boiled alive in big pots – an old Uzbek tradition, apparently). Independent only since 1991, and ruled in the iron grip of Islam Karimov, Uzbekistan is practically a police state. The President makes encouraging noises about democracy and then fails spectacularly to carry them out. A few weeks before I arrived, troops opened fire on peaceful protesters in the eastern city of Andijan, with anywhere between two hundred and five hundred people killed. Karimov was in charge in the final years of the Soviet Union, and has remained there since, keeping a firm control of the media and the police. He doesn't sound like a fun guy. Unlike his former counterpart in Japan, it's doubtful whether he has ever sung 'Baby Let's Play House' at karaoke. If he has, it was probably more along the lines of 'Baby Let's Ransack the House in Search of Dissidents and Light a Fire Under the Cauldron'.

As in most Soviet-bloc countries, Elvis was banned for years, making Uzbekistan probably, on the face of it, one of the most un-rock 'n' roll places in the world. No one ever wrote a song asking long-distance information to get them Samarkand. Nobody has ever lamented on record being twenty-four hours from Tashkent. Uzbekistan is more Silk Road slippers than blue suede shoes. So you can imagine my surprise when I learned via a friend living in Kazakhstan that she'd heard Uzbekistan's biggest pop star had opened an Elvis-themed café in Tashkent, the Uzbek capital. I was intrigued enough by the concept of the nation having pop stars at all, let alone ones dedicated enough to Elvis to open a café in his honour. How could the King's influence have spread to such an unlikely place as distant, mysterious Tashkent, about as remote and unexpected a repository for Western popular culture as you could imagine? To find out, I was soon on a plane heading for central Asia.

Now I am not one for hot weather. Anything above about twenty-two degrees and I am no good to anyone. I'm grumpy, sweaty, whiny and uncooperative. I do not have a fun time in hot weather, and as a result people around me don't have a fun time in hot weather either. The only bearable things about hot weather for me are air-conditioned bars serving cold beer in bottles with condensation on them. Otherwise you can stick your hot weather where, er, the sun don't shine. Even slightly warm weather makes me edgy and has me scurrying indoors, pulling the curtains and attempting to climb into the fridge. Give me good, solid cloud cover and a light breeze any day. My perfect holiday would probably feature drizzle. Yet here I was, going to central Asia. In August. When the temperature rarely dips below thirty-eight degrees. At night.

It's a long way to Tashkent, especially when you have to fly there via Armenia; and when you have flown there via Armenia, where you land at a reasonable time but don't get off the aeroplane, you arrive in Tashkent at three o'clock in the morning. Needless to say, some places are quite fun at three o'clock in the morning. I can think of certain pubs in the west of Ireland that are at their most convivial at that hour, for example. Tashkent airport at three in the morning, however, didn't give me much hope of fun and larks.

As I walked out of the door of the plane, my first thought was that some wag had microwaved a duvet and launched it at me from a giant catapult. That could be the only possible explanation for the whump of heat that assailed me as I prepared to descend to the tarmac. It was very, very hot indeed. I whimpered audibly enough for the American archaeologist in front of me, on her way to a dig in Samarkand, to ask if I was OK. Well, I replied, it's so flipping hot, isn't it? She politely pointed out that for the next three months she would be sieving dust every day in the searing sun of Samarkand with nothing but a floppy hat and a bit of sun cream for protection. There was an unspoken caveat that I really should stop being such a gawd-help-us and pull myself together. I bumped into her again in the arrivals hall, where the bleary-eyed passengers were attempting to fill in the customs forms that the Uzbeks make you complete in duplicate as soon as you wobble off the plane. Most of the forms scattered around the place were in Russian, whereas most of the people trying to make sense of them were British or American. Fortunately I soon found a rare sheaf of English-language forms, which I purloined and surreptitiously slipped to my archaeologist friend in order that she may revise her opinion of me as being a whiny old drink-of-water.

'Why do we need two?' she asked.

'One's for arrival here and the other one you hand in when you leave,' I said helpfully and, it turned out, totally incorrectly. As I waited for my bag at the carousel a few minutes later I heard a small commotion at the customs desk, where the archaeologist was explaining firmly that she'd been told one form was for arrival and the other for departure so why were they asking for both, hmm? Was it money they wanted? A bribe? Hmmm? I stared fixedly at the revolving belt until she'd gone and hoped the noise I could hear above that of the carousel wasn't the sound of a big cauldron coming to the boil. I kept staring at the passing bags, until there were no bags left to stare at. Mine hadn't appeared. The machine was switched off.

As if by magic, a young woman in a British Airways uniform materialised at my side. She had piercing blue eyes, fearsomely red lipstick and blonde hair pulled back tightly in a bun. 'Have you lost your luggage?' she asked with a heavy Russian-sounding accent. Having travelled for several hours to arrive here in the middle of a roasting August night, and having just realised that I faced several days in some of the world's hottest temperatures wearing the jeans, polo shirt and, if I may be so familiar, pants I stood up in, my first instinct was to point out that, no, I hadn't lost my tugboating luggage, but British tugboating Airways evidently had, the tugboating useless tugboats. Luckily I quashed that instinct and instead replied meekly that, yes, I think I had lost my luggage.

When it comes to bureaucracy, my previous experience of former Soviet-bloc countries has not been good, so I held out little hope of seeing my luggage again. I also resigned myself to several more hours at Tashkent Airport filling out incomprehensible forms in which I'd have to detail where I'd bought every pair of underpants in my luggage and on what date. I have to say, however, that this marvellous woman was probably the most helpful member of any airport staff I've met anywhere in the world. She apologised profusely, gave me a solitary single-sheet form to fill in (on which I had to draw a little picture of my bag, which was fun) and asked for the sticky luggage label I was given when checking in at Heathrow. She explained that if my bag was, as seemed most likely, still in London, it would come out on the next BA flight to Tashkent (which, I stopped myself from pointing out with a lot of tugboats, arrived the morning I would be leaving the country). In the meantime I was entitled to fifty dollars in compensation, and it would be given to me as soon as possible. She was so nice to me in fact, that every tugboat in my armoury was decommissioned on the spot. She apologised again, explained once more that my compensation money would be delivered as soon as practicable, touched me lightly on the forearm and wished me a pleasant stay in Uzbekistan, before accompanying me to immigration to explain to them the reason why my customs form included one more bag than the physical evidence suggested. The smile she gave the officials seemed to melt even their stony hearts and I was practically waved into Uzbekistan with a cheery smile and a welcoming arm around the shoulder. Mind you, they might just have been chirpy because they knew there was a lightly poached American archaeologist waiting for them in the back room once they'd knocked off.

Happily for me, penniless, luggageless and without clean trolleys, I was being met at the airport, even at this unearthly hour. I had been put in touch with the pop star's – his name was Karen Gafurdjanov – production company. It had magnificently taken over the organisation of my whole trip despite being up to its eyeballs in organising the Samarkand Music Festival, due to begin a week or so after I left. I'd had a lengthy email exchange with a lovely person called Eldar, who had arranged my visa with the Uzbek embassy in London, booked my accommodation and even insisted on meeting me at the airport at this ridiculous time of night. Indeed, as I emerged through immigration there was Eldar, a tall young man with dark hair, and Rustam (who was either Karen's brother or cousin, I never really found out for sure and I'm not entirely sure whether Rustam himself was certain) waiting for me with big smiles and handshakes.

'Where's your luggage?' asked Eldar. I gave a brief, tugboat-free explanation of the situation, tempered with a little relief by the fact that I'd for some reason assumed Eldar was a girl's name and hence the little basket of perfumed soaps I'd brought as a thank-you were still in a warehouse at Heathrow.

We climbed into Rustam's car. After a little persuasion it started, and we set off into the hot Tashkent night for my hotel. Rustam and Eldar chatted eagerly to me from the front seat. As we went along I wondered why Rustam would regularly spin the wheel and send the car lurching this way and that, without drawing breath or seemingly noticing that he was doing it at all. I realised when driving through Tashkent in daylight hours that he was avoiding the suspension-shattering potholes strewn along the streets.

A short while later I was at last in my hotel room. With nothing to unpack, it wasn't long before I was in bed, debating whether to have a cool sleepless night thanks to the gritter-lorry rattling of the ancient air-conditioning unit juddering above the window or a hot but quiet sleepless night if I switched it off. I plumped for the former and eventually drifted off at about 5 a.m.

A sharp knock at the door roused me from my doze with a start. I leapt out of bed and looked for some clothes to throw on, before remembering I didn't have any. I opened the door, and standing there in the corridor was my heroine from Tashkent

Airport, hair and lipstick immaculate, eyes still as cheerfully piercing. 'Good morning,' she said with a smile, despite the dishevelled, sweaty, bleary figure in polo shirt and pants in front of her at this to my mind unearthly hour of eight in the morning. 'I have brought your fifty dollars compensation money. I can only apologise again about your baggage.'

She handed me four huge wads of notes held together with elastic bands. These were, it turned out, Uzbek *sym*. Momentarily feeling rich, I reminded myself that in dollar terms these weren't worth a great deal, hence the huge piles of paper that I now clutched to my chest. But they would at least buy me some toiletries and clean clothes.

After a few more hours of cursory shut-eye the phone rang in my room. It was Eldar; he'd be coming in half an hour to take me to the Elvis café so that I could meet Karen for lunch. I showered without toiletries and readministered the previous day's sweaty clothes. There were tomato juice splashes on the right leg of my jeans from some unfortunately timed turbulence during an airborne Bloody Mary. I reapplied my one pair of socks. A cursory sniff of the more sensitive parts of my polo shirt revealed nothing too whiffy yet, but today would surely be the tipping point. The inside of my mouth had not seen a toothbrush for more than twenty-four hours. My contact lenses were also in my baggage, so I would be forced to wear my stupid wonky glasses – and I was about to meet one of central Asia's biggest pop stars. The one time I could have done with looking even the tiniest bit hip and groovy, I looked instead like an especially nerdy vagrant.

Eldar arrived at reception and we strolled out into the lunchtime heat. It was sweltering. We drove the short journey through the wide, sun-baked streets to the Elvis café. Old men with leathery brown skin, white beards and small woollen hats sat in the shade outside shops, and on nearly every corner vendors heaped great stocks of watermelon for thirsty passers-by. Old women sat by the roadside with tables bearing teetering piles of circular loaves of Uzbek bread. Soon we pulled up in the leafy shade outside the building that housed both the Guli-Bonu Producer Centre, which looked after Karen's career, and the Elvis café. A small flight of stairs led up to the door, next to which was an illuminated Elvis sign in red, reminiscent of the logo from the *'68 Comeback Special* with 'Art Café' printed beneath it in swirly script. Eldar led me inside; it was a relief to pass from the baking dry heat into the cool, dark interior of the café. The walls were decorated with memorabilia – huge pictures of Elvis were everywhere, and the Beatles too. Next to the doorway, below a hip-swinging Elvis clock, was a small stage where a young band tuned up. Eldar introduced me to Gulnora, the boss of the Guli-Bonu Producer Centre. She was a small, strikingly beautiful woman who used to be a professional folk dancer in Soviet times and now ran one of the country's leading music agencies and production centres. Suddenly a plate full of salad and an enormous hamburger appeared in front of me, which, considering the last thing I'd eaten had been a British Airways chicken casserole somewhere over the Caucasus the day before, I set about with little ceremony. Once I had inhaled the contents of the plate, Karen emerged from the back of the café and introduced himself. A handsome dark-haired man with sharp features defined by stubble, clad in a fitted light-blue shirt and white linen trousers, there was a distinct look of the young Elvis about Karen (which is pronounced 'car-renn', incidentally). He was friendly and polite, speaking excellent English. He told me that shortly we would be departing for his friend's dacha outside Tashkent where we'd spend the afternoon eating, drinking and generally making merry.

Almost before I knew it, we were climbing into the back of a
4×4 with a couple of Karen's friends and he was handing me a
big bottle of Russian beer. Before long we were outside the
city, barrelling along a dusty road interrupted by a level crossing,
through which an enormous freight train was rumbling on its
way. The train blared its horn and a bell rang. We could have
been somewhere in the wilds of Mississippi. About an hour after
leaving the café we were knocking at the door of the dacha,
where Karen's friend welcomed us and showed everyone
through to a beautiful covered riverside terrace. There was a billiard table at one end and set amid some lovely rugs, a heavy, low,
dark wooden table that would fetch a small fortune in certain
London shops. A huge spread of food had been laid out: lamb
dishes, rice, chicken, vegetables, salad and the round bread of the
type I'd seen being peddled at the roadside. Beyond the terrace,
the river took my breath away. It flowed past at great speed, right
up against where we sat, but what struck me most was the colour
of the water – a striking, vibrant, opaque turquoise.

Karen's friend, our host, was a jovial man of middle age with
a typically central Asian face mapped in laughter lines. Wearing
only swimming trunks, he was in pretty good shape as well. We
sat cross-legged at the table – Karen had subtly motioned at me
to take off my shoes after I'd galumphed on to the rugs with my
size-nines still on my feet – and began to eat. Our host spoke no
English and I, obviously, spoke no Uzbek. We all had a couple
more Russian beers, except Karen who drinks no alcohol, and
then our host produced the first bottle of vodka of the afternoon.
Now in Uzbekistan there's none of that namby-pamby pouring
out small measures into a glass and mixing it with something
fizzy and non-alcoholic, some ice and a slice of lemon, before a
couple of 'chin chins'. Oh, no siree. A collection of small bowls
was produced, each filled to the brim with neat vodka and

handed to everyone around the table, including me. The bowls were raised in toast, and I took a sip. It had no effect at all, other than blowing the top of my head clean off and causing my eyeballs to shoot out of their sockets and bounce back to me off the far wall. I replaced the vodka on the table and tried to prevent myself from cartwheeling backwards into the river and draining most of it. Then I noticed that everyone else had emptied their bowls in one. Eyes turned to my near-full vessel, to me and then to Karen.

'You didn't like it?' he asked.

'No, it's lovely,' I gasped.

'Well, you have to drink it all at once,' he said with a wink. 'Otherwise it's kind of an insult.'

'Oh, right, OK,' I said. I lifted the vodka to my lips and threw my head back, swallowing it in three large gulps. And you know what? Taken like that it wasn't half bad. Karen, our host (whose name I still didn't know), and the couple of friends around the table applauded heartily. And then the bowls were refilled. And thus the pattern for the afternoon was set: more toasts, a raise of the bowl, down the hatch, welcome to Uzbekistan.

I hope you'll understand that as a result of the above, my recollection of the ensuing events becomes a little sketchy. A couple of beers in hot weather and I'm pretty much no good to anyone. Neat vodka by the bowlful? In forty-degree heat? Well, you can imagine. Anyway, some billiards was played, even though it was a version I'd never seen before, where all the balls were white. But a couple more bowlfuls of vodka and I was the tugboating world champion, I can tell you. I toasted British Airways. I toasted Uzbekistan. I toasted the particularly beautiful shade of turquoise that sped by a couple of feet from my back. I sent badly spelt and constructed text messages to everyone I knew and a few people I didn't about how bloody great Uzbekistan is, especially its vodka and its billiards and its pop stars and its turquoise rivers.

I bonded with our host. Although we spoke not a word of each other's language, I did manage to dredge up a long-forgotten piece of Russian from an abortive attempt to learn the language at university. I remembered that the word pronounced 'kharasho' meant good, great, splendid, fantastic. When my host handed me another bowl of vodka with a gesture and expression that asked if it was good, I instinctively replied, 'Kharasho!' His face creased into an enormous smile, at which he threw his arms around me like a long-lost brother and repeated, 'Kharasho! Kharasho!' For a moment I thought I had actually come up with the Russian for 'May I have your widowed mother-in law's hand in marriage?', before realising that drunk, loud, sweaty and in clothes I'd been wearing for forty-eight hours I represented no kind of catch whatsoever for anyone.

At the opposite end of the terrace from the billiard table a wooden plank bridged an inlet from the river. Water from the river was pumped up and over some rocks and on to the plank, making an ice-cold natural shower. My host marched over, shuffled sideways along the plank and placed his head under the water. He turned to me, gave a thumbs-up with both hands and bellowed, 'KHARASHO?', as the water fanned out from the top of his head. 'Kharasho!' I responded, meeting his twin-digit affirmation in kind. I knew what was coming next – he motioned me over. No way, I thought, not least because I didn't have any swimming trunks. In fact, other than what I stood up in, I didn't have any clothes at all this side of the English Channel. He shuffled off the board and poured me another bowl of vodka. And, wouldn't you know it, after a couple of fulsome gulps, some 'kharashos', some mutual clapping of shoulders and an eager imploring look from my genial host, I was stripping down to my underpants and edging gingerly along the plank. The water was absolutely freezing; certainly less inviting than it looked when viewed from the terrace after a couple of cereal bowls full of firewater, and my big-girl's-blouse cries of shock were probably causing people to look up quizzically from what they were doing in far-off Tashkent.

Thankfully, however, the shock of the cold water on my sun-baked and booze-addled bonce had a sobering effect. I lounged against the railings by the river to dry off in the afternoon sun, and soon my head cleared enough for me to realise that here I was standing by a river in the Uzbek countryside at the house of a man whose name I still didn't know, drinking vodka from a bowl and chatting amiably to one of the nation's biggest pop stars clad in just my soggy pants. Things then grew even more surreal when the pop star suggested we go and have a sauna.

For me, when you're outside in forty-degree heat and have had a skinful of strong drink, the next obvious course of action isn't necessarily to go and sit in a sauna for half an hour. But, at Karen's behest, that's what we did. Once we'd shut ourselves in and Karen had tipped water on to the stones to send the temperature even further into the stratosphere, he began to tell me a little bit about his connection to Elvis.

'When I was growing up we had no chance to listen to Elvis or groups like the Beatles, as rock and jazz music was banned here,' he explained. 'Fortunately I had a friend whose father was a seaman and he used to travel abroad and bring back records, so I would go to my friend's house and play this amazing music. I can remember the first Beatles record I heard, 'A Taste of Honey'. I didn't like it much, but the next day I asked to hear it again and realised that I'd missed the originality of the music the first time round.

'It was amazing. We couldn't hear anything like it on Soviet radio – if we were lucky we might hear Boney M, or Dean Reed, the American rock 'n' roll singer who went to live in East Germany and became a kind of Elvis figure in the Eastern Bloc, but certainly nothing like Elvis or the Beatles.'

Inspired by the illicitly acquired records, Karen and three schoolfriends formed a band, originally playing covers but ultimately writing and performing their own material.

'We were called Anor,' he said, 'which means "grenadine". We would practise for five or six hours a day on top of our studies, and once we left school the group became our main focus. We still had other jobs to start with, but things took off around 1997 when we signed with a professional producer and manager. We started playing much bigger venues and were promoted as a kind of boy band – we'd have thousands of girls, all screaming and in tears, it was amazing. Nobody else was playing the kind of folk-influenced pop that we were. In fact we were voted the best group in Uzbekistan in 1998 and 2000. We could never have dreamed of such success. Other boy bands sprung up too, but we just had some terrific luck.'

Anor rarely ventured outside Uzbekistan, which, when you consider that it is one of the largest countries in the world, isn't necessarily as parochial as it sounds. The prevailing trends in post-Soviet music were a problem, though.

'Even a decade after the end of the Soviet Union some traditions remained. The music world was very Moscow-centric. All the music radio and television were based there. It was much easier to develop as an international act if you were in Moscow than if you were in Tashkent. But we were pretty happy with our domestic success and didn't really have any wider horizons. Eventually the other guys got married and went into business and the band drifted apart. I guess that's what happens with boy bands – they have to grow up.'

While his band-mates moved away from music altogether, Karen made up his mind to stay in the business. It wasn't an easy decision – for a start the boy-band image would be a hard one to shake off – yet he couldn't imagine a fulfilled life without music being the biggest part of it. Like Elvis would with his love of the blues and gospel, Karen retained a deep love and respect for his own indigenous music. Even when Anor were at the height of their fame, Karen would still sing unabashedly traditional Uzbek songs at weddings and parties. His folk heritage was important to him, and when he decided to embark on a solo career he knew in which direction that would be heading. Rather than pander to the boy-band market, he would perform the kind of music he liked, based on traditional Uzbek songs and tunes. Ironically this meant that while Karen's profile increased internationally as interest in world music exploded in the US and Europe, despite remaining one of the biggest names in Uzbek music his star has dimmed here slightly since the screaming-teen days of Anor.

'My first solo album came out in 2003,' he said, 'and I did a massive concert at the biggest arena in Uzbekistan last year, which went really well. I'm about to record a new album which hopefully means I'll be able to tour abroad again. I still get recognised in the street in Tashkent, which is nice because I've not done anything new for a while and it's reassuring to know that people haven't forgotten me.

'If it wasn't for Elvis and hearing those records when I was a child I wouldn't be doing this now. Elvis just sounded amazing – he was the face of the fifties, sixties and the seventies. Now that his records aren't banned, he is very big here in Uzbekistan. That's why I opened the Elvis café – there really isn't a greater icon than Elvis Presley.'

We left the sauna and returned to the terrace to rinse off the sweat under the cold shower. 'Kharasho?' enquired my new best friend with his now customary double thumbs-up. 'Kharasho!' I responded. Another couple of bowls of vodka followed, before we bade our farewells and headed back to Tashkent. The evening back at the Elvis café was undoubtedly highly convivial, but after my boozy afternoon I really don't remember much about it. Indeed, one of my final lucid memories was of Eldar helping me back to the hotel and telling me he'd meet me back in the lobby at 4.30 a.m. Which couldn't be right.

As I lay on the bed watching the ceiling go round and round like a spin dryer, I marvelled at how Elvis's influence had permeated communist Uzbekistan at the height of the Cold War. While I was growing up, Elvis was pretty much everywhere, you couldn't avoid the guy, but in deepest central Asia he was nobody. When Karen first heard Elvis, there was no hype to go with it. The records brought home by his friend's father were curiosities. Elvis was just a name on a record label, so the reaction of Karen to the sounds coming out of the speakers was untainted by marketing and hype – his responses, which were to change his life, were completely natural and pure. Surely this must prove that Elvis had *something*, a possibly indefinable quality that would cement his position as the biggest cross-cultural icon of the twentieth century? I looked at the clock and thought again that Eldar meeting me in the lobby at 4.30 a.m. couldn't be right. I was still convinced even after he'd phoned me at four to make sure I was awake and to tell me he'd be on his way shortly. To say I felt rough would be an understatement: I felt rougher than the entire combined samples at a sandpaper convention. Dragging my shaky carcass to the shower, I stood under it and tried to come up with a good reason, or indeed any reason, why Eldar would want to meet me in the lobby of the hotel at that hour.

I left the shower and put on the clothes I'd now be sporting for a third sweltering day in succession. At least by now I'd somehow managed to acquire a toothbrush and toothpaste; today there really would have to be time for a bit of garment shopping. I lurched down the stairs to the lobby, and must have presented an appalling sight. Dreadfully hung-over, puffy-eyed, unshaven and in slightly stiffening clothes, you wouldn't just have crossed the street to avoid me, you'd have left town altogether. Eldar, however, looked spruce, fresh-faced and sparkly-eyed. The bastard.

We set off into the dawn, walking along deserted streets as the sky brightened enough to eclipse the dim streetlights. It was already a hot morning, which wasn't helping my near-chronically dehydrated state. Eldar explained that we were going for *plov*, a traditional occasion he felt it would be foolish for me to miss. Whenever an Uzbek girl gets married, the bride's family have to provide plov, a crack-of-dawn breakfast for anyone, or at least any man, who wants it. We were heading for a community hall about twenty minutes' walk away, where the family of one of the guys who worked at the Elvis café were providing plov ahead of the marriage of one of his sisters.

Before too long we rounded a corner and came upon the hall, outside which milled dozens of men dressed identically in open-necked white shirts and dark trousers. I, of course, was in the jeans and red polo shirt that were the only clothes I had in the world. We all stood outside for a few minutes when suddenly the huge double doors opened and another wave of identically dressed men left the building and dispersed into the morning. Once they'd gone, we all filed in. Inside was a large room filled with long tables – there must have been seating for more than two hundred and fifty people. Plov evidently ran to several sittings. Set up on a stage on one side was a folk band amplified to ear-splitting levels. The music demonstrated the melting pot that central Asia undoubtedly is – you could certainly hear traces of Indian traditional music, mixed with what you might call a Russian sound. Either way, it was hypnotic stuff, even to me in my dishevelled state.

Eldar and I took seats at one of the tables. Plates were passed down. Then huge bowls of rice mixed with vegetables were placed in the centre, followed by smaller dishes of meat, one between each two diners. Eldar, whose dish was between him and the neighbour to his left, began to break up the meat; my neighbour, a man in his fifties with nut-brown skin, a deeply lined face and meticulously trimmed moustache, looked at me expectantly. I smiled back. He continued to look at me. Eldar nudged me in the ribs and whispered, 'It's traditional for the younger man to break up the meat.' Oops, my first gaffe of the day and the sun had only just come up. I broke up the flaky meat and my neighbour nodded with satisfaction. Before we could start eating, there was what I imagined to be a short prayer of thanks. Uzbekistan is a Muslim country, but with caveats necessitated by the repressive regime. Religion was, of course, proscribed in Soviet times, and while Karimov lifted the ban and even went on a hajj pilgrimage himself, a series of car bombs in Tashkent in 1999 were blamed by him on reli gious extremists (although it's never been proven just who was responsible) and his attitude now veered between uneasy tol- erance and outright repression. Back at the dacha, Karen had told me that he is a Muslim but like most Uzbeks not a strict one.

Either way there was a short prayer at the culmination of which everyone made what I can only describe as a washing motion with their hands in front of their faces, and then it was time to eat. I spooned rice and vegetables on to my neighbour's plate and then my own, and did the same with the meat. I have to say that even in my, ahem, delicate state, the food was absolutely delicious. This was no professional catering job either, it was purely members of the bride's family cooking up great pots of stuff in the kitchens. There would have been at least three sittings, so it's possible that nearly a thousand men were fed that morning, all at no cost to the munching punters themselves. I offered my neighbour some more rice and meat, but he declined, saying something to me in Uzbek with a chuckle. 'He said this is his third plov of the day so far, so he hasn't room for any more,' Eldar explained.

Pots of tea also appeared – a light, immensely refreshing Uzbek brew for which my raisin-like carcass was extremely grateful. All the while the band continued to play their mesmerising brand of traditional music at deafening volume until everyone finished and stood up to leave. One of the religious elders, who sat at a special table on the other side of the room, said a prayer giving thanks for the wonderful food and blessing the forthcoming union. We made the washing motion again and headed back out into the street. It was now somewhere around 6 a.m. Eldar explained that the first sitting would probably have been at four and the family would have been up all night preparing the food. It was delicious, I said, what was the meat? Horse, replied Eldar.

An Uzbek wedding is obviously quite an occasion. As we strolled back through the streets, the temperature rising by the minute, Eldar told me that for an entire day a bride has to open her house and stand by the door in her wedding dress. Passing strangers are then entitled to walk into the house and the bride is obliged to serve them tea. This goes on all day, without a break. With that and the plov, it's a wonder that anyone has any energy left for the wedding itself. Eldar flagged down a passing car and negotiated a price to take us back to the hotel, common practice in Uzbekistan, apparently. Mind you, given the grumpiness of our driver it clearly wasn't the price he wanted.

'OK,' said Eldar in reception, 'I think you should get some more sleep and I'll come back at two o'clock. You have a radio interview to do this afternoon on our national station.'

'My dear fellow,' I said, clapping him on the shoulder and chuckling, 'do you know what? I could have sworn you just said I had a radio interview to do this afternoon on Uzbek national radio.'

'That's right,' said Eldar. 'You have. But don't worry, I'll be in there with you. It's with one of the most popular DJs in Uzbekistan; it'll be fine.'

Not surprisingly, when I woke up some five hours later, I presumed that a dawn meal of horse and rice to celebrate the marriage of a woman I didn't even know, followed by the news that I would be interviewed on Uzbek national radio, had just been a really weird dream. However, I'd risen with the haunting music still going around my head and the distinct taste of horsemeat in my mouth. When Eldar phoned me at one to make sure that I was awake, I asked tentatively, 'Was I having a strange dream, or did you say something about the radio?'

'Yes,' he confirmed. 'I've arranged for you to be interviewed about your Elvis journey on Uzbek national radio. Now the DJ doesn't speak English, but don't worry, he's really funny and I'll be there to translate for you.'

In a little over an hour I was back in the Elvis café chatting to Karen about music. 'Do you play?' he asked. I told him I used to play quite a bit in various bands, hawking Elvis and Hank Williams songs around the pubs and bars of London. I pointed out that I was, in truth, rubbish, which is why he's a pop star and I'm not, but he seemed to drift off into thought for a moment just as Eldar literally yanked me out of my seat by my sweaty collar and announced we were leaving for the radio station. We would be driven by Sevara, a work colleague of Eldar's from the producer centre. She was a typically beautiful Uzbek girl with olive skin, almond eyes and dark blonde hair. I squeezed into the passenger seat as she put the key in the ignition. She paused, looked me straight in the eye and said, 'Don't be afraid.'

'Sevara's quite famous for her driving,' chuckled Eldar from the back seat. I could soon see why. In fairness, it wasn't so much Sevara, as every driver in Tashkent. Rarely have I seen such extraordinary, lawless driving. Now Tashkent is a city of enormously wide boulevards, so wide indeed that you never feel like you're in the centre of a city. The width of the streets gives the drivers a perception of freedom you certainly wouldn't have in the UK. On the face of it traffic lights are to be seen as merely a suggestion rather than an instruction. If you're at a red light, but feel you can shoot across the six-lane junction without impeding the oncoming traffic too much then, hey, go for it. Waiting to turn right but the road's not that busy? Ahh, sure, you'll be fine. Need to be two lanes over from where you are in busy traffic? Cross your fingers, wish yourself luck and then turn that steering wheel!

What makes such free-form driving even more remarkable is that there are police on nearly every road, pulling people over and demanding fines (aka bribes) for minor offences. Maybe the Uzbeks think, Well, we're going to get pulled for something, might as well make it worth paying an on-the-spot fine for. Better to be hung for a six lane U-turn than a dodgy brake light, eh?

Either way, it was a pretty hair-raising journey to the radio station as Sevara giggled her way through several anecdotes about what appeared to be her daily brushes with the roadside police and answered a number of mobile phone calls, all the while apparently narrowly avoiding calamitous accidents at every slight turn of the wheel. By the end I realised that in the circumstances Sevara is actually a quite brilliant driver – obey the rules of the road in Tashkent and the chances are you'll be tomorrow's plov.

The national Uzbek radio station is at the top of a sixties tower block, which we ascended via a rickety lift. Once we'd reached the correct floor we were shown immediately into the studio, whose walls were plastered with signed posters of myriad Russian pop stars, and introduced to a DJ by the name of Johnny. Eldar and Sevara had told me in hushed tones on the way up in the lift that Johnny is one of Uzbekistan's most famous DJs, well known for being hilariously funny. I, however, was hungover and in desperate need of a pick-me-up. I was also wearing stinky clothes and felt as if I had just dived head first into a driving game at the arcade. It didn't bode well for my Uzbek radio debut.

The whole set-up was very relaxed for a national radio station. I've done a few bits of radio here and there, and at the BBC you're primed, briefed, placed in a chair and encouraged to talk with winning nods and smiles while several stern-looking fellows monitor things from the other side of a soundproof glass window. Here, no sooner had we sat down than Johnny was babbling away into his microphone in the same frantic manner that Memphis jock Dewey Phillips did when he played the acetate of Elvis's 'That's All Right' back to back over and over again the night it was recorded. My appearance on Uzbek radio would not have quite the same historic resonance, but for the next twenty minutes or so Uzbeks everywhere were treated to my bland opinions on Elvis, Karen and Uzbekistan in general, all guided through the multilingual channel of Eldar. I'm not saying that the atmosphere was over-informal, but Johnny's mobile phone rang twice during the interview. You'd think once would have been enough to remind him to switch it off. Still, at least he didn't answer it.

By now my state of mind was so frazzled I had to be virtually fireman's-lifted out of the studio. It was roughly twenty-four hours since I'd stood by a turquoise river having a civilised conversation with a pop star while just wearing a pair of damp undies, a period in which I had had a sauna, drunk about four pints of vodka, eaten horsemeat with strangers at the crack of dawn and then diced with death on the roads in order to address an entire nation. Eldar and Sevara helped me back to the lift. The doors closed and after a few seconds Eldar said, 'We should go and get you some new clothes.' This was probably the politest way possible to say that I honked worse than a sauna full of baboons.

Sevara drove us back to Elvis with her extraordinary hand-eye-oncoming-traffic co-ordination. Eldar rounded up Rustam and said that we were going clothes shopping. In all seriousness he asked if I wanted to wear traditional Uzbek dress. I replied that if I did, I would succeed only in offending the entire nation of Uzbekistan just by walking around its streets looking like I was taking the piss. I'm all for 'when in Rome', but I look daft enough in my own clothes, let alone the national dress of another country. The three of us set off for a supermarket on the edge of town. Within half an hour I was clad in a pair of linen trousers that were too tight around the thigh and too long for my, ah, abbreviated legs and a short-sleeved olive-green shirt that somehow made me look even rounder than I really am. Eldar knew a shop where I could have the trousers taken up, so we adjourned there where a friendly woman measured my inside leg (politely avoiding an audible guffaw when she realised what it was) and told us to come back in an hour. We repaired to a nearby restaurant and as the sun set we dined on shashlik, bread, spicy lamb and cold Russian beer, while sitting cross-legged again at a high outdoor table. I was finally coming back to life, which was a good thing because at that moment Rustam – who it turned out had been Uzbekistan karate champion three times and once finished third at the world championships – answered his phone, had a brief conversation and announced that it was Karen and we needed to head back to Elvis as quickly as we could. Pausing only to pick up my expertly altered trousers, Rustam barrelled us through the darkening streets as my head lolled slightly with contentment. It had been a busy couple of days, but now my hangover was finally in remission, my stomach was full of magnificent Uzbek food and I had clean clothes to climb into. I was looking forward to a quiet couple of beers at Elvis and an early night.

What I certainly didn't expect, though, was within half an hour of my arrival to be performing an Elvis song in duet with Karen on Uzbek national television. No, I wasn't expecting that in the slightest. I had not an inkling in fact, as I watched the lights of Tashkent flash by out of the car window, reflecting upon just how fulfilling the purchase of a new pair of underpants could be when you're a long way from home with no clean trolleys. They were Uzbek pants too, and I loved the Uzbeks and everything about them. Their hospitality and kindness would stay with me. These weren't the sort of people who'd stick you on national television without so much as a by your leave.

There appeared to be a stronger light than usual leaking around the door of the café as I climbed the steps. When I pushed it open and entered I discovered that in my absence the place had turned into a television studio. There were big flood-lights with flaps on the front and everything. Cables snaked around the floor. Men screwed up one eye and looked into the viewfinders of large cameras. There was a big furry sound boom, and young women with headsets and clipboards bustled around. In the middle of it all was Karen, who walked over with a big smile and shook my hand. 'How are you?' he enquired. A little taken aback, all I could do was waggle the flimsy carrier bag in my hand and say, 'I've got new pants.'

He motioned at me to sit down at a table, where Gulnora organised me a beer. 'OK,' said Karen, 'here's what we're going to do. They're going to interview both of us, you in English, and then we're going to play an Elvis song together. Here, use this guitar.' He handed me a sleek black acoustic. 'I'll play bass. Which song shall we do?'

There are some people who go to pieces in a crisis. When up against it, when their mettle is tested, they let the side down. For once, I am immensely proud to say, I didn't let the side down. My mettle was passing muster.

'Hmm, well,' I said, 'it should be a simple one, I reckon. A three-chord song. What about 'Blue Moon of Kentucky'? That's just three chords in A.'

'Perfect,' said Karen. 'Let's have a run-through.'

I'd not played 'Blue Moon of Kentucky' in a long time. The last occasion was probably a backstreet pub in King's Cross a good four years earlier for about thirty people. And now here I was about to play the same song with a proper, bona fide pop star in front of an entire central Asian nation. Now I'd really like to sound all nonchalant here, as if I was taking the whole thing in my stride, as travel writers seem to do when something unfeasi-ble happens to them, like suddenly having an audience with a monarch or inadvertently being elected prime minister. But I have to confess that, while I was unquestionably nervous, I was most of all hugely, chair-bouncingly, hat-brim-grippingly excited.

We ran through the song. My three-chord assertion proved slightly incorrect, as there is some funny stuff going on with an A seventh and a D minor near the beginning, but thankfully the digits skittered over the fretboard in the right patterns and Karen managed to allow for my rusty timekeeping. I even remembered the words.

Finally the presenter, all hair in bunches and oversized clothes in the manner of funky television presenters across the globe, came over to join us at the table, the lights went on and we were under way. First of all she asked Karen a few questions and then, slipping easily into English, turned to me and quizzed me about my Elvis mission to Uzbekistan. 'And did you find Elvis here?' she enquired. 'Well,' I said, gesturing at the huge picture of a young Elvis behind Karen's head, 'he's on the wall obviously, but also I think I found a little of Elvis in Karen. He takes the music he grew up with and gives it his own special touch. That's what Elvis did, and that's what Karen does.' A little bit clunky perhaps, but I meant it sincerely.

'And now you're both going to play something for us,' she said, 'an Elvis song, I believe?'

'That's right,' I said as if I'd been doing this for years. 'One of his earliest ones in fact, a Bill Monroe song called 'Blue Moon of Kentucky', A-one, two, three, four, Blue moon . . .'

And I was off. I thrashed away at the chords and Karen thundered out a monumental bassline. The words flew from my throat, and we even called and responded on the choruses. This wouldn't be the best version of the old bluegrass song ever broadcast, and it wouldn't be one of Karen's career highlights either, but me, I was flying, having the time of my life. As the final chord died and Karen produced a closing flurry on the bass, there was a moment of silence and the café burst into applause.

If only I hadn't been wearing my wonky old glasses and an ill-fitting supermarket shirt.

A couple of closing questions and it was, as they apparently say in the television business, a wrap. Karen shook me heartily by the hand, grinning warmly. My mouth as dry as the Aral seabed, I snatched up my bottle of beer and drained most of it. It was then that I noticed the calendar behind the bar. The date was 16 August, the anniversary of Elvis's death.

From then on, the evening took a predictable course. More drink was taken although, thankfully, not vodka by the bowlful this time, and Elvis's anniversary was toasted with appropriate respect. Uzbek hospitality is quite staggering. My memory is sketchy, but I'm pretty sure that I didn't have to pay for anything at any time in the café for the length of my stay. Now of course there is the possibility that once I'd left for London everyone looked at each other and said, 'Can you believe he never put his hand in his pocket once, the robbing bastard?', but my recollection is of every offer of payment being waved away.

After a few glasses one of the other customers came over to join me. A huge Georgian bear of a man clad entirely in sports-wear advertising various basketball and gridiron teams from the US, he clapped me so hard on the shoulder I was convinced it had popped out. I saw stars. He took my hand in the hardest handshake I've ever experienced – if the pain in my shoulder hadn't been so intense I'd have noticed my fingers being crushed.

'Charlie!' he bellowed. 'How is it going? You like Russian girls? Me, I love fucking. Every day when I finish work I just fuck, fuck, fuck. After breakfast, fucking. After lunch, fucking. After dinner, more fucking. Oh man, I love fucking.'

He went on to tell me how he'd been a sniper in the Russian Army and had killed seventeen enemy soldiers in Afghanistan. Or seventeen 'motherfuckers' as he called them. He then mimed squinting down a rifle sight, shouted, 'Die motherfuckaaaaa – ka-BLAM', and collapsed into roaring giggles, flinging his arm around me and holding me in a cross between a bear hug and a half nelson. Strangely enough, I quite liked the guy, not least when he produced a small photo album of his wife and children back in Georgia and became distinctly emotional.

As the evening wore on, Eldar, Sevara, Gulnora's right-hand woman Shakhista and her daughter Shakhlo and I piled into a car and drove into the centre of Tashkent. There we spent most of the night sitting in a Japanese garden looking up at the stars talking about music and Uzbekistan. It was peaceful, with just the gentle babbling of a couple of fountains and the panoramic starscape of the central Asian night sky. At that moment I absolutely loved Uzbekistan. Yes, it has an appalling human rights record and an oppressive government regime, but here on a hot night, lying on low benches and looking at the stars while Shakhista told me she loved coming to this place, I saw the real, everyday Uzbekistan. The real soul of a nation is in its people, and every Uzbek I had met, with the possible exception of a couple of over-zealous policemen, had been warm, friendly and genuine.

We walked down by the river, where I was implored to throw a coin into the water as 'it means you'll definitely come back to Tashkent'. Come back? Right then I didn't want to leave. As the night progressed towards day we found a bar open and went for a final beer. 'This must be owned by a policeman,' surmised Shakhista, 'because in the run up to national day all bars are supposed to close at eleven.' She also explained that the darkness in most of the streets was due to the streetlights being switched off to save electricity ahead of the impending celebrations. We watched the sun preparing to come up from the steps of the Palace of Peoples' Friendship. When the sky began to glow pink on the horizon it really was time for bed.

The next day was my last in Uzbekistan and was spent with Sevara showing me around Tashkent, climbing darkened staircases in ancient religious schools, visiting the graves of famous Uzbek poets and finally sampling nuts and spices in a huge, circular indoor bazaar packed with sacks of spices in every colour you can think of and a few you probably can't. Grizzled men with filthy hands offered nuts to try, which I accepted wholeheartedly even though they brought on a stomach bug so virulent that I would spend nearly the whole flight home in the aircraft toilet. Yet despite this, nothing could cloud my disposal towards everything Uzbek. In the evening there were tearful farewells at the Elvis café, innumerable photographs taken and yet more drink supped. In the end, with my flight taking off in the early morning, Eldar and Sevara decided it would make most sense for us to go back to the hotel and stay up all night, before they drove me to the airport. We stopped on a street corner and went midnight-melon shopping, and Eldar picked a couple of winners from a small boy who slept on a little bed among the fruit on the street. A few blocks further on we bought a couple of loaves of bread – from a woman so elderly it was almost as if Tashkent had been built around her – and decamped to the terrace of the hotel, where we sat up in the balmy open air drinking green tea, and eating bread and watermelon.

I looked up lazily at the big yellow Uzbek moon. Somewhere up in that sky at that moment a bag of my clean clothes was winging its way to Tashkent, but just then my pants, like my heart, were unashamedly Uzbek.

Porthcawl, Wales

I think it was the moment that two women opened their purses and pulled out photographs of their domestic fridges that I realised just what a strange, quasi-religious hold Elvis has over some of his fans.

It was late at night in the bar of the Fairview Hotel on the seafront at Porthcawl, and I'd just returned from an evening watching Elvis impersonators of various abilities, ages and girths going through their paces at the town's pavilion as part of the Porthcawl Elvis Festival. The weather was pretty filthy; the rain smacked against the windows and the wind howled along the seafront, whipping the sea into such a frenzy that the foaming white tips of the waves were visible from where I was sitting, two hundred paces away on the other side of the road, through the prism of double glazing and a particularly well-mixed Bloody Mary. My companions at the table were four women of middle age, all in black T-shirts with the eyes of a young Elvis gazing moodily out from each breast. They all wore gold chains hanging over their T-shirts and they all had similarly bouffanted hair. Like me, they wore their laminated festival passes around their necks.

Uzbekistan had provided an eye-opening insight into how Elvis had permeated even the most apparently resistant parts of the globe; South Wales wasn't quite as remote – nor was it as warm – but at the same time it was a place Elvis had never visited yet was now home to the largest Elvis event in Europe. If I was going to glean a sense of his influence and legacy in the UK it would surely be here.

At the table we'd been discussing the merits or otherwise of the Elvis acts we'd seen earlier in the evening, and the conversation turned to the man himself. Things hadn't started promisingly when one of the women announced in a harsh West Wales accent that she'd sit on Elvis's face any day of the week. Eventually, though, they'd started discussing the various Elvis shrines they had in their homes. And that's when the photographs came out. Two of the women carried in their purses photographs of their fridges, which were covered in Elvis memorabilia. They cooed over each other's fridge magnets and portraits, and then the talk returned briefly to what they would do to Elvis if he was a) still alive and b) in a hotel bar on the South Wales coast – a conversation that fair made me blush.

I asked what their husbands made of it all. 'Oh, who cares what he thinks?' said the West Wales correspondent. 'Ptchaw, yeah,' scoffed her friend, presumably about her own spouse rather than passing comment on her companion's. 'Mine wanted to come this weekend. No way, I said, absolutely no bloody way.' They both dissolved into cackles, putting their heads together behind their gin and tonics.

My midnight companions in the hotel bar were fairly indicative of the audience at the event, which styles itself the biggest Elvis festival in Europe. It did seem to consist largely of women, and women of a certain age at that. I had arrived at Bridgend station earlier that day, as the wind flung bullets of rain around with an abandon that could only be described as gay. Having checked in to the Fairview, I braved the elements along the seafront to the pavilion, where the festival's main business was taking place, for the welcoming reception.

My fellow festival-goers and I milled around in the lobby with a growing sense of expectation. There were, of course, plenty of middle-aged ladies in near identical T-shirts, many of whom sported handbags bearing Elvis's image too. There was also a smattering of men: old rockers whose hair had been teased into a quiff for so many years now that if they tried to pull a hat on to their head it would doubtless spring off and shoot twenty feet into the air as soon as they let go. There was a decent percentage of families, at least one of which were dressed absolutely identically in Elvis baseball caps and silk tour jackets. Every now and then an Elvis impersonator would stroll by, causing a flurry of excitement, much rummaging for cameras and the odd autograph request, before the doors to the auditorium were opened and we all filed in to be greeted with a glass of bubbly. There were big round tables scattered about and given the choice of taking one near the stage or the booze, I plumped for the latter. A large, grey-haired lady, walking uncomfortably on sticks and nervously attended by her daughter, eased her way into the seat next to me.

'I love Elvis,' she said to me, out of breath but in a lilting Welsh accent. 'He's the last thing I hear when I go to sleep and he's on the CD player as soon as I get up in the morning.'

'She's right,' said her daughter. 'My poor old dad gets banished to the other room. Elvis always comes first in her house.'

'I'm supposed to be in my wheelchair here,' continued her mother, laughing heartily, 'but I said to my daughter, there's no way I'm going to Porthcawl in the chair. I'm going to walk for Elvis. If I'm still alive next year, we're going to Graceland.'

Judging by the way she was fizzing with energy, she was going to be around for a good few years to come, let alone next year. Rarely have I seen someone so excited to be anywhere, much less at an Elvis festival. The lights went down and we were treated to a sneak preview of a few of the personalities and acts that would feature throughout the weekend. The guests of honour were Charles Stone, a likeable, bearded fellow who in the seventies worked for Elvis's manager Colonel Parker as the King's tour manager, Patsy Andersen, a former Graceland employee turned artist manager, and her main client Jerry Presley, billed as Elvis's cousin. Well, it would turn out that in reality he was Elvis's *second* cousin and never actually met Elvis, but, hey, he was a Presley. And he sang, apparently, so hats in the air.

Also in attendance was a man named Sid Shaw, who runs the Elvisly Yours shop and mail-order service from central London. Sid is most famous for taking on the might of Elvis Presley Enterprises and winning the right to use Elvis's image on his souvenirs. He gave a short speech about his excitement at the forthcoming festivities, whipping up the crowd by announcing that 'before long Porthcawl will be the world centre of Elvis Presley'. Which was quite possibly the biggest load of bollocks I've ever heard in my life, but you could see what he was driving at. Patsy Andersen tried to keep the momentum going by giving an impassioned speech about how great the festival was and how she was going to promote it in Memphis. She let herself down, however, by consistently referring to the town as 'Porth-a-cawl'.

Once the speeches were done with, a few of the acts came on to be introduced. One of the Elvis impersonators, a shyly charismatic young man who specialised in the GI numbers dressed immaculately in a replica of Elvis's army uniform, pronounced that he'd also be doing some stuff in the black leather jumpsuit Elvis wore for the *Comeback Special*. Anita, the woman with the crutches, elbowed me heartily in the side and bellowed, 'Ooh, I'll have some of that!'

Once the formalities were completed there were still a good few hours to kill before the first show of the festival proper, so I set off for an explore of Porthcawl. There wasn't, in truth, much to explore. The wind howled in off the sea and up the main shopping streets, which betrayed little evidence of the sheer Elvis-ness that we were told was going to transform this little seaside town into the 'world centre of Elvis Presley'. A couple of shops carried token references to the King, but it wasn't until I rounded a corner and came upon the hotel that was the official nerve centre of the event that I found any evidence the King and his fans were in town at all. The place had temporarily renamed itself the Heartbreak Hotel, while posters in the window boasted of the 'ELVIS FESTIVEL' (sic). Inside, the bar and lounge were packed with people, while in the centre some Elvis karaoke took place on a small round stage with those shiny multicoloured strips of foil at the back that are designed to give little round stages in hotel lounges a classy, showbiz look. I went in, ordered a pint and sat at a table with a decent view of the podium, where a young man with an impressive quiff dangling over a youthful, openly friendly face hosted proceedings. There weren't many takers at first, so with a fantastic voice he kept things going himself. Curiously he interspersed the songs with Frank Spencer impersonations, but these didn't detract from his impressively accurate renditions of some of the King's favourites. Then, at last, a woman put herself forward for a performance, proclaiming with some degree of confidence that she would sing 'Teddy Bear' without the need of a backing accompaniment. It was a bold move, some would say a cocky one. As it turned out she wasn't the most musically gifted vocalist ever to stand in front of the business end of a microphone, but if that was counterbalanced by sheer lusty enthusiasm her performance was in perfect equilibrium. A couple of songs later, another woman got up and in tribute to the King nervously read out a poem that she said she'd worked on for two weeks. It was actually very sweet.

Shortly after this, as the karaoke host was getting thoroughly and impressively stuck into an operatic 'It's Now or Never', a frisson went around the bar when two of the Sweet Inspirations walked in. The Sweets, as those of us in the know refer to them, are a female gospel trio whom Elvis incorporated into his stage show as backing singers around the turn of the seventies. It's the Sweets who sing the lines where Elvis encourages them to 'Take it' and 'Sing the song' on 'I Just Can't Help Believing', and the Sweets who feature prominently in the behind-the-scenes documentary *That's The Way It Is* and on *Aloha From Hawaii*. And here they were, walking into a hotel lounge. In South Wales. Where there was Elvis karaoke. Two strikingly beautiful (particularly when you consider they are by now well into their sixties) black women would have stood out anyway here in this all-white crowd, but the fact that these women had spent years with Elvis meant every pair of eyes in the room followed them to the bar, where they ordered orange juices, hot dogs and chips, and then crossed to a table by the window. They turned out to be completely unaffected and down to earth, chatting easily and patiently with awestruck fans, who realised that in talking to the Sweet Inspirations they were just one step from the King himself.

By this time, a couple of the Elvis impersonators appearing at the festival had arrived as well. A nineteen-year-old who had apparently been voted the best Elvis tribute act in Wales reluctantly got up and did a couple of songs, although dressed in a black shirt and trousers, white tie and sporting slicked-back hair he looked more like a Shane MacGowan tribute act than Elvis. He'd only deigned to perform after some coaxing from the compère, but when asked for a third song he muttered something about not doing his 'whole bloody act', and left the stage, handing the microphone to his manager to plug his show taking place somewhere else that evening.

I would be somewhere else in the evening too, seated in the front row of the pavilion auditorium for a show of Elvis impersonators who had impressed at the previous year's event.

Now I think this is a good place to point out that I don't really get the whole Elvis impersonator business. And it is a business. I read a statistic once that I wish I could remember accurately, but it went something like this: in 1977 there were 185 Elvis impersonators in the world. In 2005 there were 186,000. At that rate of growth, by something like the year 2060 one in four people in the world will be an Elvis impersonator. Yes, it's a funny line and one I wish I could claim as my own, but it does demonstrate the widespread growth of people prepared to curl their lip, learn some karate chops and squeeze into an often ill-advised jumpsuit.

In my thankfully brief (at least for the audiences) career as a musician I performed Elvis songs. But I didn't feel the need to put on a wig, shoehorn myself into a white one-piece suit with a high collar, and attempt to kick my legs up and do karate moves. No, the songs stood up for themselves. I never tried to sound like Elvis himself and I find it difficult to understand people who do, let alone those who also strive to look like him. Mind you, these attempts never seem to go much beyond the outfit, wig and glasses. Why is it, incidentally, that nearly all the impersonators go for the Vegas look? Yes, he was undeniably Elvis in those days, but, dang, he was a handsome dude in the

early years with his sharp pink and black threads and carefully
sculpted quiff. Why not go for that look?

Most Elvis impersonators prefer to call themselves 'tribute
artists'. If you ask me, stretching the seams of a polyester jumpsuit isn't any kind of tribute. Surely that's just pastiche? A piss
take? Stick on a pair of slacks, a jacket, wax up the old barnet,
learn how to play G, C, A and D chords on a cheap acoustic
guitar and you can't go wrong, surely? And while we're on the
subject, try learning a few chords on the guitar instead of just
holding it gingerly like you don't know what it's for.

Elvis impersonators, tribute artists, call them what you will,
divide the Elvis fan community like nothing else. One Elvis
internet mailing list to which I subscribe refers to impersonators
simply as 'assclowns', which I think is a terrific word, if a little
harsh on those who really feel they are demonstrating their love
for Elvis. But the critics feel that the King's image is desecrated
by imitators, particularly as most of them aren't actually any
good. However, the ones who ARE good, the ones with the
voice, charisma and musical talent, make me wonder why they're
not pursuing careers for themselves instead of aping other
people. I mean to say, I quite like Alan Bennett, but have never
felt the need to demonstrate this by donning horn-rimmed
glasses and reminiscing about childhood holidays in Filey in a
thin, reedy Yorkshire accent.

The first act of the evening did offer something a little different. A lack of years for a kick-off. Jamie Elvis, or Jelvis for short,
was just fourteen years old and, alleluia, chose the early Elvis
years for his act. He took to the stage dressed in black shirt and
trousers and a white jacket; which was presumably purchased for
him to grow into, and put in a mature, energetic and accomplished performance. He was still just the right end of the
teenage years not to be self-conscious about getting up on a

stage and gyrating like Elvis, and indeed he had about him a polite, shy demeanour reminiscent of the young Elvis himself. When he dedicated 'Young and Beautiful' to his mother, sitting proudly in the audience, there broke out a distinctly maternal sigh from around eighty per cent of those watching, who clearly right then could have taken him home with them, given him a cup of warm milk and tucked him up in bed with a story. Jelvis had a real naive charm about him – I wondered how much longer it would be until the advancement of teenage years would lead to doors slamming in the Jelvis household, shouts of 'I'm not doing that Elvis stuff anymore, it's embarrassing', and visible piercings.

Given the maternal make-up of most of the audience, Jelvis was going to be a tough act to follow. Unfortunately the next act on the bill wasn't up to the task. Things started promisingly as the opening strains of *Also Sprach Zarathustra*, with which Elvis began his Vegas-era shows, gave way to the thunderous drum break and stinging brass stabs that announced 'See See Rider'. Then the impersonator sauntered apparently reluctantly on to the stage. He was the most immobile Elvis you've ever seen. He wasn't the youngest on the bill by a long way, so maybe he was sporting an uncomfortable truss beneath his jumpsuit or something. Either way, every step around the platform appeared to be an unwelcome effort, as he plodded through the first number. At its conclusion there was loud applause – this audience genuinely wanted the acts to do well – and I got a little bit carried away and found myself emitting an involuntary whoop. The woman next to me in the front row, around my age and there with her mother, turned in my direction, her gold jewellery glinting under the lights and while still applauding just said the word 'Crap.'

During 'Can't Help Falling in Love', the impersonator managed with some difficulty to descend the steps at the side of the stage and move along the front row kissing women at random. My neighbour turned to me and announced levelly, 'If he comes anywhere near me, I'm going to kick him in the bollocks.' Now this, I thought, would be worth the admission money on its own. She seemed just the kind of woman who would administer a fly-kick to the fly region at the slightest provocation, and I had no reason to doubt otherwise. Almost subconsciously I crossed my legs away from her. As he moved nearer I guessed, correctly as it turned out, that with my neighbour being one of the few women in the room well under the age of fifty, he would be puckering up as soon as she hoved into his crosshairs. Sure enough, he made a beeline for her (inasmuch as his speed progressed beyond glacial) and I prepared myself for the testicular pinball that would inevitably follow. He leaned forward, expecting her to do likewise with the attendant blushing and giggling of his previous victims. Instead she sat impassively still, a little Welsh Mount Rushmore, her steely gaze honed to perfection no doubt on countless drunken suitors late on a Friday night in the nightspots of her home town. Still bent over, given his general lack of mobility a task that was no laughing matter, the Elvis instead took her hand from her lap and kissed the back of it. My neighbour's expression didn't change, but to my disappointment there was no sudden movement from below the knee to deliver a gold-braid-enhanced pointy shoe to jumpsuited scrotum, and the impersonator ascended the stairs at our side of the stage in a manner that called to mind those Sunday supplement magazine adverts featuring the late Thora Hird.

After the interval, however, came the real showstopper. Dressed in a replica of Elvis's famous gold lamé suit from the 1950s, Colbert Hamilton was billed as the 'Black Elvis', the name by which he made himself known in a fit of camp giggling at the start of his set. Colbert clearly didn't take himself or the whole Elvis impersonation shtick too seriously, and hence put on a great show.

One of my criticisms of these tribute acts is that they nearly all use a karaoke backing, making it difficult for them to put any energy or vitality into the performance, thanks to the constraints of a bland, soulless accompaniment. Colbert completely blew my theory out of the water by throwing himself around the stage and clearly having the time of his life. He had fits of giggles mid-song, he twisted and contorted his skinny frame into brilliant pastiches of the early Elvis, and left the stage at the end of his set to a huge ovation, even from my hard-to-please neighbour.

The Black Elvis was a tough act to follow, and for the second time that evening the act following the tough act to follow found it too tough to follow the tough act. To follow. Or something. Which was a shame because the closing act had come a long way and had a considerable pre-festival reputation to uphold. Calling himself Martin Elvis, this guy had come all the way from Malta with quite an impressive entourage. A section of the crowd sat there cheering his every move and waving little Maltese flags, while a full-size flag had been taped to the front of the stage. Alas, Martin Elvis appeared to believe the hype. He began by completely deflating the buoyant mood left by Colbert Hamilton and bringing everyone down with a frankly turgid rendition of 'Peace in the Valley'. Not an atten-tion-grabbing show-opener at the best of times, and on this occasion everyone's attention, bar the Maltese contingent, soon wandered pretty much anywhere but the stage. As he reeled out a seemingly endless roster of little-known Elvis gospel tunes, I found myself at one point mentally naming Charlton Athletic's 1947 FA Cup-winning team. So wrapped up in himself and his followers was he that at one point he stopped at the edge of the stage in mid-song to kiss goodbye a woman, who was presumably an elderly relative of some kind.

But then came the moment of the night, possibly even the weekend. To this day I still haven't worked out quite what it was all about. We reached the end of another lengthy gospel number, when Martin Elvis started to thank his manager. Then he paused for a moment and announced, 'OK, sorry, I have to get this off my chest. In the last few weeks I've been getting phone calls and text messages saying, "Don't go to Porthcawl", and "If you go to Porthcawl your legs will be broken".' There was a pause. Someone from the Maltese contingent gave a nervous whoop. We all leaned forward expectantly for the punchline of what we assumed was an elaborate gag. It didn't come. Instead he just added, 'Well, that's what love means', and cued the next song.

Everyone looked at each other in bemusement. My bollock-kicking neighbour turned to me and enquired, 'What the fuck was that all about?', the question that was, in truth, on all our minds and in those exact words. Was it a very strange gag? Or was he really risking taking a bullet simply by appearing at the Porthcawl Elvis Festival? And why would anyone want to bump off the Maltese Elvis? Granted, much more interminable adagio gospel and I wouldn't have ruled out scrambling over the lip of the stage armed with a table leg myself, but even so it all seemed a bit over the top. The bewildered glances among the audience lasted well into 'An American Trilogy', before Martin Elvis left the stage, either a very brave man who had risked some kind of Maltese mob-hit to bring us his gospel marathon, or a complete loon. I really couldn't decide which, and neither could most people in the room.

It seemed to me that Martin Elvis had somewhere along the line acquired himself a substantial ego. This became particularly evident during the ad-libbed encore when all four Elvises gathered around the microphone for an a cappella version of 'The Wonder of You'. He appeared to have it in for Colbert, at whom he pointed, then declared to the audience, 'He turned up half-pissed and late and drank lager on stage!' Even if that were true, he was still better than you, old son. He then attempted to dominate the encore and left the podium seemingly under the impression that it had been his show. It was a quite extraordinary performance that will live long in my memory, that's for sure.

Then it was back to the hotel for the fridge-photograph display, and a chat with Anita, the woman on crutches from the opening event earlier in the day who was staying with her daughter in the same hotel. Anita was, it turned out, a really startlingly amazing woman. She'd been a foundling raised in a children's home. She had endured three years in borstal after running away from the home and spending her last sixpence putting an Elvis song on the jukebox of a pub. Another girl kicked the jukebox to stop the record and Anita had knocked her out cold. Despite this, she went on to be a pillar of her South Wales community, had served on the local council, was now a proud grandmother, and was quite possibly the biggest Elvis fan I have ever met. I've never seen anyone so happy and excited to be anywhere as Anita was at this festival, something even more remarkable considering the pain she was in with her legs. But as we knew there was no way she was coming to Porthcawl in a wheelchair, she was going to walk for Elvis. As the clock struck midnight in the lounge it became her birthday too, and her daughter Maxine produced a mountain of cards from home. We all sang 'Happy Birthday'.

The following lunchtime there was an Elvis question-and-answer session featuring Charles Stone, Patsy Andersen and Jerry Presley. What struck me most about this was how little the discussion mentioned Elvis himself. Most of it revolved around the behind-the-scenes machinations at Graceland, and Jerry Presley's tales of, er, never actually meeting Elvis. Once again, however, the highlight was Martin Elvis from Malta. Rising from his seat in the audience to ask a question, he stood to inform the panel that walking around Porthcawl he had seen 'kids and even young adults' wearing Elvis-style wigs and sunglasses. Surely, he proffered, these people were mocking Elvis, disrespecting his memory. This from a man who imitates Elvis for a living and who was standing in the hall with quiff rampant and wearing a jacket that had his own name and Elvis's in big letters on the back.

The panel made noises about how it was great that a new generation of fans were being introduced to Elvis, even if it did mean they were wearing wigs and glasses, and Martin Elvis, the self-appointed guardian of the memory of the King, sat down again. To be fair to him, he did sort of have a point. The so-called Elvis wigs are quite frankly ridiculous. The thing is, Elvis never had a giant, gravity-defying quiff, certainly not in his jumpsuit days, which, if the gold sunglasses that accompany the wigs are anything to go by, is what they're implying. In his early years he had a rock 'n' roll pompadour, but nothing like the crouching gorillas that Elvis wigs resemble today. In the seventies he had formidable sideburns and a bit of a bouffant, but so did every man under forty in that sartorially extreme decade. Elvis's hair was, if anything, quite sober for the time.

That afternoon there was an Elvis wedding on the seafront. Two fans climbed out of a Cadillac and shivered on the promenade while an Irish Elvis impersonator recited a well-crafted wedding blessing that featured countless Elvis song titles. From the wedding I took a stroll along the front to the Elvis-themed funfair, which was just the regular funfair but with Elvis records playing over the tannoy. Admittedly it was just about out of season and a windy, chilly day, but there really wasn't much fun about this fair. The ghost train, for instance, was about as scary as watching Christopher Biggins play draughts in a Wendy house with Geoffrey from *Rainbow*.

In the evening there was another concert of Elvis impersonators. The GI Elvis did his stuff to great effect and went down a storm; the Emerald Elvis, the guy who'd 'married' the couple amid the gales earlier, was particularly entertaining; while the Shane MacGowanesque Welsh Elvis, last seen grumpily skulking from the stage of the Heartbreak Hotel, might have been better advised that dark-blue underpants do not go well beneath a tight-fitting white jumpsuit.

Next to me sat a woman of late middle-age sporting a diamanté Elvis baseball cap. On her lap rested an Elvis biscuit tin from which at various intervals she would extract a number of items to wave around. It was an impressive feat of preparation. When Jerry Presley emerged after the interval wearing one of Elvis's own jumpsuits, one that must have taken some altering, as Jerry Presley is tiny, she opened her tin and unfurled a silky white banner that read, 'Elvis – That's The Way It Was'. Having held it aloft like a football fan, she folded it back up with the sort of reverence accorded to a holy relic and replaced it in the tin. Later in the show she again opened the tin and produced a small Confederate flag with the face of Elvis superimposed on it, which she waved regally for a while before it too was put back in the holy biscuit tin.

The best part of the occasion, though, related to the fact that it was still Anita's birthday. She and Maxine had front row seats, and even though I was a good few rows away I could see her dancing in her seat, probably much to the chagrin of her neighbour. No one applauded louder or with more gusto between every song than Anita. At one point Jerry Presley descended into the audience to hand out roses, and there was no way he was getting past Anita even if he had wanted to. From my vantage point I saw him bend towards her to administer rose and kiss, and then, like Jaws emerging from the sea to swallow a couple of small children, Anita's meaty arm came out and wrapped itself around his neck for a long embrace. After a time he managed to extricate himself, leaving Anita with her birthday rose and a smile as big as the distance between Porthcawl and Graceland.

After the concert I was detailed to divert Anita while Maxine organised the birthday cake she'd somehow kept a secret from her mother despite them sharing the same hotel room. It wasn't hard as all I had to do was mention the words 'Jerry' and 'Presley', and she was away, describing every last moment of their off-stage encounter. Eventually one of the organisers came and fetched us, telling Anita she was wanted in the bar. Her progress was slow and painful on the crutches, but when we arrived, there sat Jerry Presley behind an enormous cake adorned with candles, singing the opening lines of 'Happy Birthday'. I don't think I can remember seeing someone so overwhelmed with emotion as Anita just then. By good fortune somebody produced a chair for her, into which she half sat and half collapsed, her mouth open in wonder. Jerry finished the song and leaned over to give her a birthday kiss, at which point the arm came out and clamped itself around his neck once again. This was a moment that one of Elvis's biggest fans would never, ever forget.

The next morning saw an early start. I was heading for the Elvis gospel service at a local church. Unsurprisingly the small, modern building was packed to the doors and the only seat I could find was near the back of the balcony. It was an impressive occasion, with terrific performances from Jerry Presley and from Dallas Kraig Parker, regarded by many as the best Elvis impersonator on the circuit. The Sweet Inspirations did a breathtaking a cappella gospel version of the Lord's Prayer. Oh, and Martin Elvis did a song too, but that was nothing compared to what happened next, when the priest announced that Martin and his wife had asked to renew their wedding vows. A noble sentiment indeed, though surely one for a private, family occasion in your home country. But no, the place to do it is in a church that's not even of your denomination in front of a crowd of strangers in a foreign country.

From the gospel service I went in search of Porthcawl's rugby ground, where the local team were I was told due to take on fifteen Elvis lookalikes wearing a gold lamé kit. There had been an appeal on the festival website for some months for rugby-playing Elvises to come forward and, I might say, this was probably the part of the weekend to which I was looking forward the most. I am not a rugby fan by any stretch of the imagination; to me it just seems to be a load of fat blokes running into each other, but a team of Elvises was something not to be missed, whether the sport was rugby, hockey, kabaddi or synchronised judo on ice.

Naturally I got completely lost looking for the place, but this allowed me to think up some tortuous puns with which I could pepper this chapter. Maul Shook Up, Good Rucking Tonight, A Little Less Conversion – they were getting worse by the minute – when I finally stumbled across the rugby ground, via a small, brambly opening in a hedge rather than the traditional and well-signposted main entrance.

Porthcawl Rugby Club on a Sunday lunchtime is a pleasant place to hang out. It's exactly how I imagined a local rugby club to be, with its railing around the pitch, its concrete dressing-room block and the warm, inviting prefabricated clubhouse beneath an old 'Courage Best' sign announcing that you are welcome to Porthcawl RFC.

Inside the walls were covered with pennants, honours boards and the obligatory team photographs from the seventies when everyone had far too much hair for their own good. The air hung thick with that cosy, familiar clubhouse brew of stale cigarette smoke, frying fat and bleach. I ordered a pint at the timber-effect bar, went outside and took up position by the touchline. A few of the Porthcawl players were on the pitch kicking a football around. There was a decent smattering of spectators and even a television crew fronted by a bemused-looking man in a tan suit and impressive bouffant, but there was as yet no sign of the Elvises.

Kick-off time came and went, and still there was no opposition. A woman in full Vegas jumpsuit, sunglasses and wig sat at one of the pub tables, but looked unwilling to pit herself against the might of Porthcawl's finest. Which was a little bit selfish if you ask me. Some of us had given up our Sunday lunchtimes for this, after all.

On the pitch, the footballing Porthcawl players threw occasional glances in the direction of the dressing rooms in the hope that fifteen bequiffed, rugby-playing Elvises would burst forth in a cloud of dry ice to the thunderous strains of *Also Sprach Zarathustra*. But it soon became clear that Elvis hadn't just left the building so much as not arrived in the first place. There was to be no Elvis-related rugby match, and it wouldn't be enlivened by the carefully timed shouts of punning song titles I'd been rehearsing since I got there, either.

The final event of the festival was a coruscating performance by Kraig Parker and his band – not to mention the Sweet

Inspirations – in the pavilion that evening, which only served to illustrate for me that a live backing is essential to be a decent Elvis impersonator. Elvis never performed to backing tapes, so why go to all the trouble of acquiring an outfit and hairstyle accurate to the last detail if you're just going to do glorified karaoke? Maybe this is why impersonating Elvis has become so popular – it's so easy to do. Anyone of any shape, size or colouring only has to don a white jumpsuit with optional sunglasses, curl their top lip slightly and, hey presto, there's no mistaking who they are. It's even fairly simple to sound vaguely like Elvis, you just sing from somewhere beneath your tongue. Maybe that's also the problem. So ubiquitous is Elvis's image that you only have to hint at it for people to know exactly who you're driving at – hence there are a lot of very bad Elvis imitators out there. The thing is, so powerful is the image of Elvis that people forget what's important, the thing that made Elvis the cultural juggernaut he is: the music. The bland, soulless karaoke backing CDs that permeated the festival just made everyone sound the same (which, I suppose, is the object of the exercise in a way, but you know what I mean), and not a single impersonator seemed to be able or willing to play a note on the guitar. Granted Elvis was a singer first and foremost, but in the early years at least, his driving rhythm guitar is what gave the music its energy. If you listen to Arthur Crudup's original 'That's All Right' and then compare it to Elvis's high octane, guitar-flailing version, you can hear the difference instantly. It's Elvis's guitar that gives it the impetus.

Porthcawl, I felt, didn't bring me any closer to Elvis. Instead it hammered home a perception of Elvis that seems to bear little relation to the man. For an Elvis festival, there was very little of the man himself in evidence. I left South Wales a little deflated; further even from the King than when I'd arrived. It was time, I decided, to go to some of the places where Elvis had lived, worked and played. To the US, then, the country that produced, raised and venerated the king of rock 'n' roll.

If I left Porthcawl disillusioned, my Elvis journey had none the less been invigorated by the extraordinary devotion and indomitable spirit of the amazing Anita.

Tupelo, USA

Gate forty-eight at Gatwick Airport's south terminal one freezing January morning. It was a hideously early hour and the orange light of dawn was only just heating the edges of the clouds through the giant plate-glass window opposite. I had a dry mouth full of morning breath, my eyes were swollen through lack of sleep, and the omissions from my packing, left of course to the very last minute, were popping into my mind with the regular thudding of a piledriver. Electric shaver. Shower stuff. The favourite shirt I'd washed and ironed specially that was still hanging on the back of the bedroom door.

A small boy was running around being really unnecessarily noisy. I swivelled my bloodshot eyes towards him. Oh great, he was heading my way. He was about four years old, dressed in jeans and a little matching denim jacket, beneath which I could see the face of Elvis on his T-shirt. He was now running towards me. At this time of the morning I am grumpy and misanthropic, especially towards cheerful, noisy small children. I took my hand from my pocket ready to hasten his progress past me with a light skelp to the back of the head, when he was stopped dead in his tracks by a shout from his mother.

'Presley!' she barked. 'Come back here!'

It was shortly before Elvis's birthday, and my flight to Atlanta was packed with Elvis fans. Most, if not all, were heading for a connecting flight to Memphis, while I was going for the surely much more hardcore option of his birthplace at Tupelo in northeast Mississippi.

My fellow passengers at the gate were almost a carbon copy of the crowd at Porthcawl: mainly middle-aged women in black T-shirts with Elvis's face on the front, elaborately coiffed hair, ostentatious gold jewellery, and handbags portraying the famous shot of a young Elvis dressed in dark shirt and trousers reaching out to a crowd from an outdoor stage that I knew for a fact was taken at a show in the little town to which I was heading.

Away to my right sat a family. An American accent said, 'Really? Memphis is where I'm from', at which point the English mother exhorted her teenage son, 'Go on, show him.' The boy needed no second asking and leapt from his seat, buckled his knees and launched into a near-authentic rendition of 'Blue Suede Shoes'. People clapped politely when he finished. The flight was called, and the family scrambled to get their things together. As they walked past me, I noticed that the boy who sang the song had a white stick in one hand and his other arm linked through his mother's as she led him to the plane.

A large amount of hours later I touched down at Tupelo Regional Airport. It's a small affair, so small in fact that there is no baggage carousel as such. A man drives the bags from the plane, opens a hatch, and pushes them through the gap. Everyone's bags thudded through the hole and were collected. Except mine. Again. The young man driving the baggage truck gave me a smile of genuine regret through the hatch, spread his arms wide as if to prove he wasn't hiding anything behind his back and said, 'That's all of 'em.'

With a sigh of inevitability, I approached the desk, which appeared to be the ticket office, check-in and general enquiries counter all rolled into one. A sturdy, square-jawed man stood behind it in T-shirt and jeans, and appeared momentarily startled to see me. From the arrivals and departures board behind him I could tell that only four flights arrived and left here each day, so no wonder that, now all the bags had been unloaded and the passengers dispersed, he was a little surprised to see floating in front of his counter the head and shoulders of a scruffy, unshaven Englishman with a look of exhausted resignation on his face.

'Kunnah help yew sur?' he said in a proper, slow Mississippi drawl.

'My bags haven't shown up,' I mumbled wearily.

'Y'on the flight from Atlanta, sur?' he replied, as if I could possibly have arrived any other way. I was briefly tempted to reply 'No, the magic bus from Marrakesh', but was by now too tired and already jetlagged even to think clearly.

'Yes.'

I handed over my baggage reference label, whose number he typed into a computer using one index finger. 'OK,' he said reassuringly. 'Char-rules Cahnnelly?'

'Yes.'

'OK, you started yurr journey in Kansas City.'

'Erm, no. London, actually. Gatwick.'

'Oh,' he said, furrowing a brow and indulging in a bit more single-digit typing. 'Oh, here y'are, ah gotcha.'

The man, whose name was Perry, all but reached out and clapped me reassuringly on the upper arm as he looked directly into my eyes and explained in a soothing tone that there was one more flight to come in that evening and that my bags would 'sure as hell' be on it.

'We deliver between eleven a.m. and four p.m. tomorrow, so God willing you should have your stuff then. Oh, and welcome to Tupelo, Char-rules.'

Meanwhile, the young man who'd unloaded everyone else's bags had appeared behind the counter. He was young, with innocent eyes shining between a Tupelo Regional Airport base-ball cap and an eager smile. His name was Jason.

'So how's London?' he asked. 'Ah sure would lahk to go there someday.'

We made small talk while Perry copied my details from the screen on to a piece of paper. I furnished Jason with the startling news I always impart in this situation, namely that London is very big because lots of people live there and the weather is changeable. That's the sort of insight you can offer when you've lived in a place all your life.

Perry handed me the piece of paper on which he had painstakingly written my details.

'Don't worry, Char-rules,' he said with a firm set to his jaw. 'We'll have yurr stuff to ya as soon as we can, hopefully tomor-row.'

'Hey,' said Jason brightly, 'if it comes in on the ten o'clock then I could drop it over to ya tonight.'

I've never wanted to marry a man before, yet standing there after the best part of a day travelling through a number of time zones to find no luggage again, I all but dropped to one knee and popped the question.

I took a taxi to the motel, driven by a man who when I asked what goes on in Tupelo replied after a short pause, 'Ain't nuthin' goin' on here', as if it was the stupidest question he'd ever heard. After checking in I went to my room. To my excitement it was one of those places I'd always thought typically American, where the door opens direct on to the car park. Huge SUVs nosed up against my window. If the films I'd seen were anything to go by, the neighbouring rooms would be occupied by vest-wearing criminals on the run, who had leapt to the side of the window and loosened the safety catches on very large guns as they'd heard me approach.

I was absolutely exhausted, but much as I would have liked to collapse into bed and send out enough zeds to be picked up on satellite photos of north-east Mississippi, I knew that I had to stay up in case my stuff arrived on the later flight. Ten o'clock came, the time the last flight of the day arrived from Atlanta. At ten-fifteen the phone by my bed chirruped. I had inadvertently fallen into a light doze in front of, bizarrely, the first-ever episode of *As Time Goes By* starring Geoffrey Palmer and Judi Dench, and woke with a start.

'Hello?' I croaked.

'Char-rules?' burred a voice.

'Pardon?'

'Char-rules Cahnnelly?'

'Oh, yes, sorry, hello.'

'It's Perry here, at the airport. How ya doin' over there?'

'Oh, you know, fine.' Apart from the prospect of several weeks in the US in the clothes I was wearing right now, of course.

'Well, ah gaht some good nooze for ya, yur baggage was on the late flight. Jason's picked it up fur ya, and he's a-heading over to ya now. He shouldn't be morr 'un ten minutes.'

Sure enough, barely twenty-five minutes after the late plane's wheels had hit the Tupelo tarmac, there pulled into the motel car park a pick-up truck, from within which a thumb jerked towards the back seat while above the throaty tickover of the engine a familiar grin called triumphantly, 'Ah got 'em, ah got 'em.'

I thanked Jason profusely, handed him what I guessed was enough money to get him and Perry a large cold beer and told him that I'd see him in London one day. His eyes sparkled again, while the incredulous look on his face suggested that I'd actually said I'd see him windsurfing on the rings of Saturn sometime.

'Ah shurr would like that,' he said, before driving off into the starry Mississippi night.

I fell into a deep sleep within minutes.

It didn't last long, as the vagaries of jetlag conspired to wake me at 4.30 a.m. I counted the hours until breakfast, watching from beneath the covers as the morning glow emerged slowly around the edge of the curtains. By the time a civilised hour arrived the idea of breakfast had reached mythical proportions. I'd not eaten anything since the flight from Gatwick – the Tupelo leg was so short we got only a packet of about half a dozen peanuts and a small bottle of water – and I was starving. Breakfast, I thought, would be a tremendous thing. Indeed, the girl who'd checked me in at the motel had mentioned twice, between jaw-cracking yawns, that a 'deluxe breakfast' would be served. Americans were famous for their breakfasts and I pictured plate-fuls of steaming pancakes and syrup, scrambled eggs, bacon, the works. The receptionist had given me the very definite impression that the Mississippi breakfast was something to behold – you'd need something substantial after a long night's lynching and cross-burning, I'd thought – and this one would be a deluxe version. I showered, dressed and went in search of sustenance.

Doughnuts. That's about all it was. Doughnuts. Doughnuts and a coffee machine for your deluxe breakfast, sir, served on crockery of the finest polystyrene and cutlery of exquisitely crafted white plastic. If this was the deluxe version, I shuddered to think what the regular one was like. Maybe someone threw the doughnuts at you and flung the coffee in your face.

After munching on a couple of sorry specimens of the great American doughnut, I noticed two smaller baskets I'd missed that contained what appeared to be little beefburgers and some cheesy, eggy things. I ate them, cold, and they were probably quite the most disgusting things I've tasted since I once accidentally sprayed hairspray in my mouth. It was only when a fellow guest arrived, piled his plate with the things and took them to a rectangular metal machine with buttons which went 'beep' when you pressed them that I realised you were supposed to cook them in the microwave first

Americans, it seems, don't walk anywhere. I discovered this when I attempted to walk into the centre of Tupelo. The motel was north of town, on one of the main roads through Tupelo, but when I left the tarmac of the motel car park there was nothing to walk on. At least nothing in the way of a pavement, just spongy, dry, scrubby yellow grass. I tramped alongside the road as some big cars and frighteningly large trucks thundered past barely four feet from my right ear.

Then I reached a junction. A big one. Slip roads, a bridge, the lot, and no obvious way for the pedestrian to get across. I walked this way and that. I stood and scratched the back of my head. I even bent down and squinted into a couple of storm drains to see if there was a way through. I looked up and down the highway. I glanced up to see if there were telephone wires that would allow me to abseil across using a rolled up copy of the *Northeast Mississippi Daily Journal*. I knew little of American law, but I did know about jaywalking. Knowing my luck as soon as I crossed a slip road a police car would ease up next to me and a cop with mirror shades, moustache and doughnut sugar down the front of his shirt would have me up against the vehicle with the barrel of his pistol in the small of my back.

I sat down for a few minutes. There appeared to be no way across. I was in a strange country and a strange time zone and I couldn't even get across the bloody road. I had visions of spending my time in Tupelo in the motel watching the entire run of *As Time Goes By*, with the occasional two-hundred-yard stroll to the junction for a change of scenery. I tore at some grass by my side and saw that I'd sat next to a very large bird in the advanced stages of decomposition.

The question popped into my head. What would Elvis do? He spent the first thirteen years of his life here; he must have crossed a road at some point. I pulled out a map from my bag and realised I could get around the junction by heading in the opposite direction and taking a very long way around. There would be some minor road-crossing involved, but nothing like the duel with instant death or sharing of a cell with Big Bubba that appeared to be the only options in front of me here.

I picked myself up and headed north. I passed the motel, an insurance company, a couple of steak houses and a place called Shoneys whose first 'S' failed to illuminate on the sign, so at night would appear to promise 'honeys'.

As I prepared to cross a petrol station forecourt a large green pick-up pulled up, blocking my path. The window wound down and a young man with a crewcut looked out at me. He said something I couldn't understand due to the roar of the passing traffic and the fact that my ear was not yet tuned to the laidback, tongue-chewing Southern way of speaking. In most countries where you can't understand someone you'd ask them to speak slower. In Mississippi you're better off asking them to speak faster.

I made a twirling motion with my index fingers by my ears,

shook my head slightly and rolled my eyes while grinning in that idiotic way you do sometimes when you can't understand a complete stranger.

'Did you get yurr luggage?' he asked, and I twigged that the man in the truck had been on security duty at the airport the previous night while Perry the one-fingered typist was deducing that I'd travelled from Kansas.

'Oh, yes, I did thanks.'

'Where you headed?'

'Into town.'

'Walking?'

'Yes'

'Yurr going the wrong way.'

'Yeah, I know, I tried the right way but couldn't get across the junction. I thought if I came back this way and went up and round North Green Street I'd find a way through that didn't involve crossing big roads.' Even as I said it I realised just how stupid that must have sounded.

'Aw, you don't wanna go to North Green Street, that's a bad area, yurr liable to get jumped. Tell you what, hop in, I'll take you into town.'

At that point I became very British. I spluttered. I demurred. I gibbered. I raised both my palms to face him. I may even have addressed him as 'my dear chap'. Either way, I told him that he couldn't possibly do that. His brow furrowed with a mixture of confusion and hurt.

'Wha' not?' he asked, with genuine curiosity. The Southern sense of hospitality was one I'd have to get used to, clearly.

I slid on to the passenger seat and the truck swung out to join the traffic. My new friend was called Ricky, and in the short time it took for him to drive me into Tupelo I learned that despite being barely twenty-four years old, he had already been married, divorced and was about to marry again, a woman who was now expecting their second child. Somehow he'd also found time for a spell in the US Army, where he'd done a tour of duty in Afghanistan. He loved his job at the airport, and in his spare time bred and sold Great Danes. 'Big dogs,' he said, adopting the same tactics as me when asked, 'How's London?' After I told him why I was in town and where I was heading he adopted the same wistful expression Jason sported when we parted. 'Ah shurr would love to do something like that,' he said, before dropping me outside the Tupelo Hardware Store, where Gladys Presley bought her young son his first guitar. 'Ah never knew that was where Elvis got his first guitar,' said Ricky as I climbed down from the passenger seat to ground level. 'Lived here all this time, too.'

He gave me a self-deprecating chuckle, threw the truck into a large U-turn and sped off up the street, waving out of the window. I waved back, turned around and walked through the door of Tupelo Hardware. Now this was a proper shop. It was quiet, with no piped music. Boxes of screws, nails and so on were piled high up the walls as far as the high ceiling. The counters and floors were old and wooden, lit dimly by ancient-looking lights hanging from above. It was about as far from Homebase as you could possibly get.

'Can I help you, friend?'

A kindly looking man with grey hair, wearing a blue-and-white striped shirt, dark-blue jerkin and a pair of spectacles on a chain around his neck, walked over to me. I said that as I understood it, this was where Elvis bought his first guitar.

'Why, that's right,' he said, brightening. 'Tell you what, c'mon over here and we'll have a talk all about Elvis.' I followed him across the shop, weaving between displays of cleaning cloths, screwdrivers and lots of metal things whose use I couldn't even guess at. He walked behind an old-looking, glass-fronted-and-topped counter that contained a frightening selection of hunting knives.

'Where I'm standing now is the exact spot where Mr Forrest L. Bobo stood when he sold Elvis Presley his first guitar. The guitar was right here, on the top shelf inside this cabinet which, incidentally, is still the original cabinet and the floor is still the original floor.' Without thinking, I reached out and touched the wooden edge of the cabinet with, I realised later, a reverence that bordered on the religious.

'If you look down at the floor, you'll see a marking,' continued my new friend, whose name was Howard. Sure enough, right between my feet was a small 'X' of grey masking tape. 'That is the exact spot where the young Elvis stood,' he said. I tried to picture the young man, puppy fat still around his face, clad possibly in dungarees, standing right here, probably with his arms folded and his bottom lip thrust out, having been refused the gun he'd really wanted. Who knows, if Forrest L. Bobo had actually sold him a gun, maybe Elvis Presley would have gone on to win a minor medal in the Olympic rifle shooting events. Or perhaps he would have ended up in jail for shooting out streetlights on a drunken joyride through the centre of town.

Howard was a big Elvis fan, it transpired. He'd been at the famous show in 1956 at the Tupelo Fairgrounds, no more than four hundred yards from where we stood, and at a show the same year in Memphis. His father had been in the Army, and Howard had been at an Elvis concert at Schofield Barracks in Hawaii. In 1974 Howard and his wife went to see Elvis in Memphis, a Vegas-style show that was recorded and released as *Elvis Recorded Live on Stage in Memphis*.

'What a fantastic entertainer,' said Howard. 'I love the early stuff, the Sun Records material, but I also love the later stuff too.

The guy had it all. It's amazing to think that it all started right here, where we're standing.'

He had given this speech countless times to the trickle of Elvis fans that passes through the store, but still his eyes held mine for a moment. We stood there: Howard, a Tupelo man through and through, a man who had watched Elvis perform in person at every stage of his career, and me, who'd grown up listening to Elvis on my parents' tape deck in south London. You could tell that even now, thirty years after Elvis's death, as Howard approached retirement, he still shared the sense of wonder that I was feeling for the first time. Across generations and oceans, we both knew what this place meant.

The moment passed.

'Here,' he said, emerging from behind the counter, 'we still sell guitars too. Come see.' He led me to the other side of the shop, where a row of acoustic guitars hung on the wall. 'Maybe the next Elvis will buy his first guitar here as well. You play?' he asked, unhooking one from the wall and laying it on the counter.

'Not really,' I replied. 'I just flail away on about four chords.'

'Oh, please,' he said, 'play something. Know any Elvis songs?'

'A couple,' I replied.

'You know "Blue Moon of Kentucky"? That's one of my favourites,' he said. That song was clearly going to follow me everywhere. 'C'mon, let's sing "Blue Moon of Kentucky",' Howard implored. I laid my index finger between the second and third frets to form the A chord that starts the song, took a Tupelo Hardware plectrum from a pot on the counter and launched into it. As usual, it was a pretty horrendous rendition. If I'd been there when Gladys mulled over the guitar on the counter on the other side of the shop, it would have been enough to convince her that maybe the rifle was a good idea after all, and the history of rock 'n' roll could have been very different. I reckon she would already have been thinking of a possible use for the gun right there and then. Howard joined in on the chorus and heads appeared in the doorway. Somehow I got to the end, and he clapped his hands together. 'Let's do "That's All Right, Mama",' he cried. And so we did, with Howard backing up my strained vocal and keeping rhythm by clapping his hands.

'How about that?' he said as we ground mercifully to a halt. 'I love those songs.'

I handed Howard the guitar, and he made a couple of comments which I presumed were designed to induce me to buy it, but I settled instead for a couple of screwdrivers and a keyring. We walked back over to the counter where one of the most important events in rock 'n' roll history had taken place, I shook hands with Howard and left the shop to the sound of him humming 'That's All Right'.

It was only afterwards that I realised something. According to the experts, Gladys took Elvis to the store on the day before his tenth birthday. This meant that Howard and I were having a high old time with a guitar at Tupelo Hardware sixty-one years to the day after Elvis's historic purchase. Somehow I felt my visit wouldn't have the same long-term resonance for the world of music.

I walked up to the corner of the street and took out my map of the town again. I was looking for McDonald's, not because I was in need of dubious sustenance, but because Tupelo's McDonald's also serves as a bit of a shrine to Elvis. As I opened out the map, a sudden gust of wind blew up the street and deposited it straight on to my face. I scrabbled at it, stumbling around for a few seconds with arms outstretched like some weird cartographic Frankenstein's monster, and almost blundered off the kerb and into the street itself. By the time I'd unpeeled the diagrammatic representation of the centre of Tupelo from my panting phizog, a man in a sharp dark suit carrying books under his arm was regarding me with curiosity.

'Are you lost, friend?' he asked.

'No,' I gushed, giving up on trying to fold the map properly and shoving it instead straight into my bag, where most of it stuck out of the top like a strange mercatorial chrysanthemum. 'Well, at least not exactly. Could you tell me whether I can walk to McDonald's from here?'

'Sure you can, but it's quite a way,' he said. He thought for a moment, looked up and down the street and said, 'Look, my truck's just around the corner, tell you what, I'll drive you there myself.'

Rather than putting up a polite protest that it was far too much trouble, as I had with Ricky earlier, I did the decent thing and acquiesced immediately. On the way to his truck, the man introduced himself as Roger Tubbs, a local lawyer.

'I went to London once,' he informed me after I'd responded to his question as to my origins and I'd given my usual reply regarding size, population and weather. 'Went on something called a pub crawl. It was great. After that I was just dying to try the famous English fish and chips, but when it arrived, it was just fish and French fries. What a disappointment that was,' he said with a slight chuckle that failed to mask the indignance that clearly still rankled. Hoodwinked by a battered cod – that's got to hurt.

When I told him why I was in town, he slapped his leg and said, 'It's a damn shame that my secretary's not in today. Elvis's horse once bit her on the butt.' It turned out that Vernon Presley used to do some work for Roger's secretary's father way back when, and somehow this arrangement led to equine teeth-marks on the rear end of a Tupelo legal secretary. I would never learn the full story alas, as Roger had suddenly swung the car into a side road, informing me he'd give me what he called the 'nickel tour' and show me where Elvis went to school.

Milam Junior High has changed quite a bit since a young Elvis Presley spent just over two years behind its portals between 1946 and 1948. 'This is the back of the school now,' said Roger as we swung into the car park, 'but in Elvis's time this would have been the main entrance.' We pulled up in front of a simple stone staircase leading to a set of double doors, the very place where a young, bashful kid from the wrong side of the highway would enter in the morning and leave in the afternoon. Elvis apparently made little impression here, although a few classmates remembered that he did start bringing his guitar to school and would sit in the basement with a boy named Billy Welch working out chords and harmonics to gospel songs. Contemporaries who remembered him recalled that the hillbilly-style music Elvis favoured wasn't popular, but for all his shyness and outward lack of confidence Elvis carried on playing exactly the kind of music he wanted, even to the extent of saying that he would play at the Grand Ole Opry one day.

As we sat in silence facing the old school entrance, I tried hard to picture the reticent kid in overalls with his Tupelo Hardware guitar slung on a piece of string over his shoulder. It was his one comfort against an almost crippling shyness, the one thing that gave him any sense of self-confidence. I imagined him taking the large steps his little legs needed to get to the double doors and could almost hear his pre-pubescent voice and awkwardly fingered chords drifting up from the basement on the Mississippi breeze.

'Shall I take you to McDonald's now?' asked Roger.

A few minutes later Roger eased back out into the traffic

sounding his horn and waving out of the window. I stood and waved back. A couple of days later I'd be walking along Main Street and pass his office. 'Roger Tubbs, Lawyer', said the sign in the window, close to another sign that said, 'No soliciting', which I found quite funny.

The McDonald's on Gloster Street South was packed with Elvis memorabilia. Glass cases held photographs and record sleeves, while mirrors featured friezes of the man himself, including one giant head-and-shoulders portrait of a young Elvis that dominated the room. 'Where do you want to sit, honey?' asked a tray-carrying mother of her daughter, who could have been no more than seven years old. 'Right there,' she replied, pointing a tiny finger at the table she coveted. 'Right next to Elvis Presley.'

I pulled out my crumpled map to plan a route to Elvis's birthplace the following day. A free one produced by the town, it featured advertisements for a number of local businesses and concerns around its outer edge typical of a small town in North America: the Good News Church with its services in English and Spanish; WM Waste Management, which offered the 'complete menu of waste collection services' (the desserts must be quite something); and the slightly unfortunately named Crump Body and Paint Shop that came 'highly wreck-a-mended'. Hopefully there was nothing to be read into the fact that the adjacent advertisement was for Grayson-Porter's Mortuary, 'where families come first since 1913'. Shipley Do-Nuts of Tupelo's ad said, 'Drive thru window for your convenience', which I wasn't sure was an advert or an invitation; while I misread RSC Equipment Rental's claim to be 'Your jobsite solution' as 'Your gobshite solution', whereby when you had a problem you'd hire a bloke with a loud voice to talk self-important rubbish at you for an agreed hourly rate.

The map also had a 'Did you know?' box of facts about

Mississippi. I never knew, for example, that the official state beverage is milk, nor was I aware that Mississippi's official fossil is none other than the prehistoric whale. The state's oldest Holiday Inn is in Clarksdale, while the last home run ever hit by Babe Ruth was off the pitching of Guy Bush of Tupelo. Oh, and someone called Elvis Presley was born there too.

The eighth of January, Elvis's birthday, dawned bright, sunny and warm. I plucked up the courage to defy the jaywalking laws of the United States and vowed to cross the major intersection that threatened to limit my visit to Tupelo to an area featuring Shoney's diner and either messy death or arrest in one direction, or, according to Ricky, violent physical assault in the other. Unless another Ricky, Roger or Jason appeared, I was resigned to breaking the law and jousting with fate on the road – a contest in which fate was armed with an eighteen-wheel Mack truck while I had a Tupelo Hardware screwdriver.

The first slip road was easy enough. This was for traffic leaving Interstate 45, which bisected my road beneath the bridge, and there was a clear view of any vehicles coming up the slope. There weren't any, so I set foot on to the tarmac expecting a police helicopter to sweep up from under the bridge while a gum-chewing cop with a megaphone implored me to freeze, sonofabitch. However, I managed to reach the other side without hearing the thump and clatter of rotors, and crossed the spongy yellow turf to the next challenge. This was busier, and therefore harder: the slip road for cars approaching me to sweep down on to Interstate 78 and head for Memphis. Before long there was a break in the traffic and I was able to cross with a faintly ridiculous-looking semi-trot, the result of wanting to run

like hell for the other side while still affecting an air of nonchalance. A pick-up drove past and a man's voice shouted something
from within. I don't know if it was aimed at me and, if so, what
it was. It could have been a warning, some random abuse for
being stupid enough to want to walk somewhere in America, or
possibly something along the lines of 'What's with the faintly
ridiculous-looking semi-trot? It just looks like you want to run
like hell for the other side while still affecting an air of nonchalance. You asshole.'

Whatever he had said, and each option was equally plausible,
I was nearly halfway through my odyssey. I now had to walk
across the fifty yards of bridge over the Interstate. The bridge
carried two lanes of traffic in each direction without a pavement.
Between its three-feet-high perimeter wall and the thundering
traffic there was a patch of bare tarmac about four feet wide scattered with stones, bits of broken glass and an old baseball cap or
two. I tried to adopt a gait that suggested I did this all the time,
put my head down and set off. Nobody shouted abuse, nobody
arrested me and nobody reached out and slapped me on the back
of the head as they passed, the three things that I'd feared most.

The two slip roads beyond the bridge were negotiated suc-
cessfully and with nary a hitch, I'd done it. I had crossed the
intersection. I'd also broken the law four times in the space of
five minutes, possibly five times if crossing the bridge on foot was
also a felony. In which case, my current rate of a crime a minute
would surely get me a spot on a show along the lines of *America's
Dumbest and Most Chronologically Persistent Criminals*.

Buoyed, I carried on towards the centre of Tupelo and the
junction that sits at the heart of the town. Not only did the two
main roads through Tupelo bisect here, the railway passed
through as well. There are no passenger trains that come
through, but there are plenty of freight trains. I'd heard the

mournful minor second of their blaring hooters in the distance all through the night, and most of the day too. It was a sound that was probably quite the same as it had been in Elvis's time here. Sure enough, as I reached the junction bells started ringing and red lights flashing to indicate that a train was about to pass through. And pass through it did. And through, and through, and through. No wonder I could hear hooters at night way up at the motel – they are positively ear-splitting when you're standing at the side of the track. A huge engine unit went past, coupled to another. And then the freight trucks started passing me, the ground beneath my feet trembling as the train went through. I counted the trucks as they passed. It took several minutes and there were no fewer than 135 of them. The train was longer than Tupelo itself.

Once the traffic started moving again I turned east along Main Street, past Tupelo Hardware and then beyond the site of the old Tupelo Fairgrounds, which hold terrific significance in the history of rock 'n' roll. There's nothing to see now because the old showground has been demolished and built upon, but it was here when the site featured a small wooden stage and a couple of grandstands that Elvis Presley made his first public appearance. He was ten years old when, in October 1945, he got up on stage at the Mississippi–Alabama state fair talent contest, stood on a chair and sang 'Old Shep' to the watching hundreds. He'd sung the mawkish Red Foley song at school a couple of weeks earlier and impressed one of his teachers so much she'd entered him for the contest, which was organised by local radio station WELO. Elvis did well too, but not quite well enough – he came second (some sources say fifth) behind the winner, a schoolmate of his called Shirley Jones Gallentine. As I walked past the site I wondered whatever became of Shirley, who would be in her seventies now. Who knows, maybe I'd even passed her on the street when I walked around town, or perhaps she'd passed me in a car, nudged her husband and said, 'Look at that dumbass trying to walk across the bridge, must want to get himself killed.'

Eleven years after that nervous entry into public performance, on 26 September 1956, Elvis took to the Tupelo Fairgrounds stage again. This time the watching hordes, numbering upward of five thousand, were there just to see him. They were a little more boisterous and vocal too, for by then Tupelo's most famous son had hit the big time. Elvis had come from Hollywood where he was filming his first picture, *Love Me Tender*. A fortnight before he'd appeared on *The Ed Sullivan Show* in a performance that was watched by more than 80 per cent of the national television audience that evening. A banner hung over Main Street declaring, 'Tupelo Welcomes Elvis Presley Home'. Imagine what they'd have done for Shirley Jones Gallentine.

As soon as he stepped on to the stage in white shoes, black trousers and a dark-blue velvet shirt, the crowd went crazy. Elvis worked them like a seasoned professional in a high-octane show interrupted only when he was presented with a key to the city. In the front row was a young Tammy Wynette and somewhere in the crowd was an equally young Howard Hite, the gentle old soul I'd duetted with at Tupelo Hardware.

A year and a day later Elvis returned to Tupelo for another show, the $10,000 fee for which he presented to the city. The performance was marred, however, by the fact that it was the first Elvis Presley show in which he wasn't backed by Scotty Moore and Bill Black, with whom Colonel Parker had fallen out temporarily in a dispute over money.

The stage was demolished years ago, but the grandstands still stood into the late nineties. Now there is nothing to mark the place where Elvis Presley first sang in public.

I kept walking east, crossing the railroad and passing beneath Interstate 45, today called Martin Luther King Drive. It was this highway that separated what was known then as East Tupelo from the rest of the town. East Tupelo in the 1930s and 1940s was poor, desperately so, and rough. It was regarded with distaste by the people who lived west of the railroad – at the time of Elvis's birth the Presleys were on the wrong side of the tracks.

After a while I arrived at what had been the Old Saltillo Road, now renamed Elvis Presley Boulevard. Trees lined the road providing welcome shade after my warm, dusty stroll. A couple of minutes later I rounded the bend and there it was, the tiny, two-roomed wooden house in which Elvis had been born. Vernon had built it himself, borrowing $180 from his sometime-employer Orville Bean to do so, on land owned by his father and next door to his parental home. The wind rustled the leaves, through which the sun filtered, and it struck me briefly that this was an idyllic place to live. My naivety soon disappeared as I remembered just how poor the Presleys had been. By all accounts, Vernon wasn't the most labour-intensive of men, and while Gladys worked for two dollars per day at the Tupelo Garment Plant, her difficult pregnancy meant that she had to give up work sooner than the young couple hoped.

I walked along the street, almost circling the house, which really is quite startlingly small, and entered the complex that surrounds the birthplace. Possibly uniquely in Elvis world, the whole thing has been tastefully done. There's a low, unostentatious modern building that houses the gift shop and museum, a fountain of thirteen spouts (one for each year Elvis spent in Tupelo) and a small chapel. A modest garden separates the chapel from the house, and the atmosphere is one of serene contemplativeness. There's none of the glitz or gaudy brouhaha that accompanies many Elvis landmarks, quite the opposite in fact.

The ambience is one of respectful reverence, as you'd expect perhaps from a significant religious place, not the birthplace of an entertainer.

I wandered into the gift shop and museum and was handed my admission ticket. Today it was free in celebration of the King's birthday. The place began to fill up, and the crowd was the usual combination of middle-aged women in Elvis T-shirts and their male counterparts, many with carefully sculpted ducktail hairstyles. Chatting to an attendant stood a family group, the typical all-American foursome except that the father, who had neatly combed hair and a carefully trimmed moustache, wore a T-shirt with the phrase 'I can smell your brains' typeset in dripping blood on the reverse.

Nearby three very tall, very good-looking young Danish men wandered around sheepishly among the souvenirs. The middle-aged, bouffanted attendants pounced on them right away.

'So where y'all from? Denmark? Wow, that's wonderful. And you came here specially for Elvis's birthday? No? Oh, you didn't know it was his birthday. Y'all are fans though, right? Oh, you're just travelling across America and happened to roll up here. So you're not fans of Elvis? No? Oh, well, I sure hope you enjoy it today and hopefully you'll be fans by the time you leave, huh?'

A trestle table was brought out from a back room and a pink tablecloth placed on it. A huge bowl of pink punch appeared alongside stacks of small plastic glasses and a mountain of pink paper plates. The crowd started to gather expectantly as two attendants fussed around the table, moving glasses pointlessly and rearranging lots of small serviettes embossed with the words 'Elvis Presley Birthplace, Tupelo, Mississippi'. One accidentally knocked against a lifesize cut-out of Elvis in his gold lamé suit. Instinctively she apologised.

'Oh my Gahd, I just spoke to him,' she said, blushing slightly, to another museum employee.

'Oh, I speak to him every day,' she replied. 'In fact, sometimes I touch him too.' They both giggled in a vaguely naughty way, touched each other's forearms in a moment of shared sexual frisson and carried on rearranging serviettes and moving piles of plates. After a few minutes a door opened behind us and two more women emerged each carrying a colossal pink birthday cake. We were instructed to form a queue, in which I stood behind the three now slightly bemused-looking Danes who eyed each other nervously with glances that said, 'Shall we just make a break for it now?'

Eventually a local dignitary made a short speech welcoming everybody and then led off a chorus of 'Happy Birthday', which we all sang lustily, even, I noticed, the Danes.

We passed reverentially along the table to be handed our piece of pink birthday cake on a pink plate and a glass of pink punch, and I adjourned to a bench outside to eat. Given how windy it was getting, this was possibly a bad idea. The wind slopped punch over the side of my glass and on to my lap and crumbs whipped off the cake like tiny flour-based machine-gun fire, strafing the family sitting two yards downwind of me. The little boy, having had his cake and punch and now full to the brim with so many E-numbers you could have used them for a game of bingo, started to run off in the direction of the house. 'Elvis,' barked the mother through a mouthful of cake, 'come back here this instant!'

I went back inside and had a quick stroll around the museum, most of which featured memorabilia collected by Tupelo resident Janelle McComb, who knew Elvis for most of his life. It was the usual array of jackets, gold discs and photographs, but the most disturbing exhibit for me was a montage of two coffee cups and a towel. They were from the hotel in which Elvis stayed in Monroe, Louisiana, after a concert in 1975. Two female fans had gone to the hotel just as Elvis was leaving, and talked the security guard into letting them into his room. There they found two coffee cups complete with dregs, and a damp towel in the bathroom. All three items were promptly half-inched. The towel was placed in one of the women's freezer compartments to preserve the sweat, where it stayed for no fewer than seventeen years before being presented to Janelle McComb for the museum. The towel was neatly folded on a pedestal next to the coffee cups which, more than thirty years later, still had faint half-moons of brown around the bottom. Again, the reverence accorded them was pseudo-religious, as if they were the relics of a saint.

From the museum I withdrew to the holiest place – the little house itself. I climbed the wooden steps up to the veranda, knocked on the screen door and was admitted by a kindly looking middle-aged woman with a bouffant. We stood smiling at each other for a few moments until some more people came in and she could launch into her patter. I looked around the first of the two rooms. It was tiny. An iron-framed double bed took up most of it, angled diagonally from the corner. A brick fireplace stood at the other end. The room was furnished as it would have been on the day in 1935 when Elvis was born, right here, a couple of feet from where I stood behind a rope. 'This', said the guide with all the deference she could muster, 'is the room where Elvis Presley was born.'

It was a difficult birth. Gladys was attended by Vernon's mother Minnie Mae, the midwife and a neighbour. She was in such difficulty overnight that the midwife called out the doctor and at around 4 a.m a baby boy was born, already dead. Some thirty-five minutes later another boy was born, this time healthy. Gladys, though, was in a bad way. Some reports say that she nearly died after Elvis was born; either way, the experience left her unable to have any more children.

The healthy child was named 'Elvis', Vernon's middle name, and given the middle name of 'Aaron', after Vernon's friend Aaron Kennedy. The dead twin was given the name 'Jesse' after Vernon's father and the middle name 'Garon', it seems in order to rhyme with Elvis's middle name. When Elvis's birth was registered, incidentally, one of the A's in Aaron was left off, leaving him with the curious spelling for the rest of his life and opening up a whole bunch of post mortem conspiracy theories after his name was spelled 'correctly' on his gravestone.

We stepped through a doorway to the right of the fireplace and progressed through to the second room of the house, where the family cooked, washed and dined. It wasn't hard to imagine them eating together here by the dim light of oil lamps, not least because three places had been laid at the old wooden table in the middle of the room. Out of the window they wouldn't have seen the neatly tended grass, rather the dirt yard that Gladys took great care to keep tidy, sweeping it daily. From climbing the couple of small steps to the veranda we'd shuffled in awe for barely ten yards before we were on the grass outside the back door.

There was just one more thing to see before heading back to Tupelo, so I popped in to the chapel, paid for by Elvis's fans, next to the museum and shop. It's a modern, soulless construction with a large stained-glass window that at first appears to be an abstract design. If you look closely, though, you can see a white-jumpsuited Elvis at its centre with a large crown suspended over his head.

Pausing only to buy an armful of souvenirs – my favourite of which was an Elvis birthplace snowstorm – I set out on the long walk back to the other side of the tracks. The fields either side of the road were flat and seemingly endless, with pylons marching from horizon to horizon. It was still a warm day and I wasn't particularly relishing the walk back, which would take me the best part of an hour. I'd gone barely a mile when a horn blared just behind me and a blue pick-up truck drew up. The passenger door opened and a voice from inside called, 'You wanna ride?' The answer was an unequivocal yes, I certainly did want a ride, so I heaved myself up into the seat and closed the door. I looked across to see a man in his forties wearing steel-rimmed glasses beneath a forehead that was just slightly too big for his head and the peak of a baseball cap. He gave every impression that he was a guy who still lived with his mother. As we pulled back into the traffic, he turned to me with a smile playing at the corners of his mouth and said, 'You look very young'.

I have to confess that I found this comment a bit unsettling. As a child I'd been warned about accepting lifts from strangers, but I thought that as a man in his mid-thirties such warnings could be disregarded. After all, I'm an experienced traveller. I've been to Uzbekistan and I've been to Bosnia. I've even been to Colchester. All so far without serious mishap. Hence I weighed the comment up in my mind. Can a man in his mid-thirties look very young? Do I in fact look very young, or is it the open, gullible expression I wear that says, 'I will believe anything you tell me and react to it with a look of awed wonder'? I was worried that his next pronouncement would be something along the lines of, 'and you have mighty purdy lips too', as we pulled off the highway and bumped along a track to some woods miles from anywhere.

Thankfully, I needn't have worried in the slightest. It was purely an innocent observation because Terry, as my lift introduced himself, was just one of life's innocents; a thoroughly decent guy.

'I gotta tell you, I don't make a habit of picking up strangers on the highway but that's a dangerous stretch, where I picked you up,' he said. 'A few months ago I was helping out a guy about your age who was a little down on his luck. Trying to help him get straightened out, you know. Well, about a month back he was walking along that exact same stretch of road as you, and a truck left the highway, ran him over and killed him. When I saw you, I couldn't risk the same thing happening again. Hope you don't mind.'

Terry asked where I'd been, and when I told him he replied that he was an Elvis fan himself. Although despite living in Tupelo he'd never been to the birthplace.

'So it's old Elvis's birthday today, huh?' he said as we passed Tupelo Hardware. 'You know, I visited Graceland a coupla years after he died. It wasn't open to the public then, but a security guard let me walk up to the graves and spend a bit of time with Elvis. I found that to be a profoundly moving experience and I appreciated it very much.'

We slowed to a halt in the middle of the road as Terry prepared to turn into the forecourt of Wendy's Hamburgers, where he would drop me off. As he started to turn from nowhere a truck came up behind us, horn blaring, and all but took the front off the pick-up. It must have missed by a matter of a couple of inches. The truck's giant radiator grille flashed past, followed by several wheels as tall as we were, and then it was quiet. It was only in those few seconds of stillness that I realised both Terry and I had screamed our heads off for the entire time the truck rumbled past. It disappeared up the street and we both looked at each other, wide-eyed and breathless. I felt like Dennis Weaver in *Duel*. 'That was mighty close,' said Terry in the same measured drawl he'd used to describe his trip to Memphis. I nodded, open-mouthed. 'Another couple of feet and we'd have been in the goddam ditch over there.' I nodded, still dumbfounded. Terry restarted the stalled engine and completed the manoeuvre into Wendy's without further mishap.

'I don't want to worry you,' he said as we pulled into the car park, 'but I've actually had three automobile accidents in the last month. None of them have been my fault, though.' Still shaking slightly, and very dry about the mouth, I hopped down from the pick-up, waved weakly at the man I now knew as 'Lucky Terry', wobbled into Wendy's, ordered a huge plate of hamburger and fries, and prayed to Elvis that when I took the Greyhound bus to Memphis the following day, Terry would not be on the road, at least until we were well clear of town.

Memphis, USA, Part 1

I checked my bags in at Tupelo Bus Station, and the large bearded man whose microwaved lunch I'd interrupted the previous day to buy my ticket (and boy, did he ever let me know that I'd interrupted his lunch) asked where I was from.

'I worked in England for a while,' he said, 'Place called Birmingham. The company was run by Joe Cocker's brother. They told us, don't do any Joe Cocker imitations, he absolutely hates that. Dang thing is, when I'm drinking, Joe Cocker's all I can do.'

I stood outside with my bags and watched the silver bus pull in, the word 'MEMPHIS' displayed above the driver's window. About five of us joined it here, and it was already pretty crowded. I threw my bags into the belly of the bus and stepped aboard, taking a seat next to a big man in a denim shirt. As we left the city limits, it became clear that my neighbour had a quite spectacular twitch. All along the two-hour journey I received a fair few elbows to the ribs, a rap on the breastbone from his knuckles and at one point a double blow to the left shoulder from his right ear. The poor guy didn't say a word, and neither did I, other than a slight involuntary yelp when he knocked on my chest, for which I felt immediately guilty.

The route to Memphis would be the same one taken by Vernon, Gladys and Elvis when they upped sticks from Tupelo. I tried to imagine their old car, packed high with their belongings, a thirteen-year-old Elvis somewhere among the detritus looking between the front seats at the highway ahead – the same highway along which I was now travelling – with a mixture of fear and excitement. No one knows the exact reason why the Presleys suddenly loaded up their 1939 Plymouth and headed for Tennessee in the autumn of 1948, but it seems likeliest that Vernon had lost his job as a driver for local wholesaler L. P. McCarty. Times were hard in Tupelo; maybe Vernon felt he had a better chance of providing for his family by moving to the big city a couple of hours up the highway. Either way, the young man in the back of the car surrounded by crates and boxes would not have had an inkling of the effect the city would have on him – nor the effect that he would have on the city.

Halfway through the Greyhound ride, the rain started to fall, washing over the bus in waves. It absolutely threw it down: huge, heavy droplets that battered the windows relentlessly. The windscreen wipers gwersh-gwershed to little effect and the traffic slowed down almost to a halt with the decreased visibility. At long last we hit the outskirts of Memphis and before long pulled into the bus station, where the water ran off the awnings in torrents. Heaving my bags from the bus, I ran around the corner, threw myself and the bags into a taxi and said, 'Heartbreak Hotel, please.'

There really was no other place I could stay. A stone's throw from Graceland on the other side of Elvis Presley Boulevard, the Heartbreak was opened in 1999 by Elvis Presley Enterprises and although the design of the place looks more like the kind of building that would have had Stalin's moustache twitching with approval, its attention to detail is rather impressive. When the taxi pulled off the boulevard to the hotel I was delighted to see through the rain-spattered windscreen that it was indeed situated at the end of Lonely Street, and when I approached the reception desk I was chuffed to notice that the desk clerk was actually dressed in black. I looked around to see if the bellhop's tears kept falling, but the bellhop wasn't there.

The reception area has a fifties feel. There are a couple of period style sofas and an old television showing Elvis films on a constant loop – as I checked in an elderly couple sat there transfixed by *Follow That Dream* – and the rooms are enormous: mine was more like a suite, with a lounge area, kitchenette and a huge bedroom. The only drawback, as I would discover, is the piping of Elvis records into the hotel's public areas twenty-four hours a day. Now much as I'm a fan, retiring at night to the strains of 'Teddy Bear' (there is something faintly unsettling about hearing a man telling you he wants to be your teddy bear just as you're about to turn in for the evening) and then emerging blearily in the morning to the cheerful sound of 'Rock-a-Hula Baby', before breakfasting to an accompaniment of 'Return to Sender', can get a little bit wearing when you're staying there for as long as I did.

The rain abated in the late afternoon, so I ventured out through the puddles to have a quick look around. Turning right out of the hotel, I wandered through an empty car park, its surface shiny with rain, and into the row of shops and diners opposite Graceland. Everywhere seemed to be deserted – this was the week after the birthday celebrations, the second busiest time of year behind 'Elvis Week' in August commemorating his death – and everyone had gone home, including, presumably, young Presley, about whom I'd been so misanthropic at Gatwick.

I mooched in and out of a couple of souvenir shops and ate a chilli cheeseburger as the only customer in a fifties-style diner. I wiped some of the condensation from the spattery, steamed-up window and looked through to the road outside where cars and trucks hissed along the sodden tarmac and, behind some trees on the other side of the street, the unmistakable white porticoed Graceland mansion gleamed in the gloaming. To be honest it was a bit of a surprise to find that it sits on a normal, busy road flanked by regular buildings. Yet even on this grey, overcast January afternoon, as I mulled over just how tawdry the whole place was, Graceland sat there among the trees, a dignified, old-fashioned Southern mansion. If it's possible for a building to have charisma, even from the outside on a rainy day, Graceland has it in spades.

It's quite a way from the centre of Memphis to Graceland, the best part of ten miles in fact. Indeed, when the house was built in 1939 it wasn't actually part of Memphis at all, rather a satellite town called Whitehaven. It was constructed for a Dr and Mrs Thomas D. Moore and named Graceland after Mrs Moore's great aunt Grace. Elvis paid a hundred thousand dollars for the house and its fourteen acres of land in 1957, and would spend the next twenty years until his death with it as his main home. If I was going to find Elvis, I mused as I drained my plastic tumbler of Coke, it would surely be at Graceland, the house that was the one constant in his life from the moment he hit the big time until his death in one of the upstairs bathrooms. Given its significance to my journey, I decided to save visiting the second most-visited house in the US after the White House until the very end of my time in Memphis.

☆

The next morning I found myself outside the place where rock 'n' roll was born. It's not often that a cultural phenomenon can be traced to a precise spot – rugby union has Rugby School, but that's the only one I can think of – yet the building outside which I stood on an otherwise anonymous junction on one of the main roads into Memphis from the east has probably the best claim as any to be the birthplace of rock 'n' roll. I confess to being absolutely awestruck as I stood in front of this building – in truth I'd been more excited about coming here than visiting Graceland itself. In fact I'd probably been more excited about coming here than I had about any of the places I was visiting on my travels. The address 706 Union Avenue had been the home of the Memphis Recording Service and later Sun Studio, and the walls of this little building had reverberated to some of the earliest, rawest and most significant performances in the history of popular music.

The exterior has been restored to just how it looked in the fifties when the likes of Johnny Cash, Carl Perkins, Jerry Lee Lewis, Roy Orbison and Elvis cut their earliest records here. The Memphis Recording Service sign is illuminated in the window in front of the venetian blinds, permanently closed as they were on the day in the summer of 1953 that Elvis Presley went in and made the first recording of his career. He was barely eighteen years old when he finally plucked up the courage to walk through the door with the old guitar bought from Tupelo Hardware and ask Sam Phillips's secretary Marion Keisker if he could record an acetate, a present for his mother, he said, at a cost of $3.98 plus tax. In later years Keisker would tell of how when she asked the timid kid with the spotty neck and greasy pompadour who he sounded like, he replied, 'I don't sound like nobody.'

The song he recorded was a 1948 hit for Jon and Sandra

Steele called 'My Happiness', a sentimental, faintly cheesy ballad that Elvis knew well. Listening to the crackly acetate today it is unmistakably Elvis. The guitar sounds tinny, but over it, even in this primitive recording, the young voice sounds warm and rich. It's a little thinner than in his later recordings, even the Sun sides that were just over a year away, but the tender vibrato draws you in, giving the song a depth that comes through the half-century-old acetate, taking the listener beyond the ham lyrics into the very soul of its sentiments. It was an extraordinarily assured performance, one that emphasised the big contradiction in Elvis's character. There is no sign of the crippling shyness that several times had prevented him from walking through the studio door, and had kept him as a loner throughout his schooldays. Yet there is an innate confidence burning through the record which was, remember, Elvis's first time in a studio. The surroundings were quite different from the porches and steps where he'd normally sit strumming his guitar – he was boxed into a booth and singing into a big grey microphone, while people he'd never met before fussed around with the recording process outside. All the same, from the first chord on the guitar, Elvis is lost in the song. It's just him, the guitar and 'My Happiness'.

Marion Keisker gave him his acetate, took his money, made a note of his name, and wrote, 'Good ballad singer' next to it. Maybe one day there'd be something for him to record if the right kind of song came up.

It was a curious feeling standing outside the door through which Elvis himself had passed with his cheap old battered guitar that hot Memphis afternoon more than fifty years earlier. The studio tour begins in the café next door. In the Sun heyday it was Miss Taylor's Diner, where Sam Phillips had his unofficial office in the third booth by the window and the likes of Johnny Cash and Elvis would hang out between sessions. Today the walls are festooned with Sun merchandise and memorabilia but it's been subtly done, and the place retains much of the shabby charm of the original fifties venue where Sam Phillips first told Scotty Moore of the new young singer he'd had in the studio.

The tour takes you to a room full of display cabinets that include Elvis's guitar – the acoustic with the leather surround on the body that accompanied him through his early tours and television appearances – and the original acetate of 'Rocket 88' by Jackie Brenston and his Delta Cats. This is the record that, with its thunderous, shuffling rhythm and throaty vocals, many argue was the original rock 'n' roll song. Like nearly all rock 'n' roll's pioneering recordings, 'Rocket 88' had been cut at Sun.

From there, we descended a narrow staircase, went through a door and stepped back fifty years in time. We'd emerged into the tiny front office behind the venetian blinds where Marion Keisker sat and listened patiently as a trickle of youngsters with guitars shyly asked if they could record a song or audition for Mr Phillips. The simple wooden desk that filled much of the small space between the street and the studio itself was where dreams were laid out, and Marion Keisker handled them with maternal gentleness. Some were cocky, some were shy, but all shared the same dream. It was a strange feeling to stand on the spot, the exact spot, where a young Elvis conquered his reticence to announce, 'I don't sound like nobody.'

From the office, we were shown through another door directly into the studio itself. Although Sun had changed hands several times since the days of Sun Records – including, bizarrely enough, a stint as a scuba diving equipment shop (you couldn't really be much further from the sea) the studio itself was the same as it had been the day Elvis first arrived. Whitewashed baffling adorned the walls of what was, essentially, just a medium-sized, high-ceilinged room. For a place of such almost ecclesiastical standing in popular music, Sun Studio is as simple as it gets. Modern recording studios have all sorts of paraphernalia – baffle boards, air conditioning, special fabric on the walls – but Sun, which still functions as a studio when the tours have finished, is a basic empty rectangular room with white walls scuffed by the necessary logistics of the recording process, and a floor scattered with guitars, amps, microphones and assorted cables.

Our guide, a young man with glasses and enormous muttonchop sideburns, indicated three crosses of gaffer tape on the floor, where Elvis, Scotty and Bill stood as they recorded that first famous take of 'That's All Right', and a chill ran up my spine. While 'Rocket 88' does have a strong claim on being the first rock 'n' roll record, for me it all started with 'That's All Right'. The night of Monday, 5 July 1955 is, for me, the birthdate of popular music.

Sam Phillips had called Elvis into the studio a couple of times at Marion's suggestion, but the sessions had not gone well. Phillips clearly saw potential in the young man with the sideburns who he'd see staring in at the windows while driving slowly past the studio in a Crown Electric Company truck, as if hoping the record boss would go haring out into the street shouting, 'Thank goodness you're here.' There was something about the kid. Phillips just had to work out what. For some years the Sun supremo had thought that if he could find a white singer who sounded like a black singer he would make a fortune, and, who knows, maybe from the start he saw that in Elvis. But it wasn't until that hot summer night in July 1955 that all the journeys made by the various strands of American music came together, right where I stood in this little room, no more than twenty feet by thirty, on Union Avenue in Memphis.

Sam had assigned Elvis to young guitar player Scotty Moore

and stand-up bass player Bill Black – arguably the 'star' musicians of the Sun stable. Would Phillips have asked Scotty and Bill to work with any old teenage shouter? Probably not, which suggests that he really had seen something special in Elvis. After some cursory rehearsals, the three turned up at Sun that summer evening and worked through a couple of songs while Phillips listened from behind the plate-glass window of the control room, in front of which I now stood. First there was an old Bob Hope hit 'Harbor Lights', and then several attempts at 'I Love You Because'. Elvis gave it his best shot, knowing that this could be his big chance. He was determined not to blow it, and threw everything into each attempt. Perhaps he was trying too hard. With every take he tried that little bit more, and hence began to lose the rawness, the feeling, the passion of the song. Sam called for a break; things weren't really going anywhere. When you listen to the recording today, both songs plod along. Elvis tries to make his voice soar, but he sounds constricted. The spoken-word section of 'I Love You Because' sounds almost bored. Even Scotty Moore's guitar runs seem barely interested.

Scotty and Bill put down their instruments and lit cigarettes. Sam Phillips in the control room began rewinding the tapes, and the session looked to have ground to a temporary halt. Now whether Elvis seized the silence as the chance to play what he'd really wanted to play all along, or whether he was just trying to release his anxiety and burn off some energy, we'll never know. But what happened next changed the course of popular music for ever.

Suddenly the young man who had overcome his shyness to record 'My Happiness', who had nervously kept in touch with Marion Keisker and who had hitherto merely hinted at some kind of potential beneath the curious mix of bashfulness and iron self-confidence, picked up his guitar and began flailing at an A chord, arguably the most simple chord in the guitar player's canon. All at once a raw, passionate voice started singing the opening lines to a song Sam recognised as an old Arthur 'Big Boy' Crudup blues tune called 'That's All Right'. Yet this was no slow blues number; this was a young man careering through a coruscating version of the song that was unlike any that had been played before. Elvis later claimed, with characteristic self-deprecation, that he was just fooling around, but Elvis never just fooled around with songs, at least not in his early days. His whole body was racked with the intensity of the performance. Scotty and Bill picked up their instruments and joined in, Bill slapping the strings of his bass and Scotty interspersing Elvis's singing with simple yet brilliantly effective guitar licks.

Phillips emerged from the control room and asked what they were doing. The three musicians replied that they didn't really know. 'Well,' said Sam, 'back up, find a place to start and do it again.'

A few takes later and the song was in the can. There was none of the awkwardness that had cloaked a mounting sense of irritability in the earlier session. In its place was a freshness, a revitalised energy from three musicians still to appreciate just what it was they were creating.

That two minutes of intense musicianship was the catalyst, more than half a century later, for me to be standing on the very spot where the three young men had exchanged delighted, excited glances as the song took off with a momentum seemingly of its own – one that came from somewhere within the young Elvis Presley and which had swept up the not much older but experienced guitarist and bass player with it.

The rest of our little tour group posed for awed pictures at what is reputed to be the microphone Elvis used that day. There was a respectful hush, as if we were straining to hear whether any of the remarkable sounds that had been absorbed by the cursory soundproofing all those years ago might leak back into the room.

We all stood for a few moments trying to appreciate the significance of what happened in this room. Not just in terms of what Elvis did here, but also the likes of Johnny Cash, B. B. King, Roy Orbison, Carl Perkins, Muddy Waters and Jerry Lee Lewis, all of whom poured their very souls into the slowly revolving wheels of Sam Phillips's tape decks to produce songs that changed the world of popular culture. A large picture dominates one end of the room. In it Elvis sits at the piano, his fingers spread for an unseen chord. He's half turning to look at the trio of men behind him, his lips slightly pursed as he sings a song. His eyes are focused on Jerry Lee Lewis, in high-waisted slacks and casual sweater, arms behind his back, curls flopping over his forehead as he joins in the singing. Next to him, Carl Perkins leans forward in his dark shirt, lips tight with concentration as he watches Elvis's fingers to follow the chord progression he's imitating on the guitar. Behind Perkins Johnny Cash leans forward, slightly apart from the other three, mouth enunciating whatever song Elvis has started playing. It's an iconic image, and the picture hangs over where the legendary 'Million Dollar Quartet' session actually took place. Four of Sun's biggest stars happened to be at the studio at the same time one afternoon in December 1956, the end of the most meteoric year of Elvis's entire career. Jerry Lee Lewis, then relatively unknown, was playing piano for Carl Perkins when Elvis dropped by and led a session at the piano. Johnny Cash, at Phillips's behest, dropped in briefly to complete arguably the most stellar gathering of popular musical talent in history.

The things that struck me most about the picture as I stood looking at it were Elvis's eyes. There's a happiness in them that would largely disappear in the ensuing years, but here it's the thing that draws you into the photograph. Here is Elvis at his happiest – he's at the piano playing the gospel music he loves more than anything else. They might be the biggest rock 'n' roll stars of the moment, but in Elvis's eyes they're just a bunch of guys around a piano. This picture more than any shows that despite the hype, despite the controversy (1956 was the year of his waist-up television appearances), despite the unprecedented celebrity, it was in the music itself that Elvis was happiest. Nowhere was it better illustrated than in this image, with his peers, at the height of his powers, in the place that launched him on to an unsuspecting world.

This otherwise nondescript building tacked on to the side of a diner at a junction on the outskirts of Memphis city centre now attracts pilgrims from all over the world. It's probably too sweeping a generalisation to say that without Sun Elvis would not have happened, but it doesn't really bear thinking about. Elvis and Sun will always be inextricably linked.

Still awed, I went back to the café. The third booth from the window, Sam Phillips's unofficial office, isn't there any more so I ordered a cup of coffee and sat down at the closest table to where it would have been, with a view of the counter where the tour guides took bookings and cash. I noticed a sign behind the till. Record a song at Sun Studio, it said, for thirty dollars. For your thirty smackers you got to pick a song out of a big karaoke folder and go into the studio itself and record it, taking home a CD with your very own Sun Records label on it.

Sun Studio gets it right, every time. Although it's an absolute must for the thousands of people who come to Memphis and could have become a typical, tacky, pack 'em in, turn 'em upside down and shake out every last bit of loose change then ship 'em out affair, Sun seems to retain the relaxed openness that characterised its heyday. The staff are all young, and share tour guide and counter-service duties; most are musicians themselves and have a quiet respect for the place. You can sit and have a coffee in the diner and stare into space, and no one gives you the skunk-eye about taking up space for too long. Once you finish the tour, the guide actually encourages you to hang around in the studio and savour the atmosphere, rather than herding you out into the street. I imagine it's a similar ethos to Sun in its prime, when Sam Phillips's door was always open even to a greasy-haired kid with curious sideburns and a battered old guitar. It's a cheesy old word, especially when used by a badly dressed man in his thirties, but for me Sun is the epitome of cool. They get it right.

As I finished my coffee, I realised that the chance to record a song in the same studio that Elvis made his first recordings was too good an opportunity to miss. And there was only really one song I could possibly do – I had, after all, performed it on Uzbek television, and of course with Howard at Tupelo Hardware. It had to be 'Blue Moon of Kentucky'.

One of the tour guides, Dave, led me back into the studio and directed me into a little recording booth with a microphone on a stand. He sat at the console in the control room, and I attempted a little muso to muso conversation. Casually, I dropped in my stone-cold winner of an anecdote about singing this very song on Uzbek television with that country's biggest pop star, but Dave was less than overwhelmed, probably because it turned out that his own band is a very successful one and would be touring the UK shortly.

'OK,' he said after a spot of knob-twiddling at the console, 'we'll go for one run-through, and then we'll do the take itself.'

He started the backing track, and I completely missed where I was supposed to come in. Not only that, when I did come in I realised that the song was in a much higher key than the one I used to employ to clear pubs in Hackney and which had the nation of Uzbekistan lunging for their remote controls. I missed the high notes by such a distance I almost met them coming the other way. It was probably the worst vocal performance the old walls of Sun Studio had ever had the misfortune to absorb.

'Well, heh heh,' I chuckled, desperate to put across to Dave that I knew just how appalling I'd been, 'that, er, that sucked.'

Dave said nothing. He didn't have to. 'Cool,' he said through the headphones after changing a few levels on the console. 'OK, let's do the take now. Just relax.'

This time I managed to hear the four clicks that counted the song in and hit the first note with a reasonable degree of proximity to its proper pitch and timing. Given my spectacular inability to reach even halfway to the high notes on my previous effort, I completely bottled out and went for a lower pitch. Determined to get it right, I stared intently at the television screen above me as the lyrics trundled across it, even though there are barely half a dozen words in the whole thing and I'd sung it a thousand times in the past.

The song was scarcely two minutes long, but it seemed to take for ever. Finally I croaked the last line and the closing chord echoed to silence. There was a faint hiss through the headphones for a few seconds, before Dave said, 'Cool', and invited me to step outside the booth. A couple of minutes of cursory shuffling and desultory self-deprecation on my part, and kind indulgence on Dave's, and I soon had my Sun Records-branded CD. We walked out of the studio together, and as I took one last look around its hallowed walls I reflected upon how rock 'n' roll was born here and how, on the very same spot, I had just killed it stone dead.

I set off along Union Avenue towards downtown Memphis and Beale Street. That one legendary venue of popular music is within comfortable walking distance of another emphasises how musically remarkable Memphis is. It's almost as if music is in the fabric of the place. As I walked the streets there was a feeling about the city that I couldn't quite put my finger on. It was only after a couple of days that I realised what: it was like those few minutes of expectancy just before a band comes on. The instruments are tuned and set up, there's a hiss coming through the PA, and the crowd is pregnant with excited tension. Memphis seemed to me to be in a constant state of this musical expectancy.

Beale Street is not, to be honest, very much to look at, but its place in the canon of popular music, not to mention African-American culture in general, cannot be overestimated. It is the home of the blues. And that's official – as designated by an Act of Congress in 1977.

Although its peak was probably the 1920s, Beale Street retains a shabby charm and a strong argument for being the beating heart of Memphis. Everyone who comes to the city is drawn here at some point, in the same way that the old bluesmen were drawn here from rural Mississippi and elsewhere. Named after a soldier of the Mexican American war of the 1840s, Beale Street first emerged as a centre of trading for ships on the nearby Mississippi river and a gathering point for freed slaves, as well as the headquarters of Ulysses S. Grant during the Civil War. By the 1860s it had become an important focal point for African-Americans, and in the 1890s was comprehensively refurbished, thanks in the main to Robert Church, the first black American millionaire, who had made a fortune from buying land cheaply during Memphis's crippling yellow fever epidemics in the late nineteenth century. He created Church Park at the corner of Fourth and Beale, where musicians would gather and speakers as notable as Woodrow Wilson and Franklin D. Roosevelt would come to hold forth.

However, it was a cornet player from Muscle Shoals, Alabama, named William Christopher Handy who was to put Memphis, and Beale Street in particular, on the musical map. Handy travelled extensively with minstrel shows, especially in the South but also as far afield as Chicago and Cuba, and became fascinated by a prototype music he found that became the blues. After several itinerant years, he settled in Memphis with his band the Mahara Minstrels and established himself and the band right here on Beale Street. That same year he wrote a campaign song for the legendary Memphis politician E. H. Crump called 'Crump's Blues', which three years later he reworked to become 'Memphis Blues'. It's for this song, the first recognisable twelve-bar blues composition, that Handy is known as the man who invented the blues. He became a prolific song composer, publishing the songs himself, and eventually moved to New York to start a record company, as well as his publishing firm. Such was his popularity that a benefit tribute concert was held at Carnegie Hall in 1938, his 'Beale Street Blues' was mentioned in F. Scott Fitzgerald's *The Great Gatsby* and Louis Armstrong played Handy's 'St Louis Blues' with the New York Philharmonic, conducted by Leonard Bernstein, at the Lewisohn Stadium in 1956. In addition, Handy and Duke Ellington are the only two people from jazz and blues to be honoured with a US postage stamp bearing their image.

The blues is a vital node on the musical journey that led to Elvis, Scotty and Bill's energetic reworking of 'That's All Right'. Ethnomusicologists have traced its roots to the western and central African traditional musics that travelled to North America with the slaves. The songs and chants mutated on the cotton plantations; the guitar and banjo became substitutes for the old African instruments like the kora and mbira; and in time the blues became the genre we know today, refined, if that's the right word, by W. C. Handy, and centred on a few yards of shambolic, sprawling buildings, juke joints and shops in Memphis, the final destination of pure blues after its long journey across the Atlantic.

In the 1920s the blues was transformed from a well-kept secret on the cotton fields and in tumbledown bars into a nationwide phenomenon. Beale Street was rough and dangerous – murder and violence were everyday occurrences. In fact a club called The Monarch became known as 'the castle of missing men', owing to the ease with which corpses produced by the often trivial disagreements could be disposed of, thanks to the back alley the place shared with an undertakers.

Things calmed down a little in the ensuing years, but by the 1960s Beale Street had gone into decline. It was only a concerted effort to preserve it in the 1980s that stopped the slide being terminal, and today the Beale Street pedestrian can appreciate a little of what made the place so special.

For a real flavour of the old Beale Street, however, I slipped through a door at the centre of an old glass-fronted shop front into one of the most amazing places I've ever seen. Admittedly it was a drizzly January afternoon and Beale Street wasn't exactly at its most bustlingly hedonistic. There was no traffic and only a few people mooched about hunched against the drizzle, but compared to the silence inside the building I had just entered the street was a cacophony of noisy roister-doistering.

Schwab's General Store is the oldest shop on Beale Street, having been there since 1876. By the looks of it, so has most of the stock. Inside the atmosphere is cool and quiet, and has the distinct mustiness of an ill-kempt museum. The wooden floorboards are old and creaky, and so are most of the staff. Still, it's not just age that makes Schwab's so extraordinary, it's the stuff it sells. Well, actually, maybe sells is the wrong word, as it soon became clear that my fellow shoppers, of whom there were just a handful, were there, like me, to gawp rather than purchase. Schwab's stocks some of the most bizarre tat you'll ever see; the sort of items my late cockney grandmother would have called 'a load of old toot'. Clothes in styles that no one has worn since about 1934, for example. Racks of postcards featuring Memphis landmarks pulled down years ago. Big buckets full of assorted rusty screws and lumps of metal of indeterminate purpose and origin. There are bottles and bottles of voodoo potions, and racks of elaborately alarming knives and swords, outsized denim overalls and hats. Lots and lots of hats.

Now I am someone blessed with a head of a distinctly odd shape, compounded by a not inconsiderable size. When I wore a morning suit to a wedding once, so vast was the size of my top hat that the local council insisted I install a flashing light on the top to warn approaching aircraft. Even an approximate gauging of the circumference of my bonce just above the ears requires several tape measures tied together. Local schools have sponsored bike rides around my head. If I met Joseph Merrick at a party, he would feel instantly better about himself.

Hats, then, are a problem for me. The frankly odd dimensions of my napper render most headgear ridiculous, which is a shame because I like hats. Nevertheless, on me hats sit tilted back on the very top of my crown, 'like a pimple on a football' as my mum used to say for a cheap laugh at the expense of my ensuing noggin-related psychological traumas.

I have never found a hat to fit me. They're either ridiculously small, or so big as to accommodate a small circus. Any peak or brim would take out whole buildings with a sudden turn of the head. Schwab's, though, seemed designed for a sideshow freak like me. Piles of hats of all sizes teetered alarmingly on tables. It seemed to be the kind of place that would stock outlandish sizes on the grounds that the law of averages guarantees that sometime over the next century someone of exactly those proportions would walk through the door. And here I was. Freaky Head Boy.

I began rummaging, upending piles of hats with the idea that the biggest would be at the bottom. I was tempted to put the entire stack on top of my head and wobble around the store like a millinerial caber-tosser, but elected instead just to make a mess. I tried on the biggest hat at the bottom of each pile, scattering the rest across the ranks of tables. Trilbies, fedoras, flat caps, panamas, I went through the lot. Some perched on the back of my head while others' brims brushed both end-walls of the shop simultaneously. I was whipping hats back and forth faster than a find-the-lady trickster on Charing Cross Road.

And finally it happened. Just as the assistants began to think I had some kind of psychotic grudge against millinery, I plonked a green fedora on top of my head. As I went to whip it off again, something felt weird. It was a new feeling I hadn't had before. The fedora's band clung to the right bits of my head. It didn't tilt back to look like a felt-green halo and its brim wasn't threatening passers-by with decapitation. I looked in the mirror. The hat fitted me. Properly. It even served to make my head look vaguely in proportion with the rest of me. I tilted it to a jaunty angle. It didn't fall off. I was stunned. For the first time in my life I had on my head a hat that fitted, was comfortable, and looked vaguely in proportion. Schwab's had come up trumps. There was just one problem. I looked like a complete twat.

I laid the hat back on the chaotic mess of titfers I'd created, and walked away whistling softly to myself, before trying to look inconspicuous among some piles of large women's pants gathering dust over in the corner.

Schwab's is about as close as you'll get to the original Beale Street these days, and even then there are no fights or casual murders (although if I'd messed with the hats for much longer

there might have been). It's also the only original building left on
the street that Elvis would have visited. Having grown up close
to the black areas of Tupelo and then Memphis, Elvis was about
as integrated an American citizen as there was in the early 1950s.
He was a regular visitor to Beale Street, and many people claim
to have met him. Their stories might sound spurious, but a
white kid hanging out on Beale Street would have been a rare
occurrence back then, and Elvis would have stood out, not least
dressed the way he was. His, for the time, outlandish appearance
was to a great extent the result of his regular shopping trips to
Lansky Brothers, a clothes emporium on a junction towards the
Mississippi end of the street founded by Guy and Bernard Lansky
shortly after the end of the Second World War. They specialised
in the sort of clothes the musicians of the time would have worn
on stage, the kind of sharp, colourful threads that Elvis favoured.

It was the Lansky Brothers who provided Elvis with his early
stage outfits, usually in the pink and black designs he liked most.
I walked along Beale Street from Schwab's, crossed the street and
found the corner premises that used to belong to Lansky's. The
shop moved out some years ago, to a location in the lobby of
Memphis's famous Peabody Hotel, and the hoardings outside
advertised the place currently as a diner and music venue called
'Elvis Presley's Memphis'. Elvis, mind you, appeared to have left
the building. Along with everyone else. And whoever was last
out had padlocked the doors. Curiously such a guaranteed
moneyspinner as an Elvis diner on the most musical, tourist-
mecca street of his home town had closed down, and some time
ago too by the looks of things. Even the Elvis statue across the
street, based on a famous early photograph of him with his guitar
swinging his hips and the focus of the tidy little Elvis Presley
Plaza, seemed deliberately to be looking the other way.

I stood outside the abandoned building wondering how such

a gold-mine as an Elvis diner here could fail, and headed back down Beale Street. All was quiet, other than the light speckling of drizzle on tarmac. There were fewer than half a dozen people on the street as I passed the various blues clubs and souvenir shops, before crossing to Handy Park, named for the great W. C. Handy himself and featuring a marvellous statue of the man, holding his cornet to his chest as if he'd just stopped playing, a wide smile across his lips. Nearby is the memorial to soul legend Rufus Thomas, a man as irrevocably linked to Memphis's musical heritage as Handy and Elvis. In fact these three men are arguably the most influential people in the groundbreaking music to come out of Memphis and it's no coincidence that all three have statues on Beale. Like Elvis and Handy, Rufus Thomas was not a Memphis native but grew to be closely linked to the city.

Born in Cayce, Mississippi, in 1917, Thomas's parents moved to Memphis when he was two years old. Originally a child tap dancer, Thomas joined the travelling vaudeville-style show the Rabbit's Foot Minstrels, but it was as a DJ that he made his first significant contribution to Memphis music. Thomas anchored a show on WDIA, a station that became legendary in the promotion of African-American culture and music. Although it began as a white, country music station in 1947, WDIA struggled to compete with other similar stations and almost in desperation offered a show to local black schoolteacher and impresario Nat D. Williams – the first show to be anchored by a black presenter in the US. Although nearly half of Memphis's population at the time was black, the institutionalised racism of the day meant that the community had, among numerous other disadvantages, no radio station or even dedicated programme before Williams took to the microphone (accompanied by bomb threats from local rednecks) in October 1948. The show was such a success that the station gradually became almost wholly staffed and presented by African-Americans, including Rufus Thomas. It was like Beale Street on the radio, which wasn't surprising given that it was just a couple of blocks away from Memphis's home of the blues. B. B. King got his first break on WDIA, having literally knocked on the door and asked for an audition, winning the right to record a jingle for an indigestion remedy.

WDIA became, by its own description, 'the mother station of negroes'. As the sole service aimed at African-Americans, it inevitably became a community station, whose role often went beyond simple announcements and good music. While in Memphis I visited the frankly amazing Stax Museum of Soul Music (Stax was a Memphis label, and a legendary studio where Elvis himself recorded later in his career) and noted down the following story about the role of WDIA word for word from a wall display; it was that astounding. It comes from WDIA DJ Dwight 'Gatemouth' Moore, and is reproduced in his words, demonstrating the grim reality of life under segregation and the difference that a simple radio station could make:

> I remember when the black ambulances could not haul
> white people. They had a white company, I'll never
> forget, called Thompson's. I was on my way to the
> station, and when I come around the curve there was the
> ambulance from S. W. Qualls with the door open, and
> there was a white lady laying in the ditch, bleeding. And
> they were waiting for Thompson's to come and pick her
> up. Qualls couldn't pick her up. I guess I waited thirty or
> forty minutes and still no ambulance. They tell me that
> the lady died. So I came to WDIA and told the tale. I
> said, 'Look here.' I said, 'Black folks put their hands in
> your flour and make your bread, they cook the meat,

they clean up your house, and here's this fine aristocratic white lady laying in the ditch bleeding and they won't let black hands pick her up and rush her to the hospital.' And the next week, they changed that law where a black ambulance could pick up anybody. I got that changed on WDIA.

Rufus Thomas became a key figure at WDIA, and broadcast on the station for the best part of thirty years. But it was as a recording artist that he would really make his mark. Indeed, he gave Sam Phillips his first major Sun hit with 'Bear Cat', an answer to Big Mama Thornton's 'Hound Dog' (later to be made famous by a certain pompadoured hipswinger who also started at Sun, of course). Thomas's version was close enough to the original for Sun to be sued for copyright infringement, but it set the studio and Rufus Thomas on the road to success.

He later moved to Stax, scoring a major hit in 1960 alongside his daughter Carla with ' 'Cause I Love You', and launching a successful career as one of Stax's prominent soul artistes. His late flowering and energetic stage show earned Thomas the nickname 'The World's Oldest Teenager', and he went on to have a massive hit with 'Do The Funky Chicken', which he memorably performed in 1972 at the legendary Wattstax concert (deemed the 'black Woodstock') in Los Angeles. Some 40,000 people at the stadium venue found themselves unable to resist doing the funky chicken at the behest of a fifty-five-year-old man in a bright pink jacket and matching shorts ('Ain't I clean?' he'd asked the crowd when he took the stage).

Thomas died in 2001, shortly after being inducted into the Blues Hall of Fame, and such was his influence on the music of Elvis's home town that the city named a street off Beale after him, and erected the granite memorial I now stood in front of.

As memorials go, it's probably the best I've seen. It's hard to describe what an enormous, effervescent character he was – any greatest hits compilation would give you an idea – but if I ever do anything remotely of note, I want a memorial like Rufus's. A white marble monolith, it features a smiling portrait of him encased, appropriately, in a star, above the following inscription:

RUFUS THOMAS

Ambassador of soul
The king of rhythm and blues
The funkiest chicken of the South

A star and veteran of service
To this community.

A man whose talents have endured
And whose performances have
Spanned the generations

Outspoken and outta sight.

When I go, I want a memorial stating that I too am 'the funkiest chicken of the South', even if the south is, in this case, south London.

The drizzle from the scudding Tennessee sky began to threaten full-blown rain, so I pulled up the collar of my coat and headed for one of Memphis's most famous landmarks. The Mississippi Delta, they say, begins in the lobby of the Peabody Hotel. A large Italianate building just north of Beale Street, the Peabody has for years been the venue for most of Memphis's most important gatherings, not least Elvis's 1953 high school prom, which he attended in a rented blue tux with fourteen-year-old Regis Wilson on his arm.

The lobby of the Peabody is a huge, airy space – a proper old-fashioned hotel lobby with a marble fountain at its centre. The afternoon I was there the lobby was, in contrast to Beale Street, packed with people, so I ducked through a doorway and into the place I'd really come to see, the Lansky Brothers clothes store. Signed guitars and photographs lined the walls, but the most eye-catching aspect of the shop was the racks and racks of shirts. Having spent the day under grey skies, my retinas weren't quite prepared for the assault of colour that now smacked into them. I blinked several times in order to adjust. There were shirts in every colour you could name and a few I bet you couldn't. Standing among the racks rearranging some shirts was a tall, handsome, balding man with white hair, clad in sharp black trousers and an immaculate red V-neck sweater over a shirt and tie and a tape measure around his neck. He bade me a good afternoon and continued switching coat-hangers around. I knew this had to be Bernard Lansky, the man who clothed Elvis Presley. We were the only ones in the shop and, with the glass door to the lobby closed, the only noise was the metallic tap and occasional squawk of the metal hangers being rearranged.

I wandered among the shirts, feeling a little nervous: this was, after all, a man who had known Elvis personally for many years. So far I'd not really come across anyone who had been close to the biggest cultural icon of the twentieth century. I'd hoped to meet Marty Lacker, one of the 'Memphis Mafia' and Elvis's best man at his wedding to Priscilla, but he had emailed me earlier in the day to say that due to a recent spell in hospital he wouldn't be well enough for us to get together. I stared long and hard at a nice dark-red short-sleeved shirt while trying to come up with a winning, memorable opening line to catch the attention of Mr Lansky.

'That's definitely the right colour for you,' said a deep voice from behind me. 'I'd say, looking at you, large would be your size.'

Any other total stranger approaching me and saying, 'Looking at you, large would be your size', would have received at the very least a spluttering tirade of indignance and, quite possibly, a forefinger in the eye, but I knew instantly that this was merely the professional opinion of a man who had cast his eye over countless frames and girths across the previous decades. Not least Elvis Presley's.

'Are you Mister Lansky?' I asked.

'Yes, sir, I am, Bernard Lansky.'

'The man who clothed Elvis,' I said.

'You're right about that,' he replied with a chuckle.

We stood and chatted for a while, and then I asked him if he remembered the first time he met Elvis.

'Put your arms up,' he replied. I lifted my arms without argument, and Mr Lansky pulled the tape measure from around his neck and in an instant had whipped it round me just below the armpits.

'Yeah, I remember the first time I saw Elvis,' he said. 'We were on Beale then, and there was this kid hanging around outside the window, so I invited him in. He looked around and said, "You have some beautiful merchandise in here. I don't have any money but when I get rich I'm gonna buy you out." I said, do me a favour, son, don't buy me out, just buy from me! Of course, the kid turned out to be Elvis Presley and he kept on coming back. He became almost an ambassador for me, telling everyone he got his clothes from Lansky's on Beale Street.

'Yes, sir,' he continued, examining the result of his measuring expedition around the Connelly ribcage, 'a large size would fit you just fine.'

I bought the shirt, and also on impulse picked up a pink and black one – most of Lansky's early clothes for Elvis were in pink and black. My friends might laugh up their sleeves at me, but, hey, I had a Lansky shirt, for which I was measured by the man who clothed Elvis Presley.

Clutching my Lansky's carrier bag, I shook Mr Lansky's hand and gushed about what a pleasure it had been to meet him just long enough for him to become slightly unnerved. I walked back into the Peabody with a big, stupid grin smeared across my big, stupid face. The lobby was still thronging with people, many of whom were clustered around the bar. I felt obliged to celebrate meeting the man who dressed Elvis by getting myself outside a very cold beer. Every stool was taken and I stood patiently behind the seated drinkers waiting for an opening. After a few minutes a young woman swung round and said that I was welcome to her stool as she was 'going to goose Randy'. I slid into her place and ordered a cold one.

I couldn't work out why, when the rest of the locality appeared to be practically empty, the Peabody lobby was packed. I got talking to the people next to me and asked why the bar was such a draw in the late afternoon of a drizzly midweek day in January. It turned out that most of the patrons were from the sales department of a country music station in Washington, and this was a bit of a beano for them and similar stations across the US. It was strange – the kind of corporate shenanigans you'd find in any number of hotels along the M4 corridor, only instead of the chat being about bathroom fittings, the new Lexus and the girl from reception it was about Billy Ray Cyrus, the new Lexus and the girl from reception.

They were telling me some libellous stories about some of

country music's biggest names when suddenly we became aware of a small commotion behind us. It was then I realised that the hour was approaching 5 p.m., and it was time for the famous Peabody ducks to do their thing.

I'd timed my visit to the Peabody to coincide with the ducks' twice-daily promenade 'twixt lift and fountain. If you ever visit the lobby of this hotel between the hours of eleven and five, you may be startled to see a handful of live ducks in the ornate marble fountain in its centre. It's part of a tradition dating back to the 1930s, the result of a drunken prank that helped the Peabody to achieve worldwide fame.

No one remembers exactly when the hotel's general manager Frank Schutt and his friend went hunting in Arkansas one weekend, but it was sometime during the 1930s. After an enjoyable couple of days across the state line, the two men returned to the hotel and had a few drinks. With them they had a couple of ducks that they'd been using as decoys and, boozy old roisterdoisters that they were, they thought it would be a terrific wheeze to leave the ducks in the fountain, head for bed and imagine the reaction of the guests as they emerged from the lifts in the morning to find three mallards paddling in the lobby.

The reaction of the guests was clearly a favourable one, as there have been ducks in the fountain ever since. Indeed, in 1940 a Peabody bellhop and former circus trainer named Edward Pembroke volunteered to organise the daily march of the ducks from their rooftop palace to the fountains and back again, and for some reason decided that Sousa's 'King Cotton March' should play as the birds made their daily promenade. Pembroke remained duckmaster until his retirement in 1991 (and subsequently had a square named after him at a nearby property development).

I watched from my stool as the current duckmaster Daniel

Fox, resplendent in red blazer and gold duck-head-tipped cane, placed three red-carpeted steps against the fountain and smoothed out the red carpet that led from the foot of the steps to the lift. The Sousa march blared from the speakers, the ducks hopped one by one from the fountain to the top of the steps, descended as gracefully as a mallard dropping a distance equivalent to its own height can, and made their way slowly, regally and with the occasional haughty quack to the lift, where the duckmaster waited to escort them skyward to their rooftop lodgings. A round of applause echoed around the lobby, the show was over, and the conversation returned to various girls on reception at country stations all across America. The girls on reception, presumably, were in a huddle of their own discussing sexual harassment lawsuits.

I spent the evening on Beale, dining on catfish at B. B. King's blues club and repairing to the Rum Boogie Café to hear some terrific driving blues from a stage below one of the original Stax neon signs of the legendary Soulsville USA studio. Signed guitars adorned the walls from the likes of Joe Ely, Ike Turner, Sting, Elvis, Scotty Moore and, er, Kenny Loggins. As I waited on the corner for a taxi back to the Heartbreak and looked across towards the Handy statue and Rufus Thomas memorial, my ears still ringing slightly from the music, the flashing neon of Beale to my left, I thought about the amazing global impact this slightly shabby street and the surrounding blocks had had on popular culture, even on my upbringing in the anonymous suburban streets of south-east London. Elvis himself, whose voice I first heard coming through my dad's speakers, probably once stood where I was standing now. I thought too about the blues musicians of the Mississippi Delta, whose records I used to pick up for peanuts at Greenwich market and try to learn on my cheap old guitar shut away in my bedroom. They would have arrived here at this street at the end of the physical and spiritual journeys that fuelled their music, all shabby suits, cardboard suitcases and battered guitars slung over their shoulders, looking for a place to fit in. Some of the great soul sides to which I'd danced enthusiastically badly at teenage parties were recorded a short walk away. I was definitely falling for Memphis in a big way. I loved the fact that most of its traditions had insalubrious roots – how the reputation of Beale Street was borne out of notoriety, how the long-standing tradition that made the city's poshest hotel world-famous was started by a couple of drunks mucking about – and hence made the place seem more alive, somehow.

Memphis, USA, Part 2

The next day was one of the biggest in the Memphis calendar: Martin Luther King Day, the birthday of the greatest civil rights leader the world has yet seen. King had been assassinated here in Memphis on the balcony of his room at the Lorraine Motel, now the National Civil Rights Museum. Memphians have always had a hard time dealing with the fact that Dr King was killed in their city. While there weren't the same riots that flared in other cities across the nation in the wake of 4 April 1968, there was a definite cooling of relations between the black and white communities. At Stax, for example, where black and white musicians and staff worked closely together, the King assassination was the catalyst for the gradual decline of the studio and label, and its eventual demise. There had been strong links between Stax and the Lorraine Motel – many artists recording at Stax would stay there. Indeed, Steve Cropper and Eddie Floyd wrote 'In the Midnight Hour' in Wilson Pickett's room at the Lorraine, and also penned 'Knock On Wood' there, but the divisions caused by King's death polarised the black and white neighbourhoods and contributed to the end of the great Memphis label.

The city, almost as if attempting to wash away the stigma, flattened much of the area around the motel and Beale for redevelopment (somebody once said that Memphis had bulldozed more history than other cities had history). The Lorraine itself remained open until 1982 – with King's room, 306, locked permanently – until being opened as the National Civil Rights Museum in 2002. Each year the museum, for which I was heading, stages a day of events to commemorate Martin Luther King Day.

I took the free Sun Studio shuttle bus to Union Avenue and popped into the café for a coffee and to work out the best way to get to the museum, when I heard some female English accents trying to arrange a taxi. They sounded familiar; I'd seen them at breakfast back at the Heartbreak that morning, so I lurked nearby trying to appeal to their maternal instincts with an expression that fell somewhere between boyish innocence and cheerful familiarity.

Somehow it worked and within minutes the five of us were squeezed into a taxi – me gallantly in the front seat while the four ladies crammed into the back in a fashion that would have had Picasso sucking a thoughtful tooth and reaching for his paintbox. This affected the suspension so much that when I went to close the door I found it was jammed hard against the pavement. It took considerable tugging, grunting, scraping and paint removal to shift it and allow us on our way.

My fellow travellers, it turned out, were Marje, Lena and Karen from a solicitors' office in Cirencester, and Karen's mum Eve. I asked what brought them to Memphis.

'Last summer we all happened to watch *Elvis by the Presleys* on TV,' explained Marje. 'We all went into work the next day and sat talking about the programme, how interesting it was, and one of us said how much she'd love to go to Graceland. It turned out we all did, and then Karen happened to mention that her mum was a big fan and had always wanted to go but thought she never would, so we all said, well, why don't we go then?'

'I don't think any of us were particularly great fans before we got here,' said Karen, 'apart from my mum, who's always loved him. But we were interested enough to come to Memphis and find out more, as it seemed like he was more interesting than the usual rock 'n' roll star. Plus we thought it would make a nice holiday. We're all Elvis fans now, though. He really was something special. I was only little, but I remember the day Elvis died and Mum and her friend were sitting at home with lighted candles and crying because they were so sad.'

But what, I asked from the comfort of the front seat to the tangle of limbs behind me, makes Elvis so special? What is it about him?

'Apart from the good looks, the talent, the voice, the showmanship and the sex appeal, you mean?' said Lena, triggering a quartet of giggles. 'In England we had Cliff Richard, for goodness' sake. There's really no comparison is there? I was saying the other night in the hotel bar, how can one human being be so good-looking and have so much talent? He just had everything, and more.'

'Most of us just muddle along with none of those gifts but he wasn't big-headed about it,' said Eve, picking up the baton. 'He was still polite, charming, kind and a nice person. People should remember how generous he was to his family and friends too, giving away cars, houses, money to charity – all sorts. He came from a very poor, humble background and never forgot that. He obviously got pleasure from giving and helping people out. He had no colour prejudice either, despite the segregation that went on back then; he loved working with all musicians, black or white. That's the great thing about Memphis – it's a melting pot of people and music. It's a really special place.'

'We were all very moved by Graceland, weren't we?' said Marje, to affirmative murmurs when I said I was saving a trip to Elvis's home for the end of my visit. 'Right from putting the guided-tour headphones on at the entrance and hearing Elvis singing 'Welcome to My World', we were all choked; it sent shivers down your spine, it was as if he was speaking to us and he was still there. In fact some people in our group thought he was still living upstairs, where you weren't allowed to visit. To be honest, Graceland was a lot more tasteful than we expected, not as tacky as we thought it might be, and the fact that the place was left exactly as it was made it feel as if he could have just walked out. It felt very personal and comfortable, as if you could just sit on the couch and make yourself at home.'

'Yes, it definitely made you feel very close to Elvis,' said Karen as we pulled up at the Civil Rights Museum. 'I think we have more respect and appreciation for him now, probably because we understand him a bit better, although he was obviously a very complex man. I didn't know about his charity work, what a family man he was, all that kind of stuff. The atmosphere in the house was special and quite difficult to describe.'

I sprung out of the taxi bidding the driver a cheery farewell, and waited for the ladies to extricate their limbs from each other like the aftermath of an international-standard game of Twister, and we made our way into the museum. It turned out to be probably the best museum I've ever been to. I have to confess to being largely ignorant of most of the American struggle for civil rights, and the yawning gaps in my knowledge were all filled, rendered, plastered and tastefully wallpapered by the superbly crafted displays. Starting right back at the very beginning of the slave trade in the early seventeenth century, you pass through the centuries of horrendous abuse and oppression, learning about the men and women who put the pieces into place for the likes of

Dr King to lead his people to a better world. People like Harriet Tubman, the 'Moses of the South', an escaped slave who in the middle of the nineteenth century helped countless others escape north to a measure of freedom, and Booker T. Washington, political leader and educator, who did much to advance the education of African-Americans around the turn of the twentieth century.

There was also Ida B. Wells, a fearless crusader against the lynchings of blacks that were all too common occurrences – between 1882 and 1968 there were 4743 reported lynchings in the US. The real figure is probably much higher than that. The museum pulled no punches, displaying photographs taken at lynchings of smiling white men posing beside lifeless black corpses hanging from trees or, in one case, next to the still sizzling body of a young black boy. What struck me most was the clearly casual way in which these atrocities were carried out. The white men, and it was all men, made no attempt to hide their identities. They all smiled for the camera with tangible pride, as if they were fishermen posing with a particularly spectacular catch.

The walk through the museum continued, through the foundation of the National Association for the Advancement of Colored People in 1909, the horrific 1955 murder of fourteen-year-old Emmett Till, lynched for apparently whistling at a white woman in a shop, the Freedom Rides and bus boycotts, to an inspiring Rosa Parks exhibit, where you boarded a bus to find a statue of her – she had died a matter of weeks before my visit – being harangued by the driver and ordered to move to the back of the bus. Then it was on to the 1960 sit-in by four black students at the lunch counter of a Woolworth's store in Greensboro that led to similar actions in no fewer than fifty-four cities, a major step towards integration, and then to a reconstruction of

King's famous 'I have a dream' speech at the climax of the 1964 march on Washington.

In April 1968 Martin Luther King came to Memphis to support the city's striking sanitation workers. On 3 April he gave his famous 'Go up to the mountain' speech and the following evening, just after 6 p.m., he went out on to the balcony of his room to greet a musician friend who had just arrived in the car park below. Suddenly, seemingly from nowhere, a bullet tore into his throat. He crumpled to the floor and within minutes was dead. A wreath hangs on the balcony over the spot where he fell, but the most moving aspect comes at the end of the journey through the museum, when you enter Room 306 itself.

Thanks to Walter Lane Bailey, who owned the motel and kept the room locked for so long, the museum has been able to reconstruct Dr King's room exactly as it was the moment he was assassinated. What strikes you most is the sheer banality of the scene for an incident that had worldwide ramifications. The curtains are closed. One of the beds has its orange nylon eiderdown disturbed, an unopened newspaper lies tossed casually on the other bed, never to be read. A nearly full cup of black coffee sits atop the dresser, close to an ashtray filled with butts. A carton of milk stands open, its spout gaping, and there's an abiding sense that the occupant has just popped out for a second.

The museum was absolutely heaving with people so it was impossible to linger in front of the perspex window and we filed past at a slow, respectful pace. There was a humble silence almost out of place with the everyday, unspectacular scene in front of us. This was Martin Luther King the human being we were seeing. Not the man behind a bank of microphones delivering the timeless genius oratory of the 'I have a dream' speech, nor the determined man at the head of the march to Selma, but the man who'd just had a couple of cigarettes, made himself a coffee and glanced at the front page of the newspaper not realising he had only a matter of minutes to live. Remarkably he had given a speech the previous evening in Memphis in which he made reference to his own possible demise. It's immortalised in iron on the gate across the street that leads you to the other part of the museum – the former boarding house from where the fatal shot was apparently fired.

'I may not get there with you,' he said almost exactly twenty-four hours before his murder, 'but I want you to know that we as a people will get to the promised land.'

Upstairs in the building across the street is the bathroom from where the shot was supposedly fired by James Earl Ray, although there are a number of conspiracy theories that place Ray in a similar patsy role to Lee Harvey Oswald. These theories are investigated in detail by a large display outside the shabby bathroom from where the gun was purportedly fired (the sash window remains open a fraction, just as it was discovered after King's assassination). Only two of Ray's fingerprints were found on the weapon, for example, while the bathroom itself betrayed none of his prints whatsoever. His army record showed no aptitude for marksmanship, and although he had a long record as a petty criminal, he did seem to be a distinctly rubbish one: after each incident it wasn't long before he had his collar felt by Mr Plod. Yet after the King assassination he was apprehended at London's Heathrow Airport travelling on an expertly forged Canadian passport. Even his alleged white-supremacist motive left acquaintances scratching their heads, as no one could recall Ray expressing any strong opinions on the subject at all.

Almost overwhelmed by the sheer weight of information about every conceivable conspiracy theory on display, I returned to the plaza between the two buildings, where a small stage and concession stalls had been set up. I lingered for hours, watching a procession of rap acts, R&B turns and gospel choirs, and gnawing at a roasted turkey leg so large the bird it used to support must have been on steroids. It took a while for me to realise it, but it dawned on me that I was just about the only white face in the place. The atmosphere was relaxed and celebratory, despite the fact it had taken many years to have King's birthday recognised as a holiday – the only public holiday dedicated to an African-American. The campaign began not long after the assassination, but it was not until 1986 that it was ratified by Congress, after Stevie Wonder's international hit 'Happy Birthday' and the largest petition in American history – six million signatures – finally persuaded the powers that be that King deserved a public holiday. It took until 2000 for all fifty US states to observe the holiday, however. Memphis, perhaps understandably, embraces the day more than most cities.

I stayed at the museum until the late afternoon. In contrast to the grey drizzle I'd experienced since arriving in Memphis, it was a spring-like day and the sun felt warm on my face as I sat on a low wall, greasy-mouthed from the turkey leg, watching the vast queue of people snake away around the corner. As they waited patiently for admission I felt a sense of contentment at the progress made since Dr King fell.

That evening I went to see my first-ever live basketball game. There were two reasons why I chose to go and see the Memphis Grizzlies play the San Antonio Spurs in the NBA. First, Elvis had been a fan and frequently attended matches in Memphis, and second, it was a special occasion – the fourth annual Martin Luther King Day celebration game.

I have never been a basketball fan, despite having played in a match that contained what may well be a unique piece of basketball history. The scene was a gymnasium at a school in south-east London, and two teams of fourteen-year-olds in out-of-shape white T-shirts, shorts and squeaky plimsolls were going through the motions of lumbering up and down the court trying, and usually failing, to lob a big orange ball through a hoop. Half-time arrived and the game remained predictably low-scoring. Right from the second-half whistle, however, Richard Williams grabbed the ball and hared off towards the end of the court. After some impressive technique, a hop, a skip and a flick of the wrist, the ball kissed the backboard and dropped through the hoop. Richard turned away in triumph to the expected acclaim of his teammates, but instead was greeted with open-mouthed amazement by everyone in the place. He'd forgotten we'd changed ends, and hence had just scored what might be the only 'own basket' in the history of the game.

Otherwise basketball has always left me a little bit cold. It seems to me that the game starts and each team takes it in turns to dunk the ball in the basket until the final whistle goes. Games are, I think, contractually bound to finish with the teams no more than two points apart. Why not save everyone a lot of time and trouble and just play the last thirty seconds? Or at least find other ways of making things interesting – introducing an angry warthog on to the court when play starts to drag particularly badly, for instance. Other dull sports could be livened up in similar ways. Every boxing match could have a monkey with a soda siphon sitting in each corner, squirting the combatants whenever they came near, while the drivers in Grand Prix races should each do one nominated lap of the race on a skateboard. Trust me, the public would love it.

Having grown up watching football in England, the American sporting experience proved to be something quite different. Well, obviously basketball's indoors for a start, but the entire culture is completely different. I'm not used to being treated,

well, like a human being at a sporting event. The main difference, though, is that the game itself is viewed as the main focus
of a whole evening's entertainment, not the be-all and end-all.
Having been hanging around town all day, I arrived at the FedEx
Arena, a stone's throw from Beale, very early. At an English
football ground you'd most likely be greeted by padlocked gates,
or at the very least grumpy, shaven-headed stewards in fluores-
cent jackets. At the FedEx you're welcomed into the building,
given a free, glossy programme (for which you'd be lucky to get
change from a fiver in England) and offered a range of dining and
drinking experiences. At random I picked the Jack Daniel's
Sports Bar, not far from the main entrance. As soon as I walked
in, a camp man with a Village People moustache called out from
behind the bar, 'Say, buddy, you ready for a cold beer?' Now at
Charlton Athletic you'd have been served, eventually, by a pasty-
faced teenager who wouldn't have said a word to you. Here it's
different. Given that I evidently looked like a man in need of a
cold beer, I thought it would be rude not to indulge. I perched
on a stool at the bar and he started to chat about the intricacies
of the game I was about to see. It was all off-fence, dee-fence,
steals and assists, and while I politely nodded and smiled, I hadn't
the foggiest what he was on about. He soon realised that his tac-
tical nous was falling on stony ground, and I explained that I
wasn't really a basketball fan. He asked if I knew where I was sitting and once I'd shown him my ticket, he produced a diagram
of the arena and pointed out my seat with the tip of a cocktail
stirrer.

Two middle-aged women next to me then pulled out their
tickets and asked where they were sitting. He glanced at the
small pieces of card and said, 'Oh, you have *good* seats.'

I soon found out why. I wasn't just up in the gods, the gods
themselves had to crane their necks upwards to catch a glimpse

of me. The arena consisted of three large steeply banked tiers and
I was three rows from the back of the top one. The court seemed
a long, giddy way below, like a small panel of pine flooring at the
bottom of a well and as someone with a notoriously bad head for
heights I decided to while away the time before kick-off, or
whatever they call it in basketball, by burying my head in the
programme, whose cover was a simple close-up picture of
Martin Luther King's face. I tried to gen-up on the game I was
about to see, and learned that this was the back-end of a home-
and-home series. Opponents San Antonio Spurs' 89.2 allowed
per game ranked second in the NBA, while two lightning-quick
guards would be running the point, and Michael Finley, originally the team's sixth man, had been starting at the two-guard.
So that cleared everything up nicely.

The FedEx was beginning to fill up, with the courtside cameras picking out random faces in the crowd and beaming them to
the arena via the big screens. There's always a certain ritual
involved with this, whereby a person appears on the screen reading the programme, picking their nose, or just staring vacantly
into the middle distance, suddenly catches sight of their phizog
in giant glorious Technicolor, jumps slightly, tugs at the sleeve of
their neighbour while pointing at the screen and then, and this
must be a joke among camera operators around the world
because it happens absolutely everywhere, as soon as the companion is about to look in the direction their gibbering friend is
pointing, the shot switches to someone completely different.
You can just imagine the original screen star saying, 'But . . .
but . . . we were on there! On the screen!' and receiving merely
the slight raising of a doubtful eyebrow in response.

A blues band, naturally, played on a stage at one end of the
arena until it was time for the teams to take to the court. The
MC suddenly burst into life, announcing in a chocolate-covered

baritone that apparently it was 'grizzle time' (presumably where everyone bursts into irritable tears) and that we should welcome 'your very own Memphiiiiiiis Grrrrrrrrrrrrrrrrrizzlies'. Alarms sounded, strobes flashed, thunderous music caromed around the eaves and a handful of giants ran on to the court at which point the music faded to the throaty growl of a grizzly bear. I then realised that being up this high had its advantages – the players were gigantic. It was almost as if I could reach out and ruffle their hair.

Our MC then introduced some very special guests to sing the national anthem. When he announced them as the Blind Boys of Alabama, I all but fell off my seat. The name may not mean much to most people, but the Blind Boys are one of the greatest and most extraordinary gospel acts in the history of music. Even though they were formed as far back as 1939 at the Alabama Institute for the Negro Blind, there are still three original members in the group, who have won two Grammies and been inducted into the Gospel Music Hall of Fame. In terms of stature it was a little bit like the Rolling Stones playing during the half-time interval at Birmingham City. They produced a spine-tingling a cappella rendition of 'Hail to the Chief' before the cheerleaders and razzmatazz took over once again. There was, though, one more pause in the proceedings before the game began, in a symbolic moment of silence for Rosa Parks. At its conclusion, the camera picked out members of Parks's family, who received a heartfelt standing ovation.

The game was the usual basketball affair of unnecessarily tall men running up and down the court taking it in turns to plonk the ball in the basket, while during time-outs and the break between the first two quarters the cheerleaders came on and did their stuff and boys in Elvis jumpsuits flung souvenir T-shirts into the crowd. The real action, however, eclipsing the haemorrhage of statistics that basketball fans mistake for excitement, happened at half-time when Morgan Freeman strolled on to the court to call back the Blind Boys to deliver an incendiary a cappella 'When the Saints Go Marching In' that had the whole place jumping. Blind Boy Jimmy Carter, a sprightly member of the original 1939 line-up, exhorted the spectators to greater effort by exclaiming, 'I can't see ya, so I need to hear ya!'

The place was still buzzing when Freeman presented two Martin Luther King Sports Legacy awards, one to former Boston Celtics player Bill Russell — who spoke emotionally of how he'd been in the third row when Dr King gave his 'I have a dream' speech and said, 'Today reminds us that we should never forget the dream he had for all of us' — and the other to Mannie Jackson, the owner of the Harlem Globetrotters.

The rest of the game was an anticlimax. The Grizzlies, who had led at the halfway point, ended up getting, in basketball terms, a total battering, and most of the fans had long gone by the time things limped to a halt with the home side trailing by ten points.

Back at the hotel, I was just unpeeling my clothes, thanks to the monsoon that had half drowned me on the way back, when the phone rang in my room. I picked up the receiver and said a tentative hello. 'Charlie?' said a soft voice with a distinct Tennessee twang. I replied in the affirmative. 'Hi Charlie, it's Marty Lacker here.'

I nearly dropped the telephone. Marty was, of course, Elvis's close friend whom I'd hoped to meet while in Memphis, but whose recent illness seemed to have dictated that I'd get no closer to Elvis than his clothier. Marty had also been a major contributor to the best book about Elvis to be published in a decade, *Elvis and the Memphis Mafia*, which lay recently read on the table in front of me.

'I felt bad having said I couldn't meet you,' he said, 'so we could have a talk now over the telephone if that's OK?'

'Yes,' I gibbered, desperately scrabbling around for a notebook and pen, 'that's fine, Marty, thanks.'

When I'd regained as much composure as I could, I asked him how he and Elvis first met.

'Well, I was born in New York, in Brooklyn, and grew up in the South Bronx. We moved to Memphis not long before I was to leave high school, and I was in the same year as Elvis. We weren't actually friends then, but we dressed in a similar way and he had his pompadour hairstyle that made him stand out.'

When Marty left school he was taken on as a management trainee at a Memphis department store, and didn't give his former classmate much further thought until one July night in 1954.

'I was driving down the street in a friend's car, and we had Dewey Phillips's WHBQ show on the radio.'

Phillips, no relation to Sam, was an influential Memphis disc jockey with a manic style. Sam Phillips had given him a copy of the acetate of 'That's All Right', and on the night Marty and his friend were driving through Memphis Dewey played it over and over again, back to back. The station switchboard went into meltdown. Elvis had arrived.

'Dewey was making a big fuss about how the kid singing on this record was from Humes [High School],' said Marty, 'and as we listened we couldn't think who it could be. When he said it was Elvis, neither of us could believe it.

'The next time I actually saw him, though, was at the opening of the Lamar Airways shopping centre where I was working.

I went outside on my break and there were Elvis, Scotty and Bill playing on the back of a truck. Elvis caught sight of me, pointed and grinned, but we didn't speak, and two months later I went into the Army and was shipped to Germany. While I was away, he really hit the big time and when I got back he was a huge star.'

A few months after returning from the Army, Marty received a call from a mutual friend of his and Elvis's, asking if he fancied going over to Graceland that night.

'He only asked me because I could drive and he couldn't,' said Marty, 'and Graceland is a way out of town. So I said, sure, why not. I remember clearly that as we walked up behind the house after parking the car, Elvis and his then girlfriend Anita Wood were walking from the barn in the back to meet us. He was wearing a black and white polka dot shirt and said, "I hear you just got out of the Army." I said, "How do you know?" Elvis said, "Well, I keep track of some people." Then we went into the house and shot some pool, and after that I'd hang out with him whenever he was in Memphis. They were great times – he'd rent the skating rink or the amusement park and we'd have the places to ourselves – but then of course in fifty-eight he went into the Army himself. The last time I saw him before he went off for his training was when he'd just done some recording in Nashville and he played me some of the songs at Graceland.'

While Elvis was away in the Army, Marty continued to carve out the successful career in radio that he'd commenced on his return from the military.

'I was a DJ and a production manager at a Memphis station when Elvis came back from Germany, and I carried on hanging out with him at Graceland. One night in 1961 we were shooting some pool and out of the blue he asked me to go and work for him. Now at the time I had a wife and a young child so it was a big decision for me. A lot of the other guys had no ties so it was easier for them to go off with Elvis. I said I'd need time to think about it, which made him mad as he didn't like people saying no to him. He went off into another room, and eventually I followed. He was sitting reading a newspaper, holding it right in front of his face so I couldn't see him. I said, "Elvis, I'm married, I need time to think about this." This voice from behind the newspaper said, "Well, don't think too long as we're leaving for Hollywood at two o'clock tomorrow". Anyway, the long and the short of it was that my wife wasn't happy, but I went to Hollywood anyway.'

When superstardom hit Elvis like it had never hit anyone before, he surrounded himself with familiar and trusted people, an inner circle that became known as the 'Memphis Mafia'. Elvis was rarely out of the company of his chosen few, whom he employed as bodyguards, tour managers and gofers. Marty would become a key part of that circle.

'Elvis asked me to be the foreman of the group, his right-hand man,' he said, 'which I did for a few years, and it was great until the end of 1967 when the atmosphere changed because of Priscilla.'

Things didn't always go smoothly prior to that, though. At the end of 1966 Marty's brother-in-law was asked to redesign Elvis's bedroom – something that led to Marty being asked to perform an important duty for his friend and employer.

'He came back from making a film, and my sister and brother-in-law had this little ceremony where they placed him outside the double doors and opened them in front of him. Elvis was absolutely overwhelmed; he had tears in his eyes. Vernon hated that and later told Elvis some lies about my brother-in-law, said he'd stolen some soft toys from the house, something Elvis later found out wasn't true. I didn't know about this and the next afternoon went up to the house, obviously expecting Elvis to still be in a good mood. As soon as I walked in he leapt up and started yelling at me and calling my family all sorts of things. Well, naturally I was pretty offended. I was hurt and mad, told him what he and his father could do to themselves and just walked out, staying away from the house for about four days. Eventually I went back, entered the basement den and there were two of the guys down there, sitting on stools at the soda fountain. Elvis and Vernon were sitting watching one of Elvis's movies on the TV – which was unusual, he didn't normally watch his own films – so they had their backs to me. Suddenly Elvis got up, and I didn't know if he was going to yell at me or what. Vernon looked a little scared – he clearly didn't know what Elvis was going to say. Finally Elvis said, "Hey Moon (which was my nickname), how you doing?" I said, fine, and he said, "Well I'm glad you came up." And then he said, "Look, I'm sorry." I'd never heard him apologise before, he never said sorry to anyone, he'd just buy them something. I said to him, "Elvis, please don't ever do that again."

'Elvis told me that Priscilla's father was threatening to go to the media and reveal that Elvis'd been living with a sixteen-year-old. He also said he would sue him for breach of promise if Elvis didn't marry Priscilla. I said, "Tell him to go fuck himself." Then Elvis said, "Moon, I'm going to marry her and I want you to be my best man. Remember what happened to Jerry Lee Lewis when he married his thirteen-year-old cousin, I can't take that chance. I spoke with Colonel Parker and he advised me to do it."'

Unfortunately Marty wasn't too enamoured with his friend's choice of bride, and it appeared that the feeling was mutual.

'Priscilla never liked me because I would never do her bidding,' said Marty. 'I think she's hard and cold. Elvis never wanted her to be involved in the running of the estate, but she's been pretty slick. When Elvis died she tried to make out that she was the grieving widow, when she'd been divorced from him for four years. She wasn't in his will at all when he died, but Vernon, who was the executor, fell sick and she kept nagging at him about being in charge.

'At this time I'd moved to California, but was about to move back to Memphis; this was 1979. The night before the move Priscilla came to see me, which was weird, you know? She asked me to go to Vernon and persuade him to make her executor of Elvis's will. I didn't really say anything, and she said that Elvis had said he'd give her father a hundred thousand dollars to open a liquor store in California but, and these were her exact words, "then he went and died".

'Of course, I said no. After she said that I thought to myself, Hell no. But on his deathbed Vernon made the bank, the accountant and Priscilla joint executors, with the bank forming a team of advisers, plus businessman Jack Soden for Priscilla. Now she gets the credit for opening Graceland to the public in 1982 when it was actually this advisory board and Jack behind her. I mean, let's face it, Scatter, Elvis's pet monkey, could have opened Graceland and made money.'

It was Priscilla's increasing influence on Elvis that in the end caused Marty to leave the organisation, and although he will always be associated with the Memphis Mafia, Marty also forged a successful career in the music business himself.

'By late 1967 I'd had enough. After they got married the atmosphere at Graceland had got really bad. Priscilla was getting more and more pushy and Elvis was constantly trying to appease her. I'd had an offer to start a record company, where I discovered Rita Coolidge, incidentally. Later I became involved with running the American Recording Studios here in Memphis, and in my time there we cut 153 hits in five years. Just before I became involved full-time, I managed to get Elvis to record the sessions that would include "Suspicious Minds" and "In The Ghetto".'

Despite leaving the organisation, Marty remained on good terms with Elvis.

'Elvis and I had a relationship that lasted twenty years,' he recalled. 'Even after I left in sixty-seven I was still hanging out with him if he was in town, and I went on the many tours too. He acted like I still worked for him sometimes, but I helped him out of friendship. The last time I saw him was towards the end of 1976, by which time he'd pushed a lot of us away. I spoke to him on the phone, and was last in touch with him about a month before he died.'

The Memphis Mafia have come in for a huge amount of criticism since Elvis's death. They're accused by some of being overprotective and overindulgent, even contributing to his early end by failing to tackle, or even actively encouraging, Elvis's drug use. Marty chuckles when I ask him about the criticism he and the other guys receive.

'Yeah, we laugh about that,' he said. 'The thing is that the people who criticise us have never met us or Elvis for even one minute. He was his own man. The only two people who could influence him were his father and Priscilla while they were married.

'With the drugs, well, I was as bad as him with the pills and stuff. In fact he got me on them in the first place. But you couldn't tell him anything. I gave up cold in October 1976 after fifteen years of constant pill abuse. Before I moved to California I wrote Elvis a letter telling him I was clean and how great I felt; even my sense of smell had improved. Later I heard that he read the letter and ranted and raved for a long while about how I was trying to interfere with him. That's the kind of guy he was – he pulled a gun on Red West once, and Red was one of his closest friends.

'We could have knocked him out and taken him to hospital, but they couldn't have stopped him leaving. He'd have just walked out. The people who say we didn't help him and even contributed to his death have no idea what they're talking about. We've been called leeches, parasites and hangers-on, but Elvis told us more than once that we gave him far more than he could ever give us. If we hadn't been around he would have been dead a lot earlier.'

Conscious that Marty was still recuperating from his illness, and that he'd been doing all the talking, I finished by asking him, as someone who knew Elvis better than just about anyone in the world, why he thought Elvis became the behemoth of popular culture that he remains today.

'Well, to put it simply, Elvis changed the culture of the world,' he explained. 'He liberated the teenagers and a lot of other people too. You have to understand the times – you had this goody two-shoes white music like Sinatra, Perry Como and Tony Bennett, while black music was relegated to a couple of small radio stations in Mississippi. The white kids were kept in their place; the music was clean and uncontroversial – white parents didn't want their children exposed to black music.

'Then along comes Elvis. A lot of white evangelists at the time were saying, we don't want this nigger music, as they called it, in our homes – they thought Elvis was black. But what he was doing was singing how he felt. He'd come up with this mixture of the black music he'd grown up with in Mississippi and coun-try music and it changed the world, not least by opening the blues up to a white audience. Also, he was good to people. He never refused a request for an autograph or a picture, and the celebrities who do even today never last the distance.

'What is it about Memphis? Well, we say that the music's in

the water here. Most people gravitated towards Memphis as it was the largest city in the region, so you had the poor white musicians and the poor black musicians all from similar backgrounds, all congregating in Memphis. And Elvis, well, he had the feeling in him from both sides.'

After I'd spoken to Marty, I switched on the television in the room to find airing on the hotel channel Elvis's NBC *'68 Comeback Special*, at the time his first appearance in front of a live audience for ten years. He was seated on a small stage in an informal setting with a group of musicians, familiar compadres like Scotty Moore and DJ Fontana, who played drums for Elvis on the early tours but who on this occasion drummed on an empty guitar case. As I switched on, they were just launching into a thunderous version of Lloyd Price's 'Lawdy Miss Clawdy'. Elvis, initially slightly nervous, soon lost himself in the music, his body taut and encased in a one-piece leather jumpsuit, restricted by being seated, and thrashing at the archtop guitar on his lap with barely controlled aggression. At the end of the song, he moved seamlessly into the old Jimmy Reed blues song 'Baby What You Want Me to Do', but taking it several notches faster than the original. There's a real passion about Elvis, a confidence that belied the fact he'd been away from live performance for a decade. He also looked impossibly handsome. His hair, sculpted into a pompadour at the start of the show, had soon flopped forward on to his forehead, his cheekbones were as defined as they'd ever been, and the charisma just oozed from every pore, even as I watched nearly three decades later. I'd seen the show a hundred times before and, for me, it's probably the pinnacle of his career. For someone who had been away from the musical spotlight, Elvis produced a performance masterclass. In addition, having just come off the phone to Marty, I felt more connected to Elvis somehow. For the first time ever watching the *Comeback Special*, most of which I could probably recite word for word, I could almost empathise with how he felt that day. The relief at the enthusiastic response of his first live audience in ten years, the passion bursting out of the music, the tangibly returning confidence – suddenly I was seeing it all, rather than just watching a man in a black leather suit singing catchy songs.

I lay in bed, the huge black and white print of a young Elvis looming out of the darkness above my head. I felt as though I'd got close to my quarry. Being at Sun, hanging out on Beale as Elvis had done, and meeting Bernard Lansky had all been worthwhile, and speaking to Marty, who had known Elvis better than most, had added another dimension. He was still an elusive, enigmatic figure but I felt I was getting nearer to understanding him and his continuing appeal.

The next morning, my last in Memphis, I headed for Graceland. Surely there, more than anywhere, I would find what I was looking for. It was a warm Tennessee morning, with only the odd smear of cirrus in a deep-blue sky, as I walked from the Heartbreak Hotel to Graceland Plaza. The sumptuously pro-portioned ticket office was clearly designed for busier days than this: as I tacked through the empty lanes of crowd-control bar-riers there was just a middle-aged couple declaring proudly to the person behind the one open ticket window far in front of me that they were from Wisconsin. Having shuffled away from the booth, tickets in hand, the couple were long gone while I con-tinued my zig-zag through the barriers. By the time I'd arrived breathless at the window, the ticket-seller had had time to pop off to see relatives in Nova Scotia. Having purchased my ticket I made my way outside to join a small queue waiting to board the minibus that would take us the short distance across Elvis Presley Boulevard and deposit us at the steps of the mansion. Two middle-aged women with Yorkshire accents joined the queue behind me. 'I just can't believe I'm actually here,' said one. 'To think that any minute now we're actually going to be walking through Elvis's front door,' said the other. 'I'm gonna cry, I just know I'm gonna cry,' said the first. 'If I faint,' said her friend, 'you will try and catch me, won't you?' She wasn't joking.

There was an awed silence as a Graceland employee passed along the line handing out our self-guided tour headsets like some strange audio communion ceremony. After having our pictures taken in front of a mural of the famous Graceland gates, we climbed aboard the minibus, listened to Elvis singing 'Welcome To My World' through our headphones, pulled out of Graceland Plaza, crossed the boulevard, passed through the gates and drove slowly around the sweeping drive to the mansion. We filed quietly off of the bus and gathered at the bottom of the steps up to the front door. I'd seen these steps in countless photos, not least the one of Elvis and Vernon sitting here distraught at Gladys's death in August 1958, arms around each other, absolutely bereft with grief.

The first thing that really strikes you about Graceland is how small it is. In terms of square footage, there are probably bigger houses on mock tudor estates in Cheshire, but there is a tangible and frankly surprising dignity about the place. The four classical columns that support the portico give the frontage a distinct elegance: even the lions rampant either side of the steps didn't strike me as tacky.

Graceland has a reputation as a shrine to tack and bad taste. Let it be said I don't claim to have any taste in interior design whatsoever – I still consider that nailing cheap clip frames containing pictures of W. C. Fields, Terry Thomas and Margaret Rutherford to my office wall looks pretty snazzy, for example. In spite of this I like to think I can spot tack when I see it, and confess to having relished the prospect of laughing behind my hand at some of the garish excesses inside the portals of Graceland. A couple of minutes inside the mansion, however, and I realised that I was subscribing to the snobbery that afflicts Elvis; the patronising guffawing that greets the question as to why a poor Southern white boy suddenly presented with riches beyond his dreams would only prove the adage that money can't buy class. The decor probably isn't to everyone's taste admittedly, but it certainly isn't point-and-laugh funny either. The living room to the right of the main door is decorated in restrained seventies style, complete with fifteen-feet-long white sofa, while the dining room to the left could come from just about any wealthy home in the South. The kitchen is relatively simple too, especially considering the gargantuan amounts of food that were apparently prepared in it to assuage Elvis's legendary appetite. The so-called Jungle Room – where Elvis asked Marty to be his best man – is the most exotic, with its range of ethnic furniture and trickling waterfall at one end, but even then it's not garishly tacky. There's even something vaguely tongue-in-cheek about it.

Downstairs the pool room catches the eye thanks to the pleated fabric that adorns the ceiling and walls – it took three workmen fully ten days to install – while the den is notable for the three televisions embedded in the far wall to allow Elvis to watch three channels at once. It's decorated in blue and yellow, with Elvis's seventies logo of a lightning bolt beneath the letters 'TCB', representing the phrase 'Taking Care of Business', painted on the centre of the wall – probably the most ostentatious part of the entire house.

Despite the thousands upon thousands of people who pass

through the mansion each year, Graceland sustains the feeling that you're in somebody's home. It certainly doesn't feel like a museum: when you stand in the hallway it's almost as if Elvis is about to come trotting down the stairs. The atmosphere in the den suggests that he and the guys have just popped out to throw a football around and you've missed them by minutes. Perhaps it's because Graceland remained the one constant throughout his career that there's still such a feel to the place despite the millions of feet that have passed over its carpets since its 1982 opening to the public. After every tour, film, television special, or recording session, Elvis would always come back here. It was the one place he was out of the public gaze, even though there was a constant gathering of fans outside the gates. At Graceland, Elvis could be himself. Whatever that meant. There was a palpable sense of life in the house, a real feeling of the size and buoyancy of Elvis's personality that has not been diluted even a fraction by the decades since his death.

From the back of the house I moved on to the sparsely furnished outbuilding that served as Vernon's office. It was here that Elvis gave his first press conference after leaving the Army (and famously, despite extensive reports of his fledgling romance with the then fourteen-year-old Priscilla, declared that she was nobody special) and where Vernon took care of the household affairs. A hand-stencilled notice was still pinned to the door. 'Please read and observe,' it demanded. 'No loafing in office. Strictly employees only. If you have business here, take care of it and leave.'

A television on top of a filing cabinet played the 1960 press conference on a permanent loop. Elvis looked outwardly relaxed and happy, if a little tired, and joked with reporters. He'd only been back in Memphis for a few hours and confessed that he'd not even had the chance to eat. Nor, presumably, had he had the chance to get used to the reality of the absence from the house of his mother, who had died just after he went into the Army. Elvis was given compassionate leave, but had to head off to Germany shortly after the funeral. It was only after the brouhaha surrounding his return had subsided that he would have felt the emptiness in the house, the absence of the most important person in his life, a void that would probably take years to dissipate.

The racketball building is arguably the most poignant part of the tour. The public are not admitted upstairs in the house itself, so Elvis's bedroom and of course the bathroom where he died on 16 August 1977 are out of bounds. On the day he died, however, Elvis, a renowned night owl, spent many of the small hours in the racketball building. He played a couple of games with his cousin Billy Stanley but soon tired, hobbling off the court after giving himself a hefty whack on the shin with his own racket. He sat at the little piano in the lounge area outside the court and played some gospel songs, before finishing with a reflective rendition of 'Blue Eyes Crying in the Rain', a Willie Nelson song he'd included in his recent *From Elvis Presley Boulevard, Memphis, Tennessee* album, recorded yards away in the Jungle Room. The group went back to the house, with Elvis telling his girlfriend Ginger Alden he was going to read in the bathroom. He was found dead there later that afternoon.

The court is now given over to displaying some of Elvis's jumpsuits, and the trickle of visitors entering the building passed straight through the lounge and into the court. I found myself drawn to the split-level ante-room rather than the glass cases full of rhinestone-encrusted cotton. This room witnessed the last-ever performance by the greatest musical icon of the modern world. For all the thousands that had attended his concerts, not to mention the one and a half billion who watched the *Aloha*

From Hawaii show beamed around the world and the millions who'd bought his albums, his final performance was of a few country and gospel songs at a piano in the pre-dawn of a Memphis summer morning, lost in the music, just him, a piano, and the songs. I stood for several minutes looking at the little Schimmel piano. I thought about the first hymns he'd hollered in church in Tupelo, him picking out chords on the cheap guitar purchased at Tupelo Hardware, and the recording of 'My Happiness' at Sun that led to the session which produced 'That's All Right'. The endless touring, the epoch-making Ed Sullivan and Steve Allen television appearances, the *Comeback Special*, the Hawaii broadcast and the legendary Vegas shows – it all came to an end here. A lonesome, contemplative few minutes at the piano, as the sun rose on what turned out to be the last day of his amazing life.

A few yards from the court, to the side of the house itself, is the meditation garden where Elvis is buried. He lies between his father and grandmother Minnie Mae, who both outlived him, while his mother lies next to Vernon. All are covered by large black slabs, with Elvis's middle name famously misspelled and a heartfelt tribute from Vernon that concludes, 'God saw that he needed some rest and called him home to be with Him'.

The meditation garden, again despite the legions of people who tramp through it, lives up to its name. Designed in part by Marty Lacker, a semicircular colonnade faces the graves, its curvature echoing that of the fountain whose faint trickling masks the traffic noise from the road. Elvis would sit out here and think or read, exploring the personal spirituality that he hoped would anchor the unreality of his life. It may sound like the hoariest of clichés and the clunkiest of conclusions, but as I stood at the foot of his grave I really believed that he'd finally found peace. Nevertheless, as I stood listening to the babble of the fountain and the rustle of the dying floral tributes left there on his recent birthday, I felt that the most poignant part of the house and grounds was not here, not at his grave, nor the room, nor even the building where he died, but that little piano in the racketball lounge, where Elvis had picked out the last chords and sung the final words of the last song he'd ever sing.

Elvis is dead. There are no two ways about it. The crackpot theories, dubious sightings and smudgy photographs of fat men in sunglasses are all utter bunkum. His body lay a few feet from where I stood, placed with the three people to whom he was closest throughout his life; but inside the house he's still alive. Graceland has been open to the public for a quarter of a century, and no one has actually lived there for almost as long. Yet it's still a home somehow, not a museum. That indefinable sense of Elvis-ness endures and permeates the place, as if any moment he's going to come bounding into the room. I felt it, and the thousands of Elvis pilgrims who come here from all over the world feel it too. They cover the wall that separates the grounds from the road in their scrawled tributes – one I saw was a crudely drawn heart containing the words, 'Thank you for still being my man. Your [sic] always there for me. Samantha, England'. The impact he had on the world is still reverberating, and it's echoing in the walls of the racketball court where the final chord of that incredible musical journey is still in the fabric.

Las Vegas, USA

The first thing that struck me when I stepped off the plane at Las Vegas was the banks of slot machines lining the terminal. As soon as you walk out of the gate and into the concourse, there they are: flashing, beeping sirens seeking to snare you before you've even picked up your baggage. A man in a suit stopped at one, put his briefcase down, draped his coat over the case, rummaged in his trouser pocket for change, perched on a stool and began feeding coins into the slot. He'd not been off the plane for even a minute. Welcome to Las Vegas, where the quarter is king.

In many ways Elvis was the personification of Las Vegas: the glamour, the ostentatious bejewelled appearance, the entertainment, the excitement, the sense that what you were witnessing somehow wasn't real, that beneath the glamorous veneer there was something else, that this was an illusion. An appropriate place, then, to continue my quest to find out more about the man. Strangely, considering that he went on to become the human embodiment of the city, Elvis's first experience of Las Vegas was not a good one. He'd been booked for a two-week run in April 1956 at the New Frontier Casino, as 'the atomic-powered singer', but the cabaret crowd sitting at tables in their evening wear just didn't get it. Elvis bombed, at least at first.

Leaving the airport, I headed by taxi for the hotel where Elvis banished the memory of his flop to become the most successful artist the city has ever seen – the Las Vegas Hilton. When Elvis made his return to live performance there in 1969, capitalising on the success of the 1968 NBC television special, it was called the Las Vegas International, and was owned by Kirk Kerkorian. The International was the biggest and most opulent hotel and casino in town, which in Vegas was saying something. Although Barbra Streisand opened its two-thousand-seat auditorium – Colonel Parker didn't want Elvis to open the venue in order to avoid the inevitable first night glitches – it was Elvis who came to be almost part of the furniture, selling out an amazing 837 consecutive shows and appearing regularly between 1969 and his death in 1977.

The Hilton isn't just a hotel, it's more like a small, swanky town. With more than three thousand rooms, fifteen restaurants, several bars, a range of shops, the casino and the auditorium, you could spend a week here without leaving the place. My taxi pulled up after sweeping round the driveway, and I plunged into a lobby bigger and busier than anything I'd seen before. As someone more used to dubious bed and breakfasts than the glitzy opulence on a grand scale now displayed in front of me, my eyes were very nearly bouncing out of their sockets like a couple of poorly administered yo-yos. I checked in and headed to my twentieth-floor room, which overlooked the neon festival of the city to the Nevada desert mountains beyond. It had been a long day travelling, and I couldn't face any unadulterated hedonism beyond playing with the remote-controlled curtains for a while. I slept fitfully.

The next morning I stepped into the lift to find a short-haired man whose name-tag clipped to the breast pocket of his shirt revealed that he was Ron Mears, here for 'World of Concrete' at the convention centre next door. Ron eyed me for the first few floors of our descent, and finally said, 'Are you here for the convention? I think I recognise you.' I replied that no, alas, I wasn't here for 'World of Concrete'. 'Shame really,' I added. 'We could have, heh heh, cemented our relationship.' Ron gave me a look harder than the toughest concrete at the convention and didn't say a word. When the lift doors opened at the bottom, a small blonde woman – whose 'World of Concrete' badge identified her as the frankly magnificently named Mindy McGraw – beamed recognition at Ron, and informed him that she was popping back to her room because she'd left her samples behind. How on earth, I wondered, did you lug around samples of concrete? A ring binder full of polythene sleeves just would-n't cut it, surely? I'm glad Mindy was there, though, as the look Ron gave me after my terrible gag suggested he was that close to smacking me in the mouth.

I left the hotel but, this being America, found little provision for the pedestrian. I just wanted to have a bit of a stroll around and then head for the only place where Elvis can still be found in the constantly rejuvenating city, but it would take me twenty minutes of dodging taxis, tightrope-walking along low walls and wading through shrubbery before I got anywhere near the street. Clearly anyone suitable to be a guest at the Las Vegas Hilton wasn't the sort of person to arrive or leave on foot. Emerging from the undergrowth, I walked around to the top of the Strip, passing the New Frontier, the scene of Elvis's first dodgy gig. It's been redeveloped beyond recognition since then, and the Venus Room where he performed no longer exists, so I saw little point in exploring the place other than to have a quick look inside. It

could have been a replica of the Hilton – ranks of one-armed
bandits fluttered their glittery lashes at glassy-eyed punters robot-
ically feeding bucketloads of coins into them.

My rambling itinerary along the Strip took me to a large
shopping centre in search of coffee. On the ground floor of the
galleried mall a fashion show was in the process of being set up.
A long, synthetic grass-covered catwalk had been constructed,
and half-interested models were strolling up and down it in T-
shirts and jeans in imitation of the walk they'd be doing for real
at some point later in the day. Sitting near the tip of the catwalk
was a stubbly-chinned twentysomething man in a beret, wearing
a V-neck sweater at least two sizes too small and a pair of trousers
plainly borrowed for the occasion from a circus clown. From his
huffy, self-important, arms-folded countenance I deduced that
he was the designer. The fact that he was dressed like a complete
wanker served only to strengthen the likelihood that this was the
case. As he threw his arms in the air and delivered a petulant
stream of invective at a young and obviously nervous model that
caused her eyes to redden and her bottom lip to tremble, I
caught the eye of one of the workmen who were making the
final adjustments to the catwalk. We exchanged looks which
suggested we agreed that, yes, what this bloke needed was a
thorough and energetic twatting. And soon. He indicated the
surface of the catwalk. 'Would make a great mini-golf course,' he
said.

I ordered my coffee, the girl behind the counter asked my
name, I told her it was Charlie and she wrote it on the side of my
cardboard cup. A couple of minutes later my drink appeared, and
when I picked up the cup I saw she'd written 'Jolly'. It's possible
that she'd misheard my name, but I liked to think she had chosen
that day to describe the countenance of her customers rather
than simply utilise their nomenclature.

I turned to find only one little table vacant in the corner. I saw it at exactly the same time as a woman carrying two shopping bags clocked it. We both pretended not to have seen each other, quickened our step to a pace that looked a bit daft given the air of nonchalance we were attempting to affect, and commenced the race for the table. Admittedly she was carrying two shopping bags. However, I may have had twenty years on her in terms of youth, but I was carrying a scaldingly hot beverage in a cardboard cup with 'Jolly' written on it in black crayon. It was a pretty fair contest. We still refused to acknowledge each other, and besides I'd been walking all morning and was desperate for a sit down. Normally I would have ceded the seat with a chivalrous doff of the metaphorical trilby, but I had sore feet. Sore feet that were now quickening their step. What's more I felt I had a moral right to the table given that I'd already bought my coffee and she blatantly hadn't. We both converged on the target. I was ahead slightly, but there wasn't much in it as we entered the last five yards – clearly it would go down to a battle of wills. The way we were going, we would both collide at the table, possibly knocking it and each other flying: we had entered into a coffee-related game of chicken. My resolve was strong, my gaze didn't leave the table, my step didn't falter. Then, with barely three feet to go, the shopping bags left my peripheral vision. She'd given up the chase – victory was mine. I placed my cup on the table and resisted the strong urge to bare my backside at her and crow, 'Better luck next time, sucker.' Casually I placed my jacket over the back of the chair, sat down and lifted my coffee to my lips. I stole a glance at my erstwhile opponent, who was now looking around airily for another space as if the race had never even happened.

Comfortable in victory, I settled down to read up a little on the hows and whys of the city in which I was now known as 'Jolly'.

There had been a fort on the site of downtown Las Vegas for half a century before a sell-off of 110 acres of railroad-owned land in May 1905 led to the establishment of a town, which officially became a city six years later. For all that, it was the opening of the nearby Hoover Dam in 1936 that set Vegas on the road to prosperity, as tourists began to arrive in droves to marvel at the remarkable feat of engineering. Federal money also began to flood into the city after the installation of Nellis Air Force Base close by. But it was the opening of the Flamingo Hotel and Casino in 1946 that really put Vegas on the map. There were already a couple of establishments on the Strip, including the New Frontier, but it was Bugsy Siegel's development that kick-started Vegas's glittering future. Conceived as the world's most luxurious hotel, the Flamingo was named after Siegel's dancer girlfriend, or more specifically, her legs. A notorious gangster, Siegel was assassinated in a mob hit six months after the casino opened, after gangland investors suspected him of skimming off cash for himself.

The Strip developed slowly until the opening of the International in 1969, which sparked the era of the mega-resorts. Four years later its status as the world's biggest hotel was eclipsed by the original MGM Grand, which opened in 1973 but suffered a devastating fire seven years later that killed eighty-seven people. Other resorts followed, including a new MGM Grand in a new location on the Strip, and today around thirty-seven million people a year visit Las Vegas. The city is now home to an astonishing seventeen of the twenty biggest hotels in the world.

A few minutes later I was crossing the street to reach the place I'd set out to find – the one permanent Elvis presence in town, the Elvis-a-Rama museum. Situated a couple of blocks west of the Strip, it's a low, scruffy building next to a couple of sex shops, and boasts an incredible collection of Elvis artefacts and memorabilia. The museum started as the private collection of Elvis fan Chris Donaldson, who was converted to the ways of Elvis when aged ten he saw him in concert at the Hilton in 1975, and is the largest assemblage of Elvis memorabilia outside Graceland itself. Exhibits include an eighty-feet-long mural depicting the King's life, the 1955 Cadillac Elvis bought after signing to the RCA label in November 1955 and which Elvis, Scotty and Bill used to tour the country throughout the following year, and Elvis's social security card from the 1950s (his social security number was 409-52-2002, fact fans).

I was particularly impressed by the pair of blue suede shoes that Elvis wore on *The Steve Allen Show* in July 1956, the famous occasion when he was forced to sing 'Hound Dog' to a dozy-looking basset hound while wearing a tuxedo, in order to appease the moral majority outraged by his previous incendiary gyrations on television. Elvis hated the scenario from start to finish, and referred to it frequently in interviews for the rest of his career. In a clip I'd seen many times the shoes, made of course by Lansky's of Beale Street, were the pay-off to a weak gag about Elvis being unaccustomed to wearing a tux. The blue shoes, still a vibrant colour more than fifty years later, were even more striking considering the programme went out in black and white. In a neighbouring case sat Elvis's trunk from the Army, stencilled in white with the legend, 'Sgt Elvis A. Presley, US 53310761, 3764 Highway 51 South, Memphis, Tenn, USA', the address being Graceland before the highway was renamed Elvis Presley Boulevard.

It's an exceptional collection, with items ranging from the trousers Elvis wore while singing 'Baby I Don't Care' in *Jailhouse Rock*, to the 1965 Gibson Country Gentleman guitar he played during the very first Vegas concert, right down to a 1970 store card bearing his signature for a Palm Springs liquor store. There was also that holy grail for Elvis collectors – one of his jumpsuits, a detectably camp turquoise number with a phoenix design.

You could probably spend hours in the museum just going round and round and still see things you'd missed, but I had a finite time in which to explore. For not only is the Elvis-a-Rama a museum, it also boasts a tiny concert venue staging regular shows by Elvis impersonators, on this occasion Donny Edwards. In truth I'd really had my fill of Elvis imitators by the second night in Porthcawl, but, hey, I was in Vegas, and this was the closest I'd get to seeing Elvis here. I took my seat in the little auditorium, nearly full with about thirty people. It's done out like a club, with booth tables along two walls and a stage at one end boasting a small walkway extending from the front. Without warning there was a puff of smoke, some flashing lights and a young Elvis bounded on to the stage. Admittedly he couldn't bound far on the grounds that he might have ended up in someone's lap, but he proceeded to put on a decent show, ranging from the gold-jacketed early years right up to the jumpsuited Vegas era, and interspersing the songs with some horrifically dire gags delivered in an endearingly self-deprecating manner that had the middle-aged ladies in the audience falling madly in love with him on the spot.

After the show Donny, who bore a strong and possibly surgically enhanced resemblance to a young Elvis, posed patiently for photographs with audience members in the Elvis-a-Rama shop, at the conclusion of which I managed to have a quick chat. It turned out that his uncle had been stationed with Elvis in the Army in Germany, and he'd imitated the King from an early age. He'd appeared on national television in the States and performed on several occasions with Elvis's backing vocalists the Jordanaires, as well as, he told me, being in a commercial on telly in the UK and the creaky US daytime soap *The Bold and the Restless*.

Donny's wasn't the only show I was to see that day, mind. As well as being in the hotel in which Elvis performed his record-smashing shows and stayed himself – in a massive suite on the thirtieth floor – I wanted to see a show in the Hilton. I didn't care what it was; as long as I could see somebody on the same stage that Elvis graced I'd consider my jaunt to Sin City worthwhile. When I booked my room from an internet café a stone's throw from Sun Studio, I'd all but whooped and punched the air when I saw who was on. If you're seeing a Vegas show you want something suitably showy and glitzy, with a little high camp thrown in for good measure if possible. And boy, would you ever get that with Barry Manilow.

Heady with excitement, I had splashed out on an expensive seat, one that left me with little change out of a hundred quid, and had left the café with a spring in my step. I'd gone only a few springy steps up the street when one of the café staff drew alongside and reminded me that it's customary to settle one's bill before leaving an establishment such as theirs. A little embarrassing, but, hey, I was going to see the Manilow.

I arrived early. One of the door staff held out a green glowing tube, and I held out my ticket ready for him to ensure it wasn't a forgery. He looked at me like I was nuts. 'It's a glowstick, sir,' he said, 'for waving during "Copacabana".' Ah, yes, of course.

I entered the auditorium and stood for a moment looking around the room where Elvis performed more often than anywhere else on the planet. There wasn't much in the hotel to commemorate his groundbreaking tenure – I'd heard that there were a plaque and a statue in the lobby somewhere, but I couldn't find them – other than a couple of pictures on the wall of a small annexe room of slot machines that was close to the entrance of the theatre. There was great evidence of Barry's presence, however. A huge billboard hung on the side of the

Hilton, visible from all over Vegas, there was an advertisement for the show on my room's television every time I switched it on, and there was even a permanent Barry Manilow shop among the boutiques and jewellery stores inside the hotel. Barry had been the artiste in residence here for the best part of a year performing his show, whose name, 'Music and Passion', was beamed on to what in the old days was called the safety curtain. I wandered off to the bar – christened the 'Copacabana Bar' for the duration of Barry's engagement – and in light of the occasion eschewed the idea of a beer for a glass of white wine instead. Ooh, get me. To my delight, my seat was just three rows from the stage, ensuring a clear close-up view of the man himself. There was even a little round receptacle for my (plastic) glass, whose rim I would knock almost immediately I sat down, emptying a healthy dollop of chardonnay into my groin.

The place filled up quickly, until the room was bustling with smartly dressed middle-aged couples and me, in chardonnay-groined jeans and new Elvis-a-Rama T-shirt. The house lights dimmed and the screen curtain suddenly burst into life with a montage of memorable moments from Barry's long career. The band struck up, the curtains opened, there was a puff of smoke and there striding towards the lip of the stage was the great man, in a blue Beethoven suit, arms outstretched, beaming smile, and of course leading the whole rannygazoo the famous Manilow nose. My seat being in the third row I was barely eight feet from the Manilow himself and hence six feet from the end of his nose (badoom-TISH). However, the thing that struck me most about Barry as he launched into 'Big Fun' wasn't his nose – no, I kept ducking (badoom-TISH) – but how really, amazingly, startlingly thin his legs are. It looked like he had a couple of pipe-cleaners hanging from the hem of his jacket. From the waist down the man is practically a flamingo.

The opening song finished and the band kept up a chugging, foot-tapping rhythm as Barry addressed us from the stage. 'Wow,' he chirruped. 'It's so great to see so many beautiful friends here in fabulous Las Vegas! I'm so glad you came and, wow, we're going to have such a great time here tonight, we're gonna have a ball. Oh, but hey' – he made a camp flapping motion at us with his hand – 'I can't chat now, I gotta get on, I'll talk to you later.' And we were into the next song.

I can't say I've ever been a Manilow fan particularly, in the same way that I can't say I've ever won a Formula One Grand Prix particularly, but I have to say that this was some show. He's one of those performers who surprises you with how many of their songs you actually know, and these all translated into an hour and a half of thumpingly good entertainment. Although Barry had been treading these same boards for the best part of a year, he exuded a freshness and enthusiasm that suggested this was the first time he'd performed these numbers in public. He even managed a duet with himself. Some thirty-year-old footage of Barry's first-ever televised performance was projected on to a screen at the back of the stage, just him and a piano, singing his first hit, 'Mandy'. Halfway through the song, we could suddenly hear another piano – it was Barry, gliding out towards the front of the stage on a moving platform at a white grand piano, chiming in with his younger self (whose nose, by the way, seemed a good deal wonkier than the arrow-straight proboscis he has now. He also, to me, looked a bit boss-eyed in the old clip). It should have been the ultimate conceit, duetting with yourself, but Barry has such an engaging, charming stage persona that you couldn't scoff.

There was even an Elvis 'My Happiness' moment, as Barry related the tale of his first-ever recording. His Russian grandfather had taken the six-year-old Barry to a 25-cent booth in the

Bronx to record a version of 'Happy Birthday' as a surprise present for his mother. Only Barry wasn't having any of it, as the crackly recording showed – a couple of lines was all his patient granddad got out of him.

The show finished with a whopping ten-minute version of 'Copacabana', where we all – even me – waved our luminous green glow-sticks, a display that must have looked to Barry from the stage like a field of highly radioactive corn swaying in the breeze.

I left the performance absolutely buzzing. So much so that I walked out of the auditorium and into the casino, jumped on to a stool and dropped some quarters into a slot machine. I didn't have a clue what I was doing, but it was worth the couple of dollars' worth of coins I shoved into the slot to see the lights on the machine flash so prettily. Grinning inanely, I stayed in the casino for a bit, just wandering around filled with Vegas bonhomie. I had a couple of beers, paid a few more dollars to watch some pretty lights flash on some slot machines, and went to bed happy in the faintly nuclear green candescence of my Manilow glow-stick.

Early the next morning I descended to the lobby in search of breakfast. When I emerged from the lift, a sweaty twentysomething male walked into it carrying a bottle of beer. As I wandered through the casino in search of the buffet, I realised that although I'd been away for a good seven hours, many of the gaming tables were still hunched over by the same people as they had been when I'd ambled past, slightly drunk and beaming with Barry-induced bonhomie, the night before. The casinos are timeless places: there are no clocks and there's no daylight. Now

I'm not one to claim that I lead a healthy lifestyle. When the only person in your local high street who knows your name is the bloke from the kebab shop, you lose all pretensions of your body being a temple. However, that morning, feeling spruce and chipper and giving off the fresh whiff of toothpaste and antiperspirant, I felt like a wholesome example of clean living. I was almost inclined to barge into the middle of the games and harangue the participants about the evils of gambling. I didn't, because burly men in suits wearing earpieces would have taken me out to the bins and given me a good hiding, but I still felt a distinct moral superiority, which was a whole new experience for me, I can tell you.

After breakfast I set out on the long walk north to Fremont Street, the original good-time focus of the early Las Vegas. One of the oldest, if not *the* oldest, streets in the city, Fremont boasts many local firsts. It was the first street to be paved, the first to receive a Nevada State gambling licence and the first to install traffic lights. The fictional Grand Prix in *Viva Las Vegas* careered along Fremont Street, and its casino exteriors – the famous Golden Nugget frontage, and Vegas Vic, the cowboy apparently thumbing a lift wearing a lascivious grin – remain arguably Vegas's most recognisable landmarks. In an attempt to jazz the place up now that the Strip is the main focus for visitors, the street has been covered over with a canopy that at night is lit up like a Christmas tree. Like most things in Vegas, it wasn't done by half – more than twelve million lamps are embedded in the canopy.

For some reason, though, I felt a strange kind of melancholy as I sat outside a coffee shop watching the people go by. I'd been in Las Vegas for a few days, and felt an odd kind of loneliness tinged with sadness. People back home had told me before I left that many visitors have had enough of Vegas after three or four days; and maybe the fun fatigue was setting in for me.

Perhaps it was the sense that nothing in Vegas was real that had caused me to feel suddenly detached and slightly depressed. Even here, which was about as close to reality as you'd find in Vegas, the whole thing had been given a makeover and renamed the 'Fremont Street Experience'. I always find when something is placed in a metaphorical glass case and labelled an 'experience' it instantly ceases to be just that. Vegas was starting to look to me like a giant metaphorical glass case, and the rebranding of Fremont Street was the epitome of the madness of the city. Something already built on unreality was being pushed further into the unreal, if not the surreal. Needless to say, nobody comes to Vegas for cultural enrichment, of course. It's about the quick fix, the short blast of hedonism, a brothel for the spirit – 'What plays in Vegas stays in Vegas'. But this didn't stop me wallowing in a sense of emptiness as I sat on the Fremont Street Experience having nothing of the sort. I realised that in the short time I'd spent here it had been like walking through a strange kind of dream. This wasn't helped by visiting an extraordinary replica of Venice, even down to the tower of St Mark's Square, and a reproduction of Paris that, you guessed it, had an Eiffel Tower. Even the sky there was fake, it being an ingenious cloud-filled vista despite the fact you were actually indoors. When they're faking the sky, you know you're in a weird place.

I'd also found little of Elvis here, other than what lay in the actual glass cases of the Elvis-a-Rama. So quickly does Vegas regenerate itself that most of the places which meant something to Elvis are long gone. The Aladdin, where he was married, has been rebuilt. Most of the locations for *Viva Las Vegas* are no longer there (I searched in vain for the pool at the Flamingo into which Ann-Margret pushed Elvis), and even the statue erected by the Hilton to commemorate the King's long tenure appears to have been removed. There are the wedding chapels of course, and I had popped in to the Graceland Wedding Chapel, a Vegas institution, on my way around the Strip. Although it was a genuine looking chapel, with pews and stained-glass windows, there was still a feeling that things weren't quite genuine. There were photos on the walls of some of the celebrities who had been married there, including Jon Bon Jovi, Jay Leno and Billy Ray Cyrus, all posing with an Elvis lookalike who was absolutely nothing like Elvis other than he wore the same sunglasses and had a bit of a bouffant.

The longer I sat under the canopy of the Fremont Street Experience, the more disheartened I became. I'm sure if you looked back through history to the *real* Fremont Street Experience it would be littered with broken dreams and regret. I'd been here nary three days, and the creeping feeling of emptiness was growing by the hour, it seemed. I knew I had to do something to avoid turning into a completely misanthropic old sulkytrousers, so took the long walk back to the Strip and bought a ticket to see Tom Jones at the MGM Grand.

It was my last night in Vegas and I was determined to cheer myself up. Going to see Tom Jones would be a good way of doing just that, I thought. There was even a link to Elvis – they were friends in the early days, and it's generally accepted that the gyrating Welsh crooner was a big influence on how Elvis developed his own stage show.

The MGM Grand is, at 5044 rooms, the largest hotel in the world, and its casino is the biggest in Vegas. Hence it took me a while even to find the auditorium where Tom was playing. I eventually found it, tucked away in the corner of the giant casino, past a glass case containing two real-life, placid-looking lions.

I presented my ticket – considerably cheaper than for Barry Manilow, it must be said – and was shown to my seat. Unlike at the Hilton, the seating was club style, all tables and seats. As it was my last night, I'd emerged slightly from my earlier funk and decided to mark the occasion by treating myself to a whole bottle of wine. The waitress took my order, having asked pointedly, 'Just one glass with that, sir?', with a Jeevesian barely perceptible raising of an eyebrow. After she disappeared, I was joined by my tablemates for the evening: two grandmothers, a mother and a grown-up daughter from Philadelphia. Very nice they were too. When they twigged that I was English, and I had imparted my usual spiel about the weather in and size of London, the mother of the quartet commented that I must be really proud of my countryman. For one awful moment I thought that she meant Tony Blair, but I soon realised that it was Tom Jones she was on about. 'Ah, no, well, he's Welsh,' I said. She was beaming at me. 'I'm from England,' I added. She kept beaming. 'Yeah,' she said, 'so you must be very proud to be here watching your countryman.' I could only imagine the chorus of raucous indignation from the far side of Offa's Dyke at the very thought of me being a compatriot of Treforest's finest, so I tried to explain again that he was from Wales and I was from England. Once more I was greeted with a radiant smile. Fortunately at that moment the waitress returned to take their orders. Each of my companions had a glass of water that they made last all evening. A couple of minutes later, my bottle of wine arrived in a big bucket of ice, which in terms of size almost qualified as a skip, what amounted to a bath towel over the top and a huge wineglass that could comfortably have accommodated the contents of Lough Neagh with room for a cherry and little paper umbrella. The beaming smiles from my water-drinking chums faltered a little as they realised that there was one bottle of wine on the table and only one of me. I was probably about to imbibe more wine that evening than they'd consumed in their entire lives.

Before long the house lights went down, crashing music pumped out of the speakers and a flashing sequence of images was projected on to a screen: all satellites, photographs of Tom from all parts of his lengthy career – this engagement came one year shy of the fortieth anniversary of his Vegas debut – and frequent shots of the globe to emphasise the international nature of Tom's standing. After a while the man himself took the stage in a high-collared dark suit and, surprisingly, a goatee beard.

It was another fantastic show, lapped up by the mainly female audience. Tom would flirt outrageously in between songs in his chocolate-brown Welsh burr, whose contrast with my nasal cockney whine might have confirmed to my tablemates that we weren't from the same country, but the frequent references to my 'countryman' which peppered the conversation suggested that they were still to be persuaded.

Tom's clearly not as mobile as he used to be, which is understandable given that the man's within hailing distance of his eighth decade. For the first few songs he hardly moved, but seemed to loosen up as the show progressed. At one point he got a little bit carried away and actually jumped in the air but, from the brief look of panic on his face, immediately wished he hadn't. By the end he was moving much more easily, and for a second lifted his shirt to reveal an impressively toned stomach, much to the delight of the ladies present. And, yes, knickers were thrown: I counted half a dozen pairs arcing through the air and landing at Tom's feet. The airborne underwear display was triggered by the launching of an enormous bra, however, that whistled past Tom's head about twenty minutes into proceedings. It was a huge thing, like two pillowcases sewn together and held in place with grapple hooks. The bra looped through the air, all metal attachments and heavy-duty fabric, like some giant ninja weapon fizzing towards its target. Luckily the owner's aim wasn't true — if it had got Tom round the neck, he was a goner. It would have taken his head clean off two verses into 'The Green, Green Grass of Home'.

By the time Tom closed his set with a thunderous version of 'Kiss', I had finished my bottle of wine and given up trying to point out to my neighbours the difference between Wales and England. As we stood up to leave one of the grandmothers tugged at my sleeve and told me how wonderful my countryman was. 'Yes, lovely, there, look you, isn't it, see?' I responded, and waddled off to the monorail station whistling 'Cwm Rhondda'.

Back at the Hilton, I began to pack a bag for my next destination. Chipper though I felt after my two nights of top-class cabaret entertainment and expert wine-imbibing, I still believed that Elvis had escaped me in Las Vegas. The city's perpetual, almost organic regeneration and its air of superficial unreality had left me with little of substance to go on other than the contents of the glass cases in the Elvis-a-Rama. Apart from wine, my stomach too had little of substance to go on, and my morning flight to Hawaii would be accompanied by a spectacular hangover. After tossing my Elvis-a-Rama T-shirt into my bag and zipping it closed, I gazed out at the slight glow in the night sky on the horizon above the distant mountains. At least they were real.

Hawaii, USA

On the plane I had next to me a young but very large Hawaiian named Brad, clad in T-shirt and shorts. When he heaved himself into his seat, pulled out a phone and proceeded to work his way through every ringtone in its library I thought I was in for a nightmare flight, but Brad in fact turned out to be an infectious and extremely likeable travelling companion. He produced, and insisted I share, a large box of chocolate cookies, the kind so unhealthy that I knew each one was literally taking ten minutes off my life. Brad told me that he worked as a driver in Salt Lake City and hadn't been home to see his parents on Oahu, the main Hawaiian island and the location of the state capital Honolulu, for two years. He was going back to surprise them, but not before he had passed loud, appreciative comment on every woman under the age of forty within his field of vision on the plane. Brad was also an immensely talented sleeper. One minute he'd be pointing out the line of a finely turned calf on one of the cabin crew, only for me to look in the direction he'd indicated, then look back at Brad and find him sitting there chin on chest, eyes closed, breath deep and raspy and a small gobbet of drool dangling from his lower lip. Then as quickly as he'd nodded off, he'd be awake and jabbering again. As we neared our destination, Brad looked out of the window and went quiet for the first time in six hours, at least while awake. 'It's beautiful, isn't it?' he said, turning to me, 'the ocean?'

I looked past him, and, sure enough, the Pacific was beautiful. A deep shade of blue, it stretched away to the horizon. Ahead of us lay the nineteen Hawaiian islands, nearly two and a half thousand miles from the US mainland, the fiftieth and southernmost state of the Union. Elvis loved Hawaii. It was his favourite place in the world outside Graceland. He played several concerts here – including the 1973 *Aloha From Hawaii* show that was beamed by satellite around the world – made three films and spent several holidays on the islands. In my search for Elvis, Hawaii was an important destination. Brad switched himself off again

Elvis first came to Hawaii for a couple of concerts at Honolulu's old stadium in 1957. The Colonel had noticed that some 21,000 of Elvis's 1956 Christmas cards came from the islands, which out of a population of 600,000 wasn't insignificant. Hawaii was quite different then. It was still two years away from becoming a state, for one thing, having been formally annexed by the US as far back as 1898, and was far from the tourist honeypot it is today. In fact the population couldn't even vote in US elections and the White House appointed the governor. The Hawaiian tourist industry wasn't so much in its infancy as barely smoking a post-conception cigarette.

Elvis stayed, as he would on most of his Hawaiian visits, at the Hilton Hawaiian Village on Waikiki Beach, which is where I'd booked myself into for my stay in Waikiki. The hotel is intimately linked with Elvis – as well as staying there, scenes in *Blue Hawaii* were shot in and around the place, and Elvis also gave press conferences there ahead of the *Aloha From Hawaii* show. In fact the opening scenes of *Aloha* show Elvis arriving in the grounds of the hotel by helicopter.

It was *Blue Hawaii*, though, that not only established Elvis's relationship with the islands, but also thrust Hawaii into public attention. In the years following the Second World War, Hawaii was associated in the American public consciousness with Pearl Harbor. Hal Wallis's 1961 story of Chad Gates returning from the Army and working as a tour guide served as a ninety-minute infomercial for the US's newly crowned fifti-eth state. Although it cemented the blueprint for the rest of Elvis's film career – bland plot, catchy but largely forgettable songs – *Blue Hawaii* still stands up as a decent, enjoyable film. The soundtrack album turned out to be Elvis's biggest-selling studio album of all time, which when you consider it contained the likes of the anodyne 'Rock-a-Hula Baby' and the bizarre 'Ito Eats' is a frankly amazing achievement. Granted it also included 'Can't Help Falling in Love' and the title track from the film, but even so, 'Ito Eats'?

I bade farewell to Brad, who would clearly have given Ito a run for his money in the eating stakes. Shaking his huge meaty hand, I left him at baggage claim grinning at the women bend-ing down to pick their bags up from the carousel. I took the shuttle bus from the airport to the Hilton Hawaiian Village. Right on Waikiki Beach, it's an enormous complex consisting of six towers over twenty-two acres. At check-in I was assigned a room in Rainbow Tower, the same one that Elvis would occupy whenever he was in residence. I lugged my bags – considerably heavier than when Jason had rescued them in Tupelo, now that they were crammed with accumulated Elvis memorabilia – to Rainbow, went up in the lift to the seventeenth floor, found my room and put the key card in the door.

Now normally when I travel alone I a) don't tend to stay in Hiltons and b) am usually given a room with a completely crap view. A wall six feet away, for example, some dustbins, or the less scenic parts of an industrial estate. When I opened the door to my room here, however, my gast was well and truly flabbered. Ahead of me was a floor-to-ceiling window, the other side of which was the Pacific Ocean, darkening to black in the post-sunset, the white sand of Waikiki Beach, its shape picked out by the lights winking on and off along it and, in the distance, looming gracefully out of the gloaming, the outline of the Diamond Head volcano.

I dumped my luggage, and went straight through the room on to the balcony. It was a warm evening and above the soft splashing of the tiny waves I could hear the faint hubbub of the alfresco diners below. I slept better than I had for several nights, lulled to the Land of Nod by the eternal, gentle washing of the sand by the lapping Pacific outside my window.

The next morning dawned hot. Being an idiot, I had of course packed totally inappropriate clothing. It was January, I'd thought. Brrrr, eh? Brrrr! I'd already sent a box of useless sweaters home from Vegas, but as I looked out at the sun glistening on the water in front of a beach already filling with scantily clad bathers, then back at my bag full of jumpers and Levi's, I realised that something needed to be done, and fast. Then a glint in my bag caught my eye – it was my CD copy of the *Blue Hawaii* soundtrack. There on the cover was Elvis, looking tanned and handsome, sitting with a ukulele in his hands, a lei round his neck, and wearing a Hawaiian shirt. It was a dark-red one with a hint of a floral pattern and a white vine trailing around it. I liked it. A lot. It wasn't too garish like a lot of Hawaiian shirts and, hey, I was in Hawaii, looking for Elvis. What better way to dress than in arguably the most famous

Hawaiian garment ever seen? That would be my plan for the morning – to hunt down the same shirt.

Donning my jeans and my thinnest jumper – it would still have been more suited to a north Atlantic trawler – I made one concession to the prevailing climate: I'd brought with me an old pair of flip-flops to use when I stepped out of the shower. I slipped my feet into them and flopped off towards the lifts.

The Aloha shirt, to give its proper name, originated in the 1930s, thanks to a Hawaiian of Chinese descent named Ellery Chun. Hawaii at the time was awash with immigrants working on the islands' sugar cane plantations, and they would dress in the clothes they were used to. Filipinos would wear long Barong Tagalog workshirts, while Japanese women would knock up shirts from the colourful leftover cloth from the making of kimonos. Chun, born in Hawaii in 1909, had graduated in economics from Yale in 1931, at the height of the Great Depression, and returned to the islands to take over his father's dry goods store in the heart of Honolulu. With his sister Ethel, he began selling shirts made from the kimono cloth, which soon became hugely popular. Eventually Chun started to manufacture shirts featuring Hawaiian designs, such as pineapples, palm trees and hula girls, and the Aloha shirt was truly born. When visiting the islands film stars such as Frank Sinatra and Bing Crosby would head for Chun's and similar stores that had sprung up to buy the shirts, while American servicemen stationed on Hawaii would take them back to the mainland. In 1951 the US president Harry S. Truman appeared on the cover of *Life* magazine wearing one, and Dwight Eisenhower was known to own several. Montgomery Clift's character died in an Aloha shirt in *From Here to Eternity*, and, of course, Elvis made them even more popular in *Blue Hawaii*.

Such a famous shirt as Elvis's shouldn't be too hard to track down, I thought, as I flip-flopped away from the hotel to plunge into the clothing emporia of downtown Honolulu. I considered my best bet to be Waikiki's International Marketplace, a labyrinth of stalls and shops catering to the gullible tourist's every need. Little shops boasted racks and racks of garish colour, and I descended upon them with the gusto and enthusiasm of the first people through the door at the opening of the Harrods sale. I entered the first place and rifled through the racks like an expert chef chopping a courgette. The owner appeared at my side and asked if I needed any help. Given that I was wearing a thick jumper and jeans in thirty-degree heat, and flip-flops, it may not have been a strictly retail-based enquiry. Her English was stilted and thickly accented, and I guessed she was from the Philippines.

'Well,' I said with a slightly embarrassed chuckle. 'What I'm actually looking for is the shirt that Elvis wore on the cover of *Blue Hawaii*.'

She looked at me curiously.

'Elvis?' she said.

'Yes,' I replied. 'Elvis.'

'Elvis Presley?' she averred.

'Yes,' I said. 'Elvis Presley.'

There was a pause.

'You want CD?' she asked.

'No, no,' I said with a smile. 'I'm looking for a shirt.'

'OK,' she said hesitantly, then she rattled a couple of hangers and pulled out a bright-green number adorned with hula girls. 'This one very nice. This just your colour.'

'Ah, yes, it's a lovely shirt,' I said. 'But I'm specifically looking for the shirt that Elvis wore.'

'Elvis,' she repeated, clearly believing that she was in the presence of an idiot. My attire would not have convinced her otherwise. 'I no have CDs.'

'No, no, sorry,' I said. 'I'm looking for the shirt he wore in *Blue Hawaii*.'

'*Blue Hawaii* shirt,' she said.

'*Blue Hawaii* shirt,' I responded with an eager nod.

She moved to the other side of the shop, rummaged through a few shirts in the rack and with a flourish pulled one out and laid it on top of the racks smiling triumphantly. It was blue, and emblazoned all over with the word 'Hawaii'.

This set the tone for the rest of my day. I must have visited every shirt emporium in Honolulu, looking for a particular red-print shirt with a white flower meandering around it. The poor woman I'd bamboozled in the first place could have formed a support group for bewildered shopkeepers who'd fallen victim to a sweaty fellow dressed as a trawlerman despite the tropical heat, wearing flip-flops and gibbering about Elvis. Everywhere I went, the vendors would go quiet for a moment, look into the middle distance and say they knew exactly the shirt I meant but they'd not had one in stock for a while. I reckon I flip-flopped the entire length and breadth of the city in search of this shirt, which was now assuming grail-like status. I passed the site of the old Honolulu stadium, now a public park, and the Neal S. Blaisdell Center, from where Elvis broadcast the *Aloha From Hawaii* show to a record audience around the globe. As the afternoon wore on and one shop began to look much like another, not to mention the shirts themselves, I got to the point of just sticking my clammy head through the door and barking, 'Have you got the Elvis *Blue Hawaii* shirt?' then grunting off again when the answer came in the negative. By the time I reached the Ala Moana Center near the beachfront downtown it was late in the after-noon and I was tired, sweaty and disgruntled. Despite it being the largest open-air shopping centre in the world, and once the biggest of any kind in the United States, I'd somehow contrived to miss it on my flip-flop odyssey around Honolulu.

I tried a shop called Reyn's, which turned out to be one of Hawaii's most famous Aloha shirt retailers. If anyone would have the Elvis shirt, Reyn's would. I began to rummage along the racks with a technique perfected by a near-full day of unsuccessful shopping. An assistant, a tall silver-haired man, helpfully enquired after my potential need for assistance and I told him what I was after. He thought for a while.

'You mean the one from the *Blue Hawaii* cover?' he said.

'Yes,' I replied, my eyes starting to sparkle with hope.

'The red one, with a feint print, and white flowers leading around it?'

'That's the one!' I said.

'No, we haven't stocked that one for a year or so now,' he said, before noticing my crestfallen expression and adding, 'but they do crop up every now and again.'

I stayed crestfallen. So much so that at that point it would have taken two strong men to lift my fallen crest from the floor where it now lay. I did the only thing I could do, in the circumstances. I gave in.

'OK,' I said, dry of mouth. 'Well, do you have anything that looks like it?'

'Sure, I think we can find something,' he replied. He led me over to a rack of shirts and pulled one out that did indeed look like the Elvis shirt. It was a brighter shade of red, admittedly, and it didn't have the feint print on it, but it did have the white flower motif. With Reyn's arguably the leading place in town to buy an Aloha shirt, I thought if I was going to get one, I should probably get one from here.

'You really don't think I'll find the Elvis one then?' I asked before taking the shirt to the counter. He grimaced slightly and shrugged his shoulders. That was good enough for me.

Before heading back to the hotel, I had a walk around the rest of the shopping centre, ergonomically laid out on three floors. On the top one was a shop dedicated entirely to ukuleles, which I thought was a tremendous thing. In the UK I think we've always found the ukulele a bit of a joke, maybe because we associate it with our ukulele protagonist, the man who could eat an apple through a letterbox: George Formby.

Outside our shores, though, the ukulele has a noble and popular history, and it all started in Hawaii on 23 August 1879 when a ship called the *Ravenscrag* docked in Honolulu with a boatload of immigrants from Portugal. The story goes that one of the Portuguese, Joao Fernandes, was so excited to have arrived after his 15,000-mile, four-month voyage, he pulled out his *braguinha*, similar to the modern ukulele, and played joyful tunes on the quayside. The watching Hawaiians thought that his nimble fingers looked a little like a jumping flea, which in Hawaiian sounds a bit like ukulele, hence where the name came from. Another story, put forward by the then Queen Lili'uokalani herself, is that it means 'the gift that arrived', 'uku' meaning gift and 'lele' to come. Personally I prefer the jumping flea story.

Fernandes and a couple of other men from the boat began to make ukuleles, and the instrument soon became popular on the islands, with even the royal family learning to play. In 1915 the ukulele travelled to the US mainland for an expo, and the place went nuts. The whole country went ukulele bonkers, so much so that within a year the Victor Recording Company had no fewer than 146 Hawaiian songs on its publishing roster. Two years later *Paradise of the Pacific* magazine said, 'The ukulele signifies innocent merriment – we should take off our hats to the little Hawaiian ukulele.' In the 1950s Arthur Godfrey's show on national television brought the uke to the masses – a plastic model designed for people to play along to the show sold millions. The ukulele boom faded during the sixties, but today the instrument can still be heard everywhere in Hawaii and in many other places too. They say the real test of a good tune is if it works on the ukulele. Paul McCartney said that 'if I meet a grown-up who plays the ukulele, I love them', while no less a figure than Krusty the Clown called it 'the thinking man's violin'. The ukulele even had its very own rock 'n' roll casualty in Cliff Edwards, better known as 'Ukulele Ike'. Edwards started out on the vaudeville circuit, teaching himself the uke because it was a good accompaniment to his voice and easy to carry around, but soon became the leading light of the ukulele boom. MGM put him in several films – it's his voice singing 'When You Wish Upon a Star' in Pinocchio – and he had a national radio show. However, a drink problem and recklessness with his fortune meant that the first ukulele superstar died alone, broke and friendless in a Hollywood convalescent home in 1971 at the age of seventy-five. In fact no one claimed his body for days, and he was about to be donated to medical science when word reached the Disney Organisation, which rallied round to give him a decent send-off.

Most of this was imparted to me by a young female assistant in the 'Ukulele House'. When I entered the shop, I had no intention of buying anything, I was just intrigued by the little instrument that Elvis had wielded in *Blue Hawaii* while he'd been wearing the shirt I couldn't find. When the shop assistant invited me to try one of them I thought I'd give it a shot. I used to play a bit of mandolin in a previous abortive career, and guessed it couldn't be much different. She picked an expensive Hawaiian-made model off the wall and showed me a couple of chords. I placed my fingers between the appropriate frets and strummed the first with the back of my fingernails and it sang out with a clarity and timbre that were nothing to do with my technique and everything to do with the craftsmanship that had gone into the instrument. I fingered the second chord, to complete a cadence in the same crystal clear tone, and as I strummed, it let out a ringing sustain that seemed to take an age to die.

The ukulele was a beautiful piece of workmanship with a deep rosy grain to the wood, and was clearly that of a true craftsman. I asked how much it was and the assistant quoted a price that would probably have made a hefty deposit on a big house in Hampstead – but I'd caught the ukulele bug. From the price she quoted for the one I held in my hands, it was clear I could barely afford the strings, let alone the whole thing. I asked if she had anything more affordable, and she came out with a delightful-looking thing, a Hawaiian-made mahogany instrument that, while it didn't have the heavenly choir sound of the first one I tried, was still a decent-sounding piece of wood at a price that wouldn't unduly alarm my bank manager.

I walked back to the Hilton Hawaiian Village with a definite spring in my step that hadn't been there earlier, even though walking with a spring in your step in flip-flops is difficult to accomplish. Although I hadn't found a shirt that was the same as Elvis's, I had found a similar one and, what's more, I'd acquired a ukulele.

I also had cause to wear my new shirt, and not just because wearing a jumper in that heat was undeniably the behaviour of an imbecile. I had booked to see what was by all accounts the best Elvis show on the islands, the inevitably named Blue Hawaii at the Waikiki Beachcomber Hotel, and freshly showered and clad in my new purchase, found myself in the queue outside, feeling dapper and indigenous. On the way in, Graceland-style, each of us was photographed with the Elvis impersonator and then once inside I was shown to a table of six, where the other five people had already begun setting about the dinner that was included in the ticket price. My companions were two middle-aged couples and a woman on her own, who were all together and all engrossed in conversation when I arrived and sat down, beaming widely at everyone and expecting them at least to say hello. One of the men was opposite me, and the other was next to me on my left, but they didn't even seem to notice that I was there. Instead they carried on their conversation without acknowledging my presence. Finally, just as I was doing a thorough job of demolishing the salad starter, one of the men turned to me and, as I pitchforked a mound of lettuce into my mouth, said hi. 'Hnnfff,' I said in response, trying to do some friendly eyebrow work in lieu of the smile I'd have given him if my mouth had not been full of a medium-sized allotment. Once I'd emptied my gob enough to form words without offending onlookers and returned the greeting, the man opposite me, who was from Washington, asked if I was Australian. I corrected him and gave my customary quick guide to London's climate and size, which led to a three-way bout of tortuous small talk before with tangible relief the two men went back to what they were talking about prior to my arrival, only this time their conversation – about public transport in Vancouver, as I recall – was punctuated by me interjecting politely with 'Ohs', 'Ahhs' and 'Reallys', when I had no clue about, nor, to be truthful, any interest in, what they were saying. But, hey, at least I made the effort.

Thankfully the show started soon afterwards with an impressive swirl of dry ice, lights and dramatic music, over which a woman's voice described the geological formation of the Hawaiian islands, before the impersonator, a tall, tanned man in his forties called Jonathan Von Brana, leapt on to the stage in gold lamé jacket and black slacks. It was a good show, as these things go. Where he scored was in not attempting to sound or act exactly like Elvis. He'd flirt with the women in the audience, crack up laughing in the middle of songs and generally give the impression he was having the time of his life, even though he did this show most nights of the week and had done for about five years. He finished with a rousing 'American Trilogy' after a lengthy tribute to the US soldiers in Iraq, 'who are risking their lives so there won't be another September 11' (Guiltily I wondered briefly what they'd put between 10 and 12 September instead), and then asked any former servicemen in the audience to stand up and take a round of applause. It was really quite moving to witness the scraping of chairs as around half a dozen grey-haired men in Aloha shirts pushed their seats back and stood to attention while the whole room applauded. The patriotic bombast of 'American Trilogy' somehow seemed to have extra poignance here in the land of Pearl Harbor.

Back at the hotel I spent the rest of the evening sitting on the balcony picking out some basic chords on my ukulele. The moon scattered a million shifting silver shards on to the Pacific in front of me, and my ham-fisted strumming was accompanied by the slow, steady rhythm of the little waves breaking softly on the sand. Just sitting there brushing the strings in the quiet of a Pacific evening, I felt truly relaxed and content for the first time since arriving in the US. There was no land within thousands of miles – the islands make up the most geographically remote landmass in the world – and, sitting there then I understood a little more about why Elvis loved coming to Hawaii so much. Staying in this tower, facing the ocean the way I was and knowing that most of the chaos and brouhaha of his career lay a good couple of thousand miles away must have allowed Elvis to relax a little, maybe strum a few chords on the ukulele before the moonlit sea, with no sound but the faint lapping of the waves below.

The next time I heard the gentle murmur of lapping waves among the silence was the following morning, as I stood on a marble floor above the decomposing hulk of the USS *Arizona* in Pearl Harbor. It was a peaceful, hot morning and the water in the harbor was still allowing a clear view of the ship below the sleek white memorial at which I and a small cruiser-load of people had just disembarked. Considering the monument is one of the busiest tourist attractions in the whole of the US – unless you arrive early in the morning as I did, you can queue for any- thing up to three hours – the atmosphere of awed reverence is a gratifying one. The memorial is, after all, a grave site, sitting atop the superstructure of the destroyed vessel and the remains of 1102 of the 1177 sailors killed when the ship sank during the surprise attack on the harbour by Japanese planes on 7 December 1941. The names of those who died are inscribed on a huge marble wall at the far end. Seeing the list of the fallen, most of whom still lie beneath your feet, is a humbling experience, made all the more poignant by the stillness of the scene today. Equally poignant was a smaller plaque near the base of the wall that listed a dozen or so names, with dates ranging from 1982 to the present day. These were the *Arizona* survivors who had passed away in more peaceful times and had their ashes placed beneath the water on the ship with their fallen comrades, whose memory would have been with them for the rest of their lives after a few minutes on a sunny morning like this one that changed America irrevocably.

The memorial itself was opened in 1962. It's a rectangular structure. The roof curves with a pronounced depression in the middle to signify the power of the US before the attack, the decline it caused, and the return to prominence in the ensuing years. Each side of the memorial has seven large glassless windows to represent the date of the attack. The designer was a Honolulu architect named Alfred Preis, who at the time of the strike was in an internment camp on Sand Island because he was Austrian.

Perhaps surprisingly, it took a considerable struggle to see the memorial built. As early as 1946 a permanent marker was suggested, with a Pacific War Memorial Commission created three years later. In 1950 Admiral Arthur Radford began running the US flag up a pole attached to the semi-submerged wreck, but his requests for funding to create a more permanent monument in 1951 and 1952 were turned down because of the high cost of the war in Korea. It took until 1958 for President Eisenhower finally to give a permanent memorial the green light, but $300,000 would still need to be raised privately to meet the $500,000 cost of the structure. Subscriptions and pledges were collected but by early 1961 the appeal was stumbling. Colonel Parker, who had been stationed at Waikiki when he had served in the US Army in the 1920s, read a newspaper report about the ailing fundraising campaign and immediately set about organising a benefit concert. Elvis was just out of the Army himself and was, at twenty-six, as Parker pointed out, the same average age as the men entombed on the submerged battleship.

The concert was scheduled for 25 March 1961 at the four-thousand-seat Bloch Arena close to the entrance to Pearl Harbor. Ticket prices were set at $5, with a few at $100 for the top brass. Nobody gained free admission – even Elvis bought one of the top-price tickets. The comic hillbilly singer Minnie Pearl opened the show, followed by local comic Sterling Mossman, before

Elvis took to the stage for an electrifying performance. At nineteen songs it was by far the longest show he'd played – his set normally lasted less than half an hour – and people who saw it rate it as arguably his best live performance. Most importantly, however, ticket sales added up to $47,000, with Elvis and the Colonel contributing a further $5000, a crucial kickstart to the fundraising campaign. Significantly, the concert also raised public awareness of the appeal, and the rest of the money was soon collected. Within a little more than a year of Elvis's performance President John F. Kennedy was dedicating the memorial at its opening. After the concert Elvis remained in Hawaii to film *Blue Hawaii* and subsequently to concentrate entirely on films for the rest of the decade. The Pearl Harbor benefit would be his last public concert for eight years.

Back at the hotel I watched a DVD of the 1973 *Aloha From Hawaii* concert. It was a broadcast as inextricably linked with my visit to Hawaii as anything to do with Elvis's time on the islands. He stayed on the top floor of the tower I was in, roughly ten floors up from where I watched the show. He gave press conferences from the hotel, the band rehearsed here, and the start of the broadcast featured a staged 'arrival' by helicopter in the hotel grounds that saw Elvis greet fans before being whisked off in a jeep.

Like the *'68 Comeback Special*, I'd seen *Aloha* a number of times, but again my journey in search of Elvis had given me a new perspective. Here I was in the very place from which the concert had been sent live to forty countries around the world to an eventual total (broadcast to the US was delayed by three months) of around one and a half billion people, and for the first time I was seeing it with a feeling of enlightenment, of understanding.

I detected a sadness about Elvis. Something wasn't quite right.

There was an emptiness in his eyes. Granted these had been difficult times for him: Priscilla had recently left him for her karate instructor and he was more and more dependent on prescription medication. Yet the *Aloha* show had seemed to give him a renewed sense of purpose. He was heavily involved with the preparations, even commissioning for the occasion a special jumpsuit featuring the American eagle. He lost a lot of weight and while he never recaptured the extraordinary good looks of the comeback show five years earlier, he looked lean and handsome. It was undoubtedly the pinnacle of his career, yet something wasn't right.

Again the reality was in his eyes. In the close-ups Elvis's were dark and empty, lacking the sparkle I'd seen in the picture at Sun Studio. If anything demonstrated how far he'd come from those far-off, even innocent times, it was this. He wasn't losing himself in the power of the music the way he had in 1968 and the way he had throughout his career, whether playing in front of thousands or just sitting at the piano at Graceland with friends. The show was a masterclass in Elvis-ness, but it wasn't Elvis. It was, you might say, the first Elvis tribute show, and it was being performed by the man himself. Only once in the entire concert did the real Elvis seem to emerge and then it was just briefly. During the long and dramatic crescendo to the climax of 'American Trilogy' the camera pulls in close on Elvis's profile. A bead of sweat trickles down his cheek, and you can see the rumbling crescendo sweeping him along. He emits a couple of yelps, either of encouragement to the band or simply involuntary responses to the power of the building music.

Apart from a couple of moments during the woundingly appropriate 'I'm So Lonesome I Could Cry', the rest of the show seemed one-dimensional, as if he was going through the motions. Of course even when just going through the motions

Elvis is still an amazing performer, hence the continuing popularity of the *Aloha* several decades after its first performance; but
watching the concert as the Pacific rolled in outside my open
window on the same beach that featured prominently in the
inserts to the broadcast, I felt a curious kind of sadness for Elvis.
I sensed this as the beginning of the end. I watched the adulation
of the crowd, the thrilled faces, the thousands of pairs of twin-
kling eyes that contrasted completely with those of the object of
their affection. He would never be the same again.

As well as the fun of *Blue Hawaii* and the ebullience of Elvis's
early visits, the islands have an unhappier significance. There
was the strange, disconnected *Aloha* performance, and also the
fact that Elvis spent the last holiday of his life here just weeks
before his death. This sadness had now infected me and I wanted
somehow to mark the end of my time on the islands, and indeed
in the US. I sat on the balcony, feet up, strumming a few chords
on the uke, feeling glum and not a little lonely and wondering
what I could do to bring my time here to some kind of fitting
close. I thought about the *Aloha* concert, glanced down at the
ukulele and had an idea.

An hour or so later, after a long and hot walk through
Honolulu, I arrived at the Blaisdell Center, the curiously
designed venue of the *Aloha* concert that looks a little like a
discus cradled on an ashtray. In my hand I had my ukulele
case, and my plan was to see if someone would allow me inside
to stand on the stage and play the song that had followed me on
my journeys since the day the television cameras rolled in
Uzbekistan. I walked up to the main doors, but they were
closed and padlocked. I flip-flopped around the building, but
there was no sign of life whatsoever. The place that had been
the focus of attention for the entire globe one January night in
1973 was utterly deserted. I hung around for a while, hoping

that perhaps a caretaker might arrive and indulge my quirky request.

I lurked there for the best part of an hour, before resigning myself to the fact that I wasn't going to share the same stage as Elvis. In the end, as the shadows began to lengthen, I laid my ukulele case down by some railings, unclipped the catches, lifted the lid and took out the small, polished piece of mahogany. I sat down with my back to the railings, cradled the instrument in my hands, formed an A chord on the fingerboard and strummed it with the backs of my fingernails. On this occasion the song was more plaintive, and for the first time I actually took note of the words. I thought of the late-night show here and the strange emptiness in Elvis's eyes as I strummed the chords and sang softly of the starry night when the stars shone bright, but how the whisper up on high was of how love had said goodbye.

I replaced the ukulele in its case and began the long walk back to the hotel.

Quebec and Ontario, Canada

Canada has a proud claim: it's the only country in the world other than the United States where Elvis performed in concert. In the spring and summer of 1957, at the height of his early popularity and in response to a petition organised by a fan in Ontario, the young singer played dates in Toronto, Ottawa and Vancouver. Montreal had originally been on the schedule, but in an episode that captures the spirit and atmosphere of the times, not to mention the impact Elvis was having on the world, the show was cancelled.

It was an affair that illustrates how feared as well as venerated Elvis was when he burst on to the world stage, and one that gave an appropriate backdrop to the next part of my journey.

When the Montreal date was announced, the powerful Quebec Catholic Church released a statement that any Catholic attending the concert would be excommunicated immediately. Which is a bit harsh. There are things I'd like to do to people who support Crystal Palace, for instance, mainly involving stocks, tar and feathers, but I wouldn't drum them out of their religion just for going to watch their team.

A pair of toadying local politicians jumped on the bandwagon and declared that Elvis would perform in Montreal over their dead bodies, and the city bigwigs canned the show. Ottawa, meanwhile, is only a couple of hours from Montreal and, crucially, in a different state, so the gig was moved there instead. The Catholic Church in Quebec then uprooted the goalposts and marched them over the border by threatening anyone from their province with excommunication if they travelled to Ottawa to see Elvis. Two fans did just that, and once the word of their attendance got back to Montreal they were excommunicated instantly. Even in supposedly more liberal Ottawa, eight girls were expelled from the Notre Dame Convent School for going to the concert.

Happily, Canada has chilled out a bit in the intervening half-century, so much so indeed that I was travelling there to meet two people who believe strongly in the interconnectedness of Elvis and religion, and most strongly of all in the importance of that connection. In addition it gave me a chance to delve into the next part of my quest. Having visited the places most closely associated with Elvis, I wanted to turn my attention to the, for want of a better word, 'cult' that surrounds him, particularly the pseudo-religious following he incites and the motivations of those driven to impersonate him. I'd been left largely unconvinced and unimpressed by the impersonators in Porthcawl, and while the tribute artists in Vegas and Hawaii had been an improvement, I felt that I needed to meet people who put more of themselves into their interpretations, and in Canada I would certainly do that. I would also learn much more about how Elvis crosses religious divides – something that seemed impossible in 1957.

My first destination was Montreal, the former hotbed of religious anti-Elvism and more recently occasionally violent political separatism, but now a laidback, cosmopolitan city with an atmosphere so relaxed I would at one point immerse myself so fully in the sheer bloody niceness of the place that I actually forgot where I was. But that was still a way off as I passed through immigration at Montreal's Dorval Airport and emerged into an unseasonably warm Quebec evening. There to meet me was a man dressed from head to toe in black: shoes, slacks, shirt with a guitar motif above each breast pocket and baseball cap above a neatly trimmed black beard.

'Hey Charlie,' he smiled, shaking me warmly by the hand. 'Welcome to Canada. Boy, it's warm here at the moment, can you believe it?' He fluffed his shirt away from his body, adding, 'Man, I've been *schvitzing* all day.'

Few people know more about Elvis's Jewish heritage than Dan Hartal. A former music therapist, he is better known as Schmelvis, indisputably the world's leading Jewish Elvis impersonator.

The first serious public inkling of the King's Jewish roots came in a *Wall Street Journal* article the day after the anniversary of his death in 1998. 'All Shook Up in the Holy Land: Pilgrims Honor Elvis's Yahrzeit', read the headline (will there ever be an Elvis-related headline that doesn't include the words 'All Shook Up'? Is it in the subeditors' style guide or something?), above a piece detailing the commemorations in Israel and the lighting of *yahrzeit* candles to mark the anniversary, a traditional part of Jewish mourning rituals. The article then went on to explain how Elvis's maternal great-great-grandmother Nancy Tackett had been Jewish. Her daughter Martha Tackett had a daughter called Doll Mansell, who in turn gave birth to Gladys Love Smith, Elvis's mother. Now that all may sound a little tenuous, but as Dan explained to me in the car on the way to his house, in Judaism the line goes through the maternal side, which makes

Elvis, in the eyes of Judaism, a Jew. Dan, who has been performing as Schmelvis for more than a decade, had pursued his interest in Elvis's Jewish heritage by, in 2002, fronting a documentary film called *Schmelvis: In Search of the King's Jewish Roots*, in which he visited Graceland during the vigil to commemorate the anniversary of Elvis's death and also the Holy Land itself, where, among other things, he helped Elvis's Jewish soul ascend to heaven.

Tonight Dan was unleashing Schmelvis again, at a Montreal bar called Mizzy's. I was, it turned out, uncharacteristically lucky – my visit had been planned to coincide with a regular weekly Schmelvis show elsewhere, but, he said, 'the woman who ran the place cancelled us a couple of weeks ago because she said our fans weren't drinking enough beer'. The Mizzy's show had been arranged at short notice instead.

'I'm pretty excited at the moment,' said Dan as he nosed the car through the early evening traffic and a blood-red sunset spread across the sky in front of us. 'I've been asked to perform in New York in a few weeks' time at a big free concert, a malaria benefit. I'm going to be on the same bill as Mariah Carey and it's going to be live on the TV too, can you believe that?'

A couple of hours later I was sitting at a table on the street outside Mizzy's. Schmelvis and his backing band soundchecked inside, while I sat with Dan's wife Debbie, a journalist named Sandy who was just back from three months in East Timor investigating the murder there of her best friend, and a frail-looking elderly woman whom Dan had told me in a respectful whisper was a Holocaust survivor who had run, and continued to run, something in the region of seventy marathons. Which all served to put my Elvis odyssey into perspective, that's for sure. They were reluctant to sit inside the venue. 'It's too smoky in those places,' said Debbie, persuading me to open the glass doors that separated the bar from the kerbside tables so we could hear the show. These were the doors that the doorman had just carefully closed. Which he promptly did again. 'We're not allowed to have the doors open when there's a band on,' he said meekly. 'Only when it's jazz.'

'Well, he's kinda jazzy sometimes,' said Debbie as I opened the doors again. After a couple more rounds of peek-a-boo between the doorman and me, and some one-sided verbal jousting between him and my tablemates, he realised that, faced by three Jewish women with a common goal and determined countenance, he didn't stand a chance, and relented with a stoop-shouldered resignation. I made a mental note that whenever I came up against a seemingly unwinnable situation I should arm myself with a trio of Jewish womanhood and everything would soon be sorted out in my favour.

Before long it was time for Schmelvis to hit the stage. Still dressed in black, with a yarmulke now replacing the baseball cap, and Elvis sunglasses, Dan opened the show with his own take on Elvis's early Sun side 'Mystery Train'. 'Knishes I buuu-uuuuyyyy, a dozen or two to go,' he crooned as the band chugged along tightly behind him. 'Bagels I buuu-uuuuyyyy, a dozen or two to go. Well if I eat too many knishes, on a diet I will go.'

Seamlessly the song segued into 'Tiger Man', Schmelvis-style. 'I'm the king of the temple and they caaaaaaall me Schmelvis man,' he sang, throwing impressively accurate Elvis shapes.

It was a tremendously enjoyable show, the only drawback being that there was hardly anyone there to see it. I had moved from the pavement table into the bar itself in order to appreciate fully the Schmelvis experience, but there were barely a dozen people with me. And two of them were on the quiz machine.

'Apparently the venue forgot to put their ad in the paper,'

shrugged Dan at the interval as he sucked reflectively on a beer.
'Nothing we can do about it, but it's a real shame.'

Despite the lack of numbers Dan still put everything into the
performance. The stage was tiny, yet he managed to go through
his full repertoire of Elvis moves as he and his band played a good
two hours of top-quality Schmelvis material. 'Heartbreak Hotel'
became 'Jerusalem Hotel', 'down at the end of Jaffa Street',
while 'The Ballad of John and Yoko' became 'Circumcision
Song': 'the way things are going, they're gonna circumcise me'.
It was clear that Dan absolutely relished being up there, even
though the punterage was minimal and the venue minute. So
small was the bar that the toilets were right next to the stage,
which at one point meant that but for a vital split second of
timing, Dan almost administered an Elvis-style karate chop to
the windpipe of an unsuspecting woman emerging after her
ablutions.

Dan became a completely different person on stage from the
one I'd met off it. While we'd chatted in the car, his eyes had
twinkled brightly as he spoke of Elvis's Jewish heritage, but here,
behind the dark Elvis sunglasses, he was Schmelvis, the character he'd created a decade ago in the old people's homes of
Montreal, the character that had made pilgrimages to Memphis
and Israel in honour of the King, invigorated by the spirit of his
hero. Even though his eyes were hidden, the determination and
passion were clear beneath the desultory stage lights. Dan was
lost in the performance.

The next morning I woke in Dan's basement, a room I shared
with the leads, cables and grey hardware of recording detritus as
well as the family memorabilia – photos of Debbie with the

children blu-tacked to the wall and framed pictures of rabbis and Jewish elders. By the door was pinned a Hebrew map of Israel. Dan rose around the same time as me, after Debbie had left for work and taken the kids to school. The house was quiet, and so was Dan. Even though the previous night's gig had been low key, it had clearly taken a lot out of him. He didn't come to life until we'd walked a few blocks to his favourite coffee place.

We took the subway to the centre of town. It was a warm day, and a steady stream of people walked the streets in shirtsleeves carrying plastic-topped cardboard cups of coffee. This was the Montreal equivalent of Oxford Street yet it could hardly have been more different. People strolled with their heads up and smiles on their faces, rather than snapping along at route-march pace, eyes on the pavement and faces set with a grim, almost aggressive determination. I remarked to Dan that Montreal seemed a calm place.

'Yeah, it is, it's pretty laid back,' he said. 'If you went to Toronto from here, well, you'd really see a difference. In Montreal people work to live; in Toronto they live to work.'

A quick visit to Dan's office seemed to prove that theory. With a business partner he runs a call centre selling medical supplies. When we arrived in the late morning, every desk was empty.

Having made one or two calls and been through the morning's post, Dan picked up his keys and jacket and proclaimed that we were going to climb a mountain.

Mont Royal has a spiritual place in the hearts of Montreal folk, and not just because it gave the city its name. There are some who would scoff at the very idea that it's a mountain rather than, like, a really big hill, but its importance to the burghers of Canada's second city cannot be underestimated. It was on the mountain's lower slopes that the Iroquois established the village which grew to be Montreal, and today it keeps watch over the city. It's also barely ten minutes' walk from the centre of town, so perfect for a lunchtime escape from the hustle and bustle, or at least what passes for hustle and bustle in Montreal. In London terms, Mont Royal is a little bit like having Mount Snowdon uprooted, towed down the M4 and placed somewhere in the region of, say, Bloomsbury.

The mountain was tastefully landscaped by Frederick Law Olmsted, who also designed Central Park, but the same rabid Puritanism that put a stop to Elvis performing in the city almost did for the mountain too. In the mid-fifties a newspaper report appeared with the scandalous revelation that young people were using the mountain to, ahem, get to know each other better. Not only that, people were going up there to drink beer too. Such deplorable behaviour led to the mountain being entirely stripped of its undergrowth and hedges, anything in fact that might hide a couple of pairs of bare buttocks and a six-pack of Molson from the guardians of the city's collective morality. Naturally this had a knock-on effect on the mountain's ecosystem and the trees began to die off, necessitating some frantic replanting to restore Mont Royal to its former glory.

And rather glorious it is too. It's a strange feeling walking along a street full of offices, crossing the road at the next junction and finding yourself at the foot of a mountain – but scarcely ten minutes after leaving Dan's downtown office we were breathlessly ascending a steep footpath and beginning, to employ the evocative Yiddish vernacular used by Dan when he'd met me at the airport, to schvitz like dogs. We also became rather hopelessly lost among the pines and the intertwining footpaths, at one moment having to flag down a couple of competitors in a cross-country run to ask directions to the viewing platform Dan wanted to show me.

Once we arrived, puffing and schvitzing, the view across the city was spectacular. Dan pointed out some of Montreal's landmarks and we stood in the cool mountain air for a while drinking in the peace. Behind the platform, which was more of a plaza than a platform, there was a vast chalet, a huge hall empty save for a few tables and chairs and a snack bar tucked away at one end. I bought us a couple of bottles of ice-cold water and we sat down at a table to recover from our brave ascent. Once we'd perked up a little, I asked Dan about his background.

'I was born in Israel, and had a great childhood,' he said. 'Unlike the sheltered world of North America, growing up in Jerusalem was very outdoors-orientated, you know; the kids play in the parks and they go out to the desert and the woods and they're with the animals, the snakes and the reptiles, and the sunshine. It was a great place to grow up. Coming here to Canada, as I did when I was nine, was a complete culture shock. You can't go out alone, everybody's paranoid that someone's going to kidnap you. I missed the Israeli way of life at first, but I got used to it and I love Canada for what it is. Israel has terrible problems with surrounding countries and the Palestinian issue, which I won't get into, but here in Canada the most exciting time of the week is garbage night. Tuesday and Friday night the city collects the garbage – everybody looks forward to it. If the truck forgets to take your garbage there's a whole to-do – people get all excited, the phones are ringing off the hook. That, I think, is Canada in a nutshell: nothing happens here and they like it that way. If you ask me, garbage night should be a national holiday.

'But there have been a lot of creative souls to come out of Canada, a lot of great talent: musicians, entertainers, comedians, writers, not to mention hockey players, and basketball was invented here. I feel like my real home is Israel – I was born there and I plan to return there one day – but I love Canada, I try to make the best of it; it's a great place to raise kids and a great place to enjoy.'

I wondered when Dan first realised he was musical.

'I won a competition in my early teens,' he said, 'and the prize was three hundred dollars. With that I bought my first guitar. I'd started playing piano at the age of eight, but I'd always wanted to play guitar so I could be more like Elvis and the Beatles. I had a band at school, highly influenced by Elvis. He was a great inspiration, right from when I was around seven years old and my dad bought me *Girls! Girls! Girls!*, which I loved. I saw reruns of his appearances on *The Ed Sullivan Show*, and his *Aloha From Hawaii* special when we were still in Israel. I thought, Yeah, this guy knows what he's doing, and I could do that too. He was inspirational in every way, his voice, his moves, even the way he talked to the audience, the way he captivated people.

'The Schmelvis thing was born in old-age homes when I was a music therapist in the mid-nineties. I was working at the Hospital of Hope entertaining older people and I used to sing a lot of Elvis songs, the older ones that the people knew. I'd add a bit of schtick to the songs, change the words a little bit, like in 'Circumcision Song', making them a bit more comic. That went down well, and Schmelvis was born. A couple of years later the Schmelvis movie came about after the *Wall Street Journal* article on Elvis's Jewish heritage. The grandson of one of the residents was interested in doing a movie about it; they were looking for a protagonist, so they called me up and asked if I would go along with it. That's what really established me as Schmelvis and things went on from there.'

I'd read a bit about Elvis's apparent Jewishness before I arrived in Canada, and asked Dan to fill me in on the whole story.

'Elvis wore a *chai* and a cross. When I spoke to Elvis's friends

George Klein and Larry Geller, they said that he wore both because he believed that once he got to the gates of heaven, he'd be covered. Actually a lot of people don't know that Elvis put a Star of David on his mother's original gravestone, which is in storage somewhere at Graceland. When Vernon took over the estate and moved Gladys's body to Graceland he decided just to put a cross on the stone. But there are pictures that show the original stone.'

Elvis was aware of Judaism from an early age. When the Presleys first arrived in Memphis they lived in Lauderdale Courts, a housing scheme for the poor. Above them in their duplex were a Jewish couple, the Fruchters.

'Every *Shabbat* Elvis would go upstairs and do all the things for the couple that they couldn't on the sabbath, turning lights on and off, all that kind of thing,' said Dan. 'Sometimes Elvis would ask to borrow their records and record player while they were away. He'd listen to all this Jewish stuff, the cantorial hymns, which I think you can hear in Elvis's style of singing. So he had the black gospel influences, the country stuff and also I think the Jewish musical influence.

'Although he was aware of Elvis's Jewish heritage, Colonel Parker told him to keep it in the closet because it might have been detrimental to his career. But as George Klein pointed out, he wore the *chai* so must have known about it. Now, I'm an orthodox Jew, which means I'm God-fearing, I keep the sabbath, eat kosher and generally pray once a day. I'm very proud to be a Jew; it's a growing process of realising who I am. Same as Elvis, who did a lot of soul-searching, working out who he was and what his purpose in life was. I love being an emissary, playing live and spreading the word of peace and love among people. It's an old sixties philosophy maybe, but that's what I'm trying to promote when I'm up there. As well as having a good, comical time, of course.'

I wondered whether Dan ever came up against any criticism for his Jewish Elvis schtick.

'It's very rare that I get criticised for doing the Schmelvis show,' he said. 'Sometimes I get it from the old Jewish ladies, who say, "You look too Jewish up there, you should shave off your beard, you must be such a handsome boy without your beard", but that's pretty much it; I never get anything from people who aren't Jewish. The Jewish community is very accepting of Schmelvis and rock 'n' roll is a great vehicle to make a positive impact on people. The lyrics I sing are pretty harmless. Sometimes people think I'm actually a rabbi – they come to me for advice, I don't know why, maybe I just have that kind of face.'

But what would Elvis have made of it all?

'I think Elvis would have thought Schmelvis had a good comic kick,' mused Dan. 'I consider myself to be a tribute artist, but I do things the Schmelvis way. I try to capture the essence of Elvis on stage – his moves, his persona, the way he spoke – because that's where you find the beauty of Elvis. But nobody compares to him, he always gave a hundred and ten per cent when he was up there and nothing would come between him and his music.'

Dan has taken Schmelvis to Graceland, and while there performed a moving service for his near-namesake.

'Elvis never had a Jewish burial,' Dan pointed out, 'and to have a proper Jewish burial ten Jewish men have to say *Kaddish*, which is when you elevate the Jewish soul. There were seven of us, and miraculously we found three other Jewish guys who happened to be at Graceland that day too. There was a rabbi among us and we said *Kaddish* over his grave and helped Elvis's Jewish soul ascend. In Israel we planted a tree for him in the hills outside Jerusalem, and we also went to the Western Wall and put a note there.

'Making the film about Elvis brought me closer to his fans, especially at Graceland. That's when I really understood the reverence and respect they had for him. I just kept hearing about what a great, loving, understanding guy he was. From their point of view he was the most loving individual you could ever encounter. That's an inspiration in itself as a way of life. You read a lot about the drugs and the negative parts of his life, but when you hear about the positive effect he had on people, you realise that there's something larger than the man involved, and it remains there in the fans. It's a legacy that's really wholesome and has great foundations in religion and ethics. The guy was very special. When he was young he carried Mrs Fruchter's baby from the car to the house, and now the guy is one of the best guitar players in the United States. Who knows, maybe the fact that Elvis carried him had some kind of impact, like when a prophet or a righteous individual blesses you. It's called *siddikim* in Judaism, the belief that righteous people sustain the world. Every generation has thirty-six righteous people. They have one foot in this world and one in the world to come, so they're able to communicate with God and also to bless people. Elvis, I believe, had something of the righteous person about him.

'He was chosen in a way people are chosen to perform a mission without knowing why. He knew his powers; he knew that nobody could outdo him in his domain, the stage. That's why they call him the King. He elevated music to a new level; he took it from a diamond in the rough and polished it to make it a clear and pure diamond.'

It was time for Dan to return to the office, so I decided to go and explore the old part of Montreal until he was free again in the evening. The city is set out in a way that makes it easy to navigate even for a directionally challenged numbskull like me. It was practically a straight road through Chinatown, where the smells and sights were familiar from any Chinatown in any city in the world, to the old harbour area. I passed a porn cinema whose frontage was dominated by an illuminated sign reading 'LIFE IS ART'. Above it, and in much bigger letters, flashed the word 'MASTURBATING'. I couldn't quite work out what it meant. You could only experience life as art if you were masturbating? A life devoted to masturbation could be defined as art? You only had a life if you masturbated in an arty way? Whichever way, displaying the word 'masturbating' on the front of a porn cinema was probably the most direct way of describing the outcome of a visit inside its portals. Rather like flashing the word 'HANGOVER' above a pub doorway, or 'STOMACH CRAMPS AND ONION BREATH' over a kebab shop. I made a note that if I ever open a bongo cinema, I'll be sure to go the whole nine yards and have a flashing sign reading 'GUILT, INADEQUACY AND SELF-LOATHING' over its door.

I reached the old town without too much schvitz, and spent a thoroughly pleasant few hours doing absolutely nothing of any great import, apart from buying and consuming an enormous banana split. Old Montreal is a terrific place just to wander around to no particular purpose. There's the harbour to look at. Then the narrow streets with a range of shops from swanky art galleries to tacky souvenir places hawking T-shirts displaying cartoon images of people doing inappropriate things to moose. There is also a startling number of ice cream emporia and not normally being one for ice cream, on an impulse I strolled into one and asked for a banana split to go. I thought judging by the picture this would have been an affair comfortably held in the palm of the hand. When it was handed to me, however, I almost gave it straight back pointing out that I had merely ordered a banana split, not a medium-sized kayak topped with whipped cream.

It was probably the biggest dessert I'd ever seen, and I needed to eat it quickly, before the thing melted and left the attractive Place Jacques-Cartier up to its windowsills in liquid vanilla. Eating while walking was out of the question as it took two hands to carry, and anyway I'm a boy so am by nature incapable of multitasking. There was nothing for it other than to move as quickly as possible in search of some kind of seat. I staggered across the square with a panicky, gritted-teeth expression, holding the dessert in front of me as if it were one of those big old-fashioned round bombs with a fizzing fuse. I weaved through the square leaving a trail of yellow splodges on the cobbles behind me and lurched across the road to the greensward that separated the street from the harbour. There were picnic tables, of which but one was free. I lumbered towards it, slapped the banana split on to the table, sat down, took a firm grip of the plastic spoon and prepared for my dessert-a-thon.

It was when I took my first mouthful that I twigged why this particular table was vacant. As I inserted the brimming spoon into my open gob, I simultaneously breathed in a near-lungful of midges. I coughed as heartily as a mouthful of midge-infested ice cream would allow. People were watching, so I couldn't spit it all out, and down went the midges. After a bit of anti-insect karate, with a panache of which Elvis himself would have been proud, I attempted another mouthful. It was no good. I stood up, picked up the banana split again and hot-footed it to a recently vacated table instead.

Panting now, I parked at my new spot and began spooning the stuff into me. The midges were no fools, though, and soon arrived. And this time they'd brought reinforcements in the shape of a couple of wasps. Well, I did my best, but in the end the sheer flying-insectness of the situation caused me to admit defeat. I'd made inroads into the giant dessert, but so had my aerial adversaries. I could now hardly see the table for midges, and the wasps were performing an impressive pincer movement on my ears. 'Right,' I shouted, jumping to my feet. 'That's it, you win, I give up', much to the consternation of the early-evening promenaders who turned to look at a very angry man apparently having a loud argument with a banana split. I picked it up, marched towards the nearest bin and dumped the whole thing emphatically into it. A small fountain of melted ice cream shot upwards, taking out a good couple of insect battalions and depositing yellowy gunge on to my shoes, but my ordeal was over.

Recovering my composure, I repaired to Place Jacques-Cartier to while away the couple of hours still left before Dan finished work. I sat on a bench close to, strangely enough, Nelson's Column, an obelisk nowhere near as big as the one in Trafalgar Square but one that was erected before the London version by Anglophones determined to wind up the Francophiles. The cheeky scamps.

It was a really warm, pleasant evening as I watched the day give way to the night. A busker stood not far away, churning out impressive versions of songs, including 'Lawdy Miss Clawdy' and 'All Shook Up'. As the last rays of the day's sunshine warmed my face a strange thing happened. I completely forgot where I was. I was in such a contented reverie, and had done so much travelling in the preceding weeks that I genuinely lost track of where I was. I don't mean I just lost my bearings in Montreal, nor did I just forget which city I was in; I actually couldn't even remember what country I was in. I pondered for a while and then decided with a relieved loll of the head that I was in Leipzig, eastern Germany, where as it happens I'd been the week before. For a good few minutes I convinced myself that I was in the town Bach called home, rather than the one

Schmelvis did. I was just on the point of going and ordering a coffee in faltering German when the penny dropped that I was in Canada.

My daydream was then interrupted by a curious sound: a high-pitched wailing noise from the other end of the square. Strolling down to investigate, I found quite the most remarkable busker I've ever seen. He was nudging five feet tall, somewhere in his mid-forties, bald and clad in a turquoise T-shirt and a pair of shorts so short they practically qualified as a belt. It wasn't a pleasant sight, but could possibly explain the strange falsetto in which he sang accompanied by a man on a keyboard who himself looked as though he'd disappeared into his bedroom with an Atari games console at the age of thirteen and only recently emerged into society. As I approached I realised that they were attempting to perform the Beatles' 'Yesterday'. The singer's face was screwed up with concentration, and he held the microphone in his right hand while his left arm was extended outwards. The left hand quivered in a curious manner, as if it was in an invisible blender. It was a fairly accurate rendition, apart from the fact that the guy had no sense of rhythm or timing and had the same kind of accuracy on the high notes as a blind man trying to shoot a mime in a dark room. I have to say with some sense of shame that it was absolutely hilarious. I felt guilty for finding the whole thing hideously funny, but then noticed that nobody could pass without emitting a slight snigger, or at the very least a smirk and an elbow in the ribs of their partner.

It was almost painful to watch, particularly when he attempted that Celine Dion song from *Titanic* and couldn't even get within the same continent as the high notes. It was verging on tragic – the fellow was obviously convinced he was a tremendous singer, yet he appeared to have not a trace of musicality about him. If it were just about passion and commitment he'd have been up there with the best (although he would have had to sort out the strange wiggly hand business), as he was singing with the whole core of his being. His entire body was stiff with intensity, his eyes were closed and his face was screwed up with a passionate concentration of which Elvis would have been proud, but what came out of his mouth was a tuneless, high-pitched whine that would even have cats scattering to the four winds.

By now darkness had fallen, both literally and musically, and it was time to head back downtown for a final couple of beers with Dan ere departing for Ontario early the following morning. Before we left his office we descended to the basement of the building, where a rock band managed by his drummer Mike was battering its way through a high-octane rehearsal version of Led Zeppelin's 'When the Levee Breaks'. The singer's stage presence was evidently not hindered by his left foot being in plaster. Mike, one of Montreal's busiest and most respected musicians, sat in an old armchair directing matters, so we left for the pub and my time in Montreal finished after midnight in an all-night diner, eating pepper steak and salt-beef sandwiches.

A couple of days later, a Sunday, I was up early and sitting in the lobby of my hotel outside Toronto waiting to be driven to church. As I sat there I tried to think of the last time I'd been to church on a Sunday morning, and I couldn't remember. In fact it's distinctly possible that I haven't been to a church on a Sunday morning in my entire life. But here I was, in Canada, in an anonymous, soulless commuter town, waiting to be taken to church by an archbishop.

Considering that most Sundays I wouldn't walk to the end of the street to go to a church, it would have to be something pretty special to get me flying halfway across the world to do just that. The Reverend Dorian Baxter is certainly special. Indeed, he's one of the most extraordinary people I've ever met. As well as being a hugely popular Anglican cleric, he's an Elvis impersonator who calls himself 'Elvis Priestley'. Not only was he awarded the keys to the city of Memphis for his good works, he was also declared the Bishop of Beale Street, and proclaimed the number-one Elvis tribute artist in the world, who 'manifests the spiritual heart and soul of the king of rock 'n' roll'. The Anglican Church didn't take kindly to Dorian's Elvis persona and banned him from every Anglican pulpit in Canada, in addition revoking his licence to perform weddings. He reacted by setting up his own church in Newmarket, Ontario: the Church of Christ the King, Graceland, Independent Anglican Church of Canada.

There is, however, far more to Dorian Baxter than his ministry and his Elvis act, as I would learn while spending the day with a truly remarkable human being.

Before I'd left I arranged with Dorian that I'd call him on arrival in Ontario to arrange when and where I'd be picked up. The previous evening I had left two phone messages for him and when, by 11 p.m., I hadn't heard back I was beginning to fear that he'd forgotten I was coming. Just as I was about to give up and go to bed, the phone next to my bed rang and a deep, sonorous and very English voice apologised profusely for not returning my calls earlier, 'but I've been at the hospital all evening sitting with a very ill parishioner'. He kindly offered to collect me the next morning and take me to his church, only it would have to be early as he had a healing session with another parishioner before the service. Bearing in mind that it was the best part of an hour's drive each way, this was awfully hospitable of him.

Hence at the, ahem, ungodly hour of eight o'clock the next morning I was sitting in the hotel lobby when my mobile phone went. I could hear traffic noise in the background as a familiar voice said apologetically, 'I'm running a little late and the police here are very, very hot on speeding.' There was a slight pause. 'Not that I would do that anyway, of course. I'm terribly sorry, but I think I'm going to be about fifteen minutes later than I said I'd be,' he continued. 'May the Lord be with you.'

Dorian Baxter has had an amazing half-century of a life. Born in Kenya to British Army parents, he was the Kenyan national backstroke swimming champion at sixteen, as well as a successful amateur boxer. In 1967 he visited his sister in Canada and, despite being hospitalised with malaria when he arrived, fell in love with the country and moved there permanently the following year. He qualified as a teacher in the early seventies and became a born-again Christian around the same time after attending church at the invitation of one of his students. He married in 1975 and by the early eighties decided to train as a priest. Around the same time, worried by what he saw as the satanic messages contained in rock 'n' roll, he formed a Christian rock band called Jesus Rock of Our Salvation, wearing a red leather jacket to symbolise the blood of Christ. Posted to a church way in the frozen north of Canada, Dorian and his wife adopted two young daughters at birth through the auspices of a Christian charity, something that would lead to the events that changed his life for ever and, indeed, nearly destroyed him.

He first started impersonating Elvis in public in 1996 at the behest of his daughters, when he stole the show at the Collingwood Elvis Festival. From there he began incorporating Elvis gospel songs into his services until, in 2002, the Anglican Church barred him from the pulpit under the mistaken impression that Dorian was encouraging the worship of Elvis, by among other things officiating at weddings in his jumpsuit. That's when he started his own church, whose service I was about to attend.

After a quarter of an hour or so a large, sleek burgundy Cadillac with a white Elvis jumpsuit hanging in the rear window drew up outside the hotel. The driver's door opened and an impressive quiff appeared, followed by the rest of Dorian himself. I passed through the revolving door of the hotel as he rounded the car, cutting a striking figure in a dark suit over a mauve priest's shirt with its white dog collar. We shook hands and he apologised again for being late. As I climbed into the passenger seat I noticed that in the window opposite the jumpsuit hung his priest's robes.

'Elvis has permeated my whole life,' he told me as we set off for Newmarket. 'I've been impersonating Elvis since I was five years old when my father put a record on the hi-fi at our home in Mombasa. It was the day after my fifth birthday and I was playing with the red firetruck I'd been given, and suddenly out of the hi-fi comes 'Heartbreak Hotel'. According to my dad I just dropped the firetruck and stood there mesmerised, staring at the hi-fi. Apparently I turned to him and said, "Daddy, can I have a record by that singer?" and started singing like him from that day on. So technically I've now being impersonating him for more than fifty years, longer than Elvis did Elvis himself.

'Elvis the King of rock 'n' roll worshipped Jesus the King of Kings, and I always say Elvis appeals to everybody regardless of race, creed, religion, age – he's broken all those barriers down. At the church we have the honour of two young gentlemen in their late thirties and early forties who fall into the category of being challenged mentally and emotionally. We call one of them the young Elvis, and he'll most likely be there today in a blue cowboy shirt with Elvis's name on the back and a cowboy neck-erchief, and he often gets up to sing.'

As the car cruised along the highway towards Newmarket, I asked Dorian how the Elvis Priestley thing came about.

'In 1987 I was teaching an eighth grade class,' he said. 'They all knew I was an Elvis fan and at their graduation they asked me to sing 'If I Can Dream', the song Elvis did at the close of the *Comeback Special*. There was a cartoon soon afterwards in a news-paper in which a priest was drawn as Elvis, with the hair, the glasses and a cross around his neck, and the cartoonist had writ-ten underneath, 'Elvis Priestley'. The kids jumped on it right away and, lo and behold, as a farewell gift they gave me a copy of this picture and all signed it.

'Then in 1996 after my daughters persuaded me to enter the Collingwood Elvis Festival, I named myself Elvis Priestley and the rest is history. I was worried that I didn't look like Elvis, but Rachel went out and got me a ten-dollar wig, and Malaika, my youngest, said, Daddy, we've got a leftover Halloween outfit. The outfit cost nineteen dollars and was one-size-fits-all; it was bulgy in all the wrong places and the belt they got me had jellybeans on the front and tied at the back in a bow. I looked more like the Easter bunny than Elvis. Now there were Elvises there with suits that had cost three or four thousand dollars each, so when I got on the stage the other Elvises' jaws dropped. My wig was stuck down with aeroplane glue that was burning a hole in my cheek and it kept flipping up; I looked like Mary Tyler Moore. I sang "Teddy Bear", "Blue Suede Shoes" and finished with "Amazing Grace", the audience loved it, and I won the Canadian Showstopper award, which got me on the front page of all the local papers.

'I've led tens of thousands to Jesus Christ because of Elvis, and that's one of the main reasons I do it. I have a five-point sermon where I expound on each letter in Elvis's name, and it has a massive impact, because I'm addressing Elvis fans. I also use the story of when I met Elvis's stepbrother Rick Stanley in 1983.

'Rick says he has Elvis to thank that he is still alive today, and that he's a Christian and now an ordained minister. Elvis used to pay his entourage very handsomely and many of them, including Rick, got into cocaine. Elvis, although he ended up becoming addicted to prescription drugs, was vehemently against illicit drugs. The night he died Rick was at the house. Elvis could see that he was on cocaine, and said, "Rick, I can't preach at you, but look at what I've allowed the devil to do to me. My only hope now is the Lord Jesus Christ." He then rammed his finger into Rick's chest and said, "Rick, you have to get off that cocaine. Jesus is your only hope." With that he turned and went upstairs and that was the last time Rick saw him. Rick vowed that night that he would never touch cocaine again because of his love for Elvis, but within twenty-four hours he was doing it again, his addiction was that bad.

'Six months later, Rick was so disgusted with himself he was going to commit suicide. He said, as he was about to do it he heard, clear as anything, Elvis's voice saying, "Rick, Jesus Christ is your only hope." He fell on his knees and cried out to Jesus, had a massive conversion and at that moment his desire for cocaine was gone completely. He was so committed he studied divinity and now as the Reverend Rick Stanley has led hundreds of people to Jesus because of Elvis. Isn't that amazing?

'I told that story at the Collingwood Elvis Festival and at the end of the night they asked me to put my robes on and I did three gospel numbers in the garden, and remarkably they lined up from midnight until four in the morning to pray with me and accept Jesus Christ as their Lord and Saviour. Since then there's been a stream of people finding the Lord because, I guess, of the Elvis Priestley motif.'

As it turned out, that was just the beginning of the saga that led to Dorian founding his own Elvis-style church. Despite the obvious success of his Elvis-based ministry, the bishops began to raise quizzical eyebrows in Dorian's direction.

'I think what really brought me to wider attention was my rumble with the bishops,' said Dorian. 'I should write them a thank-you letter because now I get bookings all over the world. The Lord truly does work in mysterious ways.

'The Church took strongly against me. One particular bishop seemed to have it in for me, saying that if you rearrange the letters in the name Elvis, it spells "Evils". I happened to have a Levi's belt on and pointed out that it spelled Levi's too. As far as I was concerned I'd done nothing that could even be remotely considered as desecratory to a religious service.

'The other bishops held a meeting and banned me from preaching in every pulpit across Canada. I waited about nine months in case they reconsidered, but when the media asked me what I was going to do, I said that I would open my own church on the nearest Sunday to Elvis's birthday. In Anglicanism we believe in symbolism, and my message to the bishops would be that there was nothing wrong with Elvis's gospel music and he was a good man. Two hundred and seventy one showed up at the first service and we've never looked back. In fact it's rather a similar story to Elvis himself, when he had all that early opposition from the Church.'

The bishops may well have regretted their decision when the world's media descended on the Church of Christ the King, Graceland, for its first service.

'The first service of our new church ended up on the front page – the front page, mind – of nearly six thousand newspapers around the world,' said Dorian. My eyebrows shot up like rocketing pheasants. 'CBS called and said that never before has the same front page on nearly every newspaper in North America, including the hick towns, been the same as every national paper around the world. I couldn't believe that. Two weeks later, just before the service, somebody handed me a copy of the *South China Post* with my picture on the front. TV crews showed up from all around the world.'

We pulled off the highway and parked at a diner for breakfast before the service. Dorian led the way through the doors and I followed behind assailed by the smells of eggs, bacon and coffee. We stood inside and scanned the room for an empty table. Having been sitting next to Dorian for quite a while in the car I had forgotten just what an impact a rock 'n' roll priest with his dog collar and Elvis pompadour could have if he walked into a busy restaurant. A hush fell over the place. Even a baby near by stopped crying.

'Hi Elvis!' chirped a young waitress as she hurried over. Dorian explained to her that we were in a little bit of a hurry, and would appreciate some quick service.

'Sure, anything for you, Elvis,' she responded and, followed by every pair of eyes in the place, led us to a booth in the window. Once we'd sat down and ordered, the hubbub of conversation and the clatter of cutlery started up. The baby began crying again.

Before long a large pot of coffee and two mountainous plates of bacon and eggs arrived and were placed in front of us. At once I set about the condiments, covering the eggs in pepper and slathering the bacon in ketchup. I piled up a fulsome forkful and was just opening my mouth to a jaw-cracking aperture ready for its insertion when I noticed Dorian looking at me with his hands clasped.

'Could I have the honour of saying grace?' he asked.

'Umm, of course,' I responded, laying my fork down and bowing my head in a futile attempt to make it look as though I knew that had been the plan all along.

'Lord, I want to thank you for the honour and the privilege of meeting with Charlie and pray that you'll bless us in our meeting. Strengthen us to serve you and help us to be ever mindful of those less fortunate than we. And I pray especially for your blessing on his remaining time here, and we pray for your blessing on the service this morning, and that you'll give him a safe journey home to his family and loved ones. In Jesus Christ our Lord, amen.'

We picked up our cutlery and started dining just as 'It's Now Or Never' rose above the hubbub through the speakers. We looked at each other and both cocked our heads at the same time.

'They must have put that on for us, isn't that lovely of them?' said Dorian, and then told me the story of how Elvis saved his life.

'By 1985 my ministry was going very well and I'd been married for ten years. In those days I was the golden-haired boy with a very bright future, and at the end of April the bishop had asked me to preach on a particular verse to about five hundred people at a conference. The verse was from St Paul's letter to the Corinthians where he says sometimes life will deal you a blow. Sometimes that blow can be so hard that you're struck down. But if we trust in the Lord Jesus Christ we are not destroyed. I still have a copy of that sermon, and in it I said that you can lose all your money, you can be betrayed by those nearest and dearest to you on a level you've never met, and you will be struck down. But if you trust in Jesus, I believe you will never be destroyed. Now when I got home, and the date of 1 May 1985 will always stay with me, I found that everything I had just preached about had happened to me.

'I came home to find that the woman I loved and had been married to for so long had taken our two little girls and run off with another man. She'd taken our money, the car, everything in the house – there wasn't even a bed! All I had left in the world was $61.95, so I borrowed some money from my church wardens and started the custody battle.

'It only took a year to win custody of my girls, but during that year I was given just one hour with my daughters every two weeks, for which I travelled fourteen hours each way. I'd plug in my earphones and listen to Elvis gospel music all the way there and back on my motorcycle. I was so desperate and devastated that I actually contemplated taking my own life, but listening to one particular song, "When the Storms of Life are Raging, Stand By Me", stopped me from doing it. Little did I know at the age of five, when I stood transfixed in front of my father's hi-fi listening to Elvis singing "Heartbreak Hotel", that one day the guy would save my life.'

At the church I holed up in a back room to tune Dorian's guitar. I'd told him about my appearance on Uzbek television at the diner, and he'd asked me to address the congregation and then join him in singing 'Blue Moon of Kentucky'. Alas, two of the tuning heads were missing, meaning that it was impossible to tune the instrument. I broke the bad news to him but, as I should have guessed from our conversations during the morning, he refused to give in.

'Well, we'll just have to do it a cappella then,' he said in a tone that brooked no argument. Ulp.

Out front the congregation was arriving, with the hard core working tirelessly to change the room from the soulless Royal Canadian Legion hall into the welcoming bosom of the Church of Christ the King, Graceland. On the stage was a table adorned with a purple valance decked with flowers, two candles and a large, open Bible. Stage right was an electronic organ, and left, the lectern, propped up against which was an artist's impression of the forthcoming Church of Christ the King. Folding chairs were set out in rows with a hymn book and order of service on each. I mingled with the worshippers, most of whom were delightfully friendly couples of all ages. Even the most cursory chats revealed that they thought the world of Dorian – the affection and respect they had for him was tangible.

I took a seat near the front and flicked through the order of service. Clearly, if the announcements section was anything to go by, Dorian had built a strong community. There were plugs for women's coffee and crafts meetings, a youth group and a Bible study class. At the very bottom of the page was a letter to God from one of the younger members of the congregation. 'Dear God,' it read, 'I do not think anybody could be a better God. Well, I want you to know that I am not just saying this because you are God already. Love Ricky.'

Dorian took to the stage and it was obvious from the start that he is a born showman. His personality filled the room, whether during the sermon, the hymns, or when he performed a couple of Elvis gospel songs. During the songs he would fall to his knees, throw his arms in the air and look to the heavens in passionate affirmation of his feelings for both God and Elvis.

The time came for me to be called up from the congregation, and I was introduced by Dorian as 'a visitor from London, but not London, Ontario – London, England'. I mumbled a few words about how delighted I was to be there, what a fun church it was, the spiritual influence of Elvis around the world and wished everyone luck with the new church project. At one point someone shouted, 'Mr Bean', at me – not sure what that was about – but I managed not to put my foot in it and tried to slink back to my seat. Dorian was having none of it, however.

'I've been doing Elvis since I was five,' he disclosed, 'and I found out today that Charlie started doing Elvis when he was six', which wasn't strictly true, but the sentiment was there. 'Now unfortunately,' he continued, 'it turns out that my guitar is impossible to tune so Charlie can't accompany us, but we are going to sing "Blue Moon of Kentucky", which Charlie is going to start.'

From my point of view it was probably one of the worst performances of Elvis's early Sun recording to be unleashed on an audience. I'm bad enough with a guitar, but without I'm like a fish not just out of water, I'm a halibut in the middle of the Sahara. I had the microphone in one hand, and minus the prop of the guitar I found myself slapping my thigh in a pathetic manner allegedly in time to the music. I was way out. The congregation clapped along, but I easily shook them off by getting faster and faster. I'd also pitched the song far too low and was soon mumbling somewhere in the region of my shoes as Dorian, one of the leading Elvis tribute artists in the world with certificates to prove it, struggled manfully to keep up with my pinball timekeeping and ridiculous basso profundo. Indeed, halfway through the song Dorian tried to bring it to an end, but despite my appalling performance I had the smell of the greasepaint in my nostrils. I was Elvis up there. It was Memphis 1956 and I was in Sun Studio with Scotty Moore adding guitar chops, Bill Black slapping away at his battered old bass and Sam Phillips whooping away in the control room. Deep down I knew I was utter crap, but, blustering ego aside, I did have an inkling of the kick Elvis impersonators get when they assume the persona of the greatest rock 'n' roll singer to holler into a microphone. Eventually, thankfully, I deigned to finish the song, wresting every last moment from it. The congregation applauded politely. Or maybe they were still trying to work out the tempo I'd managed to change with every beat, I don't know. Either way, Dorian made polite noises about my showing and I strutted from the stage, head held high, to retake my seat, only twigging just how shockingly dreadful I'd been in a moment of epiphany over a takeaway in the hotel later that evening.

The service ended with the hymn 'Now Thank We All Our God' – which could have had the caveat 'That Connelly's Finally Stopped Singing' and a heartfelt benediction from Dorian. As the flock got up and prepared to leave many came up to me and said how good my rendition had been, and you know what? I believed them.

Dorian had to disappear pretty much right after the service, not as I feared as a result of my showing, but because he had a long drive ahead of him to share a few days with the daughters he fought so hard for at the lowest point of his life. As he folded himself into his wonderful burgundy Cadillac, he handed me an Elvis figurine in order that I might not forget Elvis Priestley, the Church of Christ the King, Graceland, and its wonderful community in a little town in Ontario. As he pulled out of the car park virtually the whole congregation stood to wave him off. Elvis Priestley had left the building.

Jyväskylä, Finland

I've always had a soft spot for Finland. Any country that can boast more saunas than cars, the world wife-carrying championships and the most tango dancers per head of population deserves a place in everyone's affections. Things just seem to happen by accident in Finland, like when a rubber-boot company in the little village of Nokia suddenly thought that mobile phones looked like something interesting and maybe worth mucking about with. I should have known then that such a quirky country, with its strange language unrelated to any in the world other than, wait for it, Hungarian, was guaranteed to produce an irresistibly unique link to Elvis; in Dr Jukka Ammondt, Finland boasts one of the most bizarrely appealing Elvis tribute artists in the world today. Not for him an ill-fitting jumpsuit, CD of bland karaoke backing and the tuneless crooning of all your favourite hits. No, Dr Ammondt performs and records Elvis songs in Latin and, in a new and exciting linguistic development, Sumerian.

I flew via Helsinki to Jyväskylä, a city which when I presented myself at check-in I realised I hadn't the slightest clue how to

pronounce. Now I quite fancy myself as a bit of a pronunciationist. I can be quite militant about it, in fact. In Vegas, for
example, I pompously insisted on referring to the formidably
conked performer of 'Copacabana' as 'Barry Manilov'. I used to
give a haughty harrumph every time a newsreader pronounced
Boris Yeltsin's first name to rhyme with 'Morris'. 'It's Bar-
REECE, you ignorant twonks,' I'd rail at the screen,
'Bar-REECE Yeltsin!' I can be, in short, a right pain in the arse
when it comes to pronunciation. Yet here was Mr Smug well
and truly getting his comeuppance. In answer to the question,
'Where are you travelling today, sir?', I realised that having only
seen the name of the place in print, I had no clue as to how to
say the word, with its multiple consonants and scattered umlauts.
'Erm, Jive-a-sky-la?' I mumbled, before simply handing her the
ticket I'd printed off the internet. 'Ahh,' she said, the penny
dropping. 'You're travelling to YOO-vaskula.'

Of course I was, and when I landed there later that day I
could pronounce its name like a native. Of south London. After
arriving in the dark, snowbound environs of central Finland I
was collected from the airport by a tall, square-jawed man named
Esko. Esko is Dr Ammondt's accompanist, travelling with him
around the world to various linguistic gigs. The following week,
in fact, they were off to a conference of linguistics in Brittany to
perform songs in ancient Greek. As you do. Esko looked
younger than his fifty-one years, dressed in a sharp black suit and
black polo neck jumper. We crunched through the snow to a
low, sleek sports car in the car park.

'Nice car,' I said as we left the airport and sped through the
darkness between endless lines of snow-clad pine trees heading
for Esko's motel and restaurant, where I would be staying and
where I would meet Dr Ammondt over breakfast the following
day.

'It's actually my wife's,' said Esko. 'I gave it to her for Christmas.'

He then went on to tell me the veritably heartwarming story of how his wife Silje had originally come over from Estonia to work in his restaurant as part of her hospitality qualification. Despite her being some twenty-five years his junior, they fell in love almost immediately, and Silje would come over to visit as often as she could. Sadly, but inevitably, this combination of young eastern European woman and older western European man aroused the interest of the Finnish immigration authorities, who would ask impertinently personal questions, until one day Silje and Esko were actually arrested and detained overnight. It was there, in a prison cell, that Esko asked Silje to marry him. She agreed; they were married soon afterwards in a sumptuous ceremony at the hotel, and now live there happily with their baby son Oliver.

After a while we crossed a large suspension bridge over an enormous frozen lake, glowing blue-white in the moonlight, pulled off the main road and curved around to a darkened build-ing on the lakefront. We climbed out of the car, stepped swiftly across the snow creating clouds with our breath – the tempera-ture was somewhere in the region of minus twelve – and plunged gratefully into the welcome warmth of Esko's Lossivahti motel and restaurant. At Esko's prompting I sat at a table in the bar, which was in front of a large and completely deserted restau-rant area. We were the only people there. At the height of summer when boats are bobbing by the jetty and the place is full of visitors enjoying the sunshine, the Lossivahti would be bub-bling with noise – the clink of cutlery, a joyful hubbub of nautical conversation, the throaty roar of the coffee machine – but here in the depths of the harsh, dark Finnish winter it was almost eerie. There was complete silence – what little sounds there may have been were deadened by the thick carpet of snow. The countless vacant restaurant tables, all laid in preparation of customers who were still some three or four months away, were faintly intimidating in their regimented emptiness.

'Officially we're open,' said Esko as he went behind the bar to fetch us both a beer, 'but we get hardly any business during the winter months when the lake freezes. In the summer it's amazingly busy; the pleasure boats on the lake moor at the jetty here and the place is absolutely packed. Luckily we make enough money during the summer to keep us going in the winter.'

To call it a lake probably conjures up an image of a small expanse of water with an ice cream van parked next to it. In Finland this can be something quite different, however. The country boasts more than 185,000 lakes and when you look at a map of Finland much of it seems to be submerged. Indeed, some 10 per cent is underwater which when you consider that Finland covers an area roughly the size of France is, in the perceptive words of Bananarama, really saying something. The Lossivahti is on Lake Päijänne. At more than four hundred square miles it is the second-largest in Finland and is larger than Hong Kong. The number of boats that chug up and down it during the summer months make the motel a goldmine for Esko and Silje.

The beer Esko handed me commenced one of the more uncommon evenings I think I've ever spent. After a splendid dinner he took his place behind the huge clavinova that dominates one end of the restaurant, from where he regularly entertains diners, and belted out a selection of popular hits in an impressive operatic tenor. The clavinova was an astonishing instrument that in terms of wattage and volume would have comfortably satisfied Pink Floyd at the height of their powers, and Esko's set of vocal pipes was more than a match for it, even without the added bonus of the microphone. He handed me a guitar and invited me to play along, which I did with limited success, peering over his shoulder like Carl Perkins in the picture I'd seen at Sun, until a bottle of Finnish brandy appeared and, in my mind at least, improved my performance to stadium rock levels.

'You have a great voice,' I said to Esko in a break between songs as the applause of our audience – Silje, baby Oliver and Tommy, a teenager who lives and works at the motel – died away, echoing around the vast empty restaurant.

'Well, actually, I was something of, I suppose you could have called me a child star here in Finland,' he admitted sheepishly. He indicated a large, framed poster on the wall advertising a 1960s performance of *Oliver!*, in which a sweet-looking, big-eyed little boy looked up mournfully at the camera. 'That's me,' he said. All of a sudden I could see the resemblance – although he's manifestly a highly successful businessman Esko still has the same innocent shine in his eyes as the boy in the picture. He thought for a moment, then moved over to the restaurant's stereo system and rummaged through some cassettes. Inserting one into the player, he informed me that it was a recording of a programme he made as a boy for national radio, singing a selection of Christmas songs. The young Esko's voice rang out with an orchestral backing in a gorgeous soprano so crystal clear you could reach out and polish it.

Topping up my brandy glass, he asked me if I wanted to hear something by Dr Ammondt.

'We'll try the newest one first,' he said. 'The Sumerian songs.'

He slipped the CD into the player, closed the drawer, pressed play and turned up the volume. A steady, plodding beat unfolded, before Dr Ammondt's throaty, guttural, almost menacing vocal growled through the mix.

The Sumerians were a remarkable race, inhabiting Mesopotamia, now southern Iraq, between roughly 4000 and 2000 BC. They are credited with inventing, among other things, writing, beer, mathematics and the wheel. A great deal of their language and musical legacy has been uncovered by archaeologists over the last century, including pictures of instruments and notation, hence Dr Ammondt's faithful interpretation that oozed from the speakers all around the deserted restaurant. There was something familiar about the song, but at first I couldn't quite work out what it was. Then a certain chord progression linked together in my mind and I realised that I was listening to 'Blue Suede Shoes' as I'd never heard it before.

'Obviously the Sumerians didn't have suede in those days,' explained Esko over the ominous juggernaut of the backing track, 'so the translation has to make allowances. The chorus translates from the Sumerian back into English as "On my sandals of sky-blue leather do not stand", for example.'

It was a hauntingly addictive piece of music. I'd expected it to be gimmicky, maybe tongue-in-cheek, but this was apparently the closest and most faithful representation of the ancient music of the Sumerians there had ever been. As the first recording released in Sumerian, this style of music sung in this language had not been heard in more than three millennia.

'When he first performed it live, Doctor Ammondt dressed himself and the musicians in traditional Sumerian-style clothes, so they wore leather caps and leather kilts. It looked amazing,' said Esko.

Dr Ammondt's first venture into Latin music – which is to say music performed in Latin rather than rhumbas or sambas – was an album of Finnish tangos sung in the language of the Romans. Actually, come to think of it, I guess you could call it Latin Latin. It's not clear why the tango is so hugely popular in

Finland. What's known is that dance troupes from Argentina toured Europe in the early twentieth century and sparked a craze that in time fizzled out, but that craze never died out in Finland. Some say that the dance suits the melancholic, taciturn Finns perfectly – certainly the nation boasts the second-biggest concentration of tango in the world behind the dance's country of birth, Argentina.

Then the literature professor turned his attention to Elvis, having some of the King's greatest hits translated into Latin. Esko placed the *The Legend Lives Forever in Latin* CD into the player and handed me the case. It was an ingenious idea. 'It's Now or Never' became '*Nunc hic aut numquam*', while 'Can't Help Falling in Love' was rejuvenated as '*Non adamare non possum*'.

Dr Ammondt's follow-up, produced in 1997, was *Rocking in Latin*, and included '*Ursus taddeus*' ('Teddy Bear'), '*Nunc distrahur*' ('All Shook Up') and my favourite, '*Ai, nunc laudi sis claudia*', which, as every self-respecting classics scholar would know, is Latin for 'Lawdy Miss Clawdy'. The songs coming out of the speakers were surprisingly good. I'd rather feared that the novelty of hearing Elvis in Latin might wear off fairly quickly, but the albums were highly engaging, and in contrast to the faintly unsettling growl of his Sumerian recordings, Dr Ammondt's voice had a light, lilting quality, completely different from Elvis's, which I saw as an advantage. Dr Ammondt isn't an Elvis impersonator. He doesn't wear the jumpsuits and sunglasses (indeed, as I'd just discovered, leather kilts were more his thing); he is Dr Ammondt, nothing more, singing the songs of the greatest ever rock 'n' roll singer in the greatest language in the world.

Once we'd heard most of the good doctor's repertoire, Esko and I returned to the clavinova for a few more songs, which I did my best to ruin with characteristically ham-fisted guitar playing;

my host closed the evening by letting rip a formidably operatic, window-rattling version of 'O Sole Mio' accompanied by a pre-recorded backing track courtesy of the keyboard. The evening was starting to feel to me a little like *The Shining: The Musical*, but Esko's operatic rendition served as a thunderous climax to a curious musical session.

Before showing me outside to the log cabin in which I'd be staying, Esko gave me a tour around the rest of the motel. Downstairs was a bar, which opened on to the lakefront in the summer and which he was planning on renovating before the coming season. 'I want to show you something,' he said, as we picked our way gingerly among subterranean stacks of chairs and bar tables. We passed through a doorway, where Esko revealed a room filled from floor to ceiling with hundreds and hundreds of cans of drink, all of which bore the image of Michael Jackson.

'They're an energy drink produced for Michael Jackson's HIStory tour,' said Esko with a grin. 'I bought seventeen lorry-loads for the concert he played in Helsinki, and these are all that's left. I'm going to sell them in the bar here.'

Marvelling at Esko's entrepreneurial skills (upstairs he'd shown me a cassette of Finnish Christmas songs he'd recorded with his children and sold to Finnish missions and cultural centres across the world), I then did a bit of rough mathematics in my head. I'm no Michael Jackson fan, but as I recalled it the HIStory tour had been some years ago.

'Aren't these going to be out of date?' I asked, gesturing at the neatly stacked slabs of Jacko-endorsed beverage.

'Well, yes, the expiry date on the bottom of the cans is 1999,' replied Esko, 'but I sent some away to Germany for testing and have scientific proof that they're perfectly all right. They gave them a shelf life of another two years. So I'm just wiping off the old date and putting stickers on with the new. Here, try one.'

I noted that Esko was cracking a can open as he passed me one, and deduced that this wasn't some convoluted attempt at assassinating me. I took a swig, and it honestly tasted perfectly fine. Very nice, in fact.

'I've even sold some through a Michael Jackson collectors' website,' said Esko with a chuckle, impressing me even further with his capacity to make a buck.

'Right,' he said when we'd finished our drinks. 'Let me show you to your cabin.'

We went back upstairs and out of the door. The crunching of our footsteps and the jangling of the cabin keys as Esko produced them from his pocket were the only sounds in the cloaking silence of the snow. The vast road bridge over the lake looked strangely beautiful bathed in the moonlight, and the snow-covered frozen lake stretched off into the distance.

'This cabin was used by a very famous Finnish singer,' Esko told me once we were inside. 'The previous owner knew him very well. He was called Irwin Goodman, and became popular in the 1960s singing protest songs. He was quite successful but developed a drink problem and then he got into trouble with the tax people and lost his house, so the owner here let him use this cabin free of charge. One night, in 1991 I think it was, he was coming back from Russia in a lorry and had a heart attack while queuing at the border. Seemingly the Russians wouldn't let him move out of line, they thought he was faking it to jump the queue, until they realised he was dead. It's a sad story but this,' he looked around the cosy little cabin with its fireplace and built-in sauna, 'this was his place for quite a while in the eighties. He loved it here apparently.'

☆

By the time I returned to the motel at the appointed hour in the morning – having unsuccessfully tried to light a fire in the grate and sweated out most of the evening's brandy in the sauna (which, incidentally, as a world-renowned pronunciationist who can now say 'Jyväskylä' correctly, I feel I must point out should be pronounced to rhyme with 'browner' rather than 'corner') – Dr Ammondt and his producer had already arrived. As Esko picked through a few chords on the clavinova, the professor stood near by, a short man with long grey hair swept back from his face and little round glasses. He came over and smiled a shy but kindly smile; he had the demeanour of someone who has spent much of his life alone with books. Dr Ammondt was dressed in blue jeans, a thin polo neck jumper and dark blazer and, with his hands in his pockets, looked quite cool. His English wasn't very confident – Esko would act as interpreter for our chat over breakfast – but he told me in a stilted, softly spoken voice about the little speech in Latin he gives before every performance, and which he'd kindly written out for me.

'This is what I say at the start of every concert,' he said as he handed me the handwritten sheet. 'It must always be written in capital letters, incidentally.'

'SALVETE, AUDITORES OPTIMI!' it began. 'SALUTEM PLURIMAM VOBIS DARE VOLO A FINNIA, PATRIA MEA. GAUDEO QUAM MAXIME, QUOD MIHI LICET CARMINA AB ELVISIO ILLO PRESLEY QUONDAM CANTATA NUNC VOBIS CANERE ET LATINE QUIDEM, HAEC EST LINGUA AETERNA. HAEC CARMINA NOBIS PRAEBENT GAUDIA VITAE, MEMORIAM TEMPORIS ILLIUS, QUOD PLENUM ERAT SPEI. HANC SPEM IPSAM IN CORDIBUS NOSTRIS FOVEAMUS. HUNC NUNTIUM VOBIS CARMINIBUS ELVISIANIS VOLO AFFERRE.'

'I am basically greeting the audience, and explaining to them that I sing Elvis in Latin because it's the eternal language,' he told me. 'And then the concert begins.'

He presented it to me along with some of his CDs and a copy of his new DVD, *Codex Fluitans*, a composition he'd written himself and launched recently at one of Jyväskylä's biggest churches.

We sat down at one of the tables in the restaurant, Tommy made sure that we all had enough coffee, and I prepared to hear about the Dr Ammondt phenomenon from the man himself. He sat opposite me, folded his fingers together and looked earnestly down at the table.

'Elvis saved my life,' he said. 'After my divorce, which was a very unpleasant time for me, I started to sing the Finnish tangos in Latin. They had a sad yearning for life, but it was Elvis who actually brought me back to life. I'd sung Elvis songs in English when I was young, and I wanted to play in a band but my parents made me continue with my studies instead. Academia became my career and music had to be put to one side. When I was a boy in the late fifties and early sixties Elvis was a big name, of course, and I realised that he represented possibilities for the younger generation who were being oppressed by the old fashioned structures. He offered self-awareness to the youth of the world – he was a little bit rebellious, and I could identify with that as I entered my teens. 'Rock Around the Clock' had already blown my mind, making me realise that life could be joyful. The school I went to was very authoritative, so we'd use Elvis to fight the system – there were a lot of little Elvises walking around the halls; believe me, it was quite a sight.

'When I came through my divorce I think I reached back to that time to find myself, to find the freedom I had back then.

That's why Elvis will live for ever in my heart and why I will always sing Elvis Presley songs in Latin. I was fifty years old when I rediscovered the joy of life in music again, so the times I had in the band when I was young had not been wasted.'

Many people choose to imitate Elvis, but Dr Ammondt had picked a different way of honouring the man who had given his life a new purpose and direction. But why Latin, I wondered?

'We studied Latin at school, and I always had a fascination for the language,' said Dr Ammondt. 'But the final push came from a colleague of mine called Teivas Oksala, who is a world-famous Latin specialist. He can write Latin the way it should be written, with heart and soul. My Latin isn't good enough to write it all myself, but this colleague gave me the inspiration to sing both tango and Elvis in Latin.

'Latin was the first language to have a written grammar in Europe, and the language bound together the empire to make an early European union, which I think is symbolic today, uniting all the different cultures. Elvis did the same with his music, so I think it's very appropriate that I should sing Elvis songs in the eternal language. I've done a lot of work with the Finnish Ministry of Foreign Affairs with my Latin music – they took the record of tangos to the Pope, who gave me a medal of honour for promoting the Latin language, and then came the period of true joy in my life with Elvis Presley. My first trip to America was in January 1995, to celebrate Elvis's sixtieth birthday in Memphis and launch my album *The Legend Lives Forever in Latin*, which I promoted on the radio. I met Carl Perkins and gave him a copy, but "Blue Suede Shoes", which he wrote, wasn't on that one. I put it on my next album, *Rocking in Latin*, but unfortunately Carl Perkins had passed away before I could get a copy to him.'

It was on his return from Memphis, though, that things really started to take off for this quiet academic from a frozen town in central Finland.

'I came back to Finland and discovered that the main news agency had put out a press release about *Legend*. When I came back from Memphis, they called me and said they were getting enquiries from all over the world about it, and that's when the international publicity started. It felt like travelling around the globe in twenty-four hours – the BBC called first in the morning, then the rest of Europe, then the east coast of America, the west coast, then Japan – as the sun rose in these different countries my phone would be ringing. I had to sing "Love Me Tender" in Latin over the phone to nearly all of them. I did concert tours in America every summer for five years after that, thanks to the support of the Ministry of Foreign Affairs. I never dreamed it would get so big. Us Finns are situated right up north, on the edge of the world, so it was nice to give a bit of recognition to my country too. When the spotlight is on me, I feel it's also on Finland.'

None of my tutors ever did anything quite so exciting. In fact, thinking back, none of them did anything remotely exciting at all. Hence I wondered what his students and colleagues made of his linguistically musical endeavours.

'Finns aren't demonstrative people as a rule so my students don't say a lot about my extracurricular work, but I think they are supportive of it. I don't perform at the university, my job there is to research literature and linguistics. Universities are quite conservative environments, so I have to be careful to keep the two sides of my life apart. The principal is positive about it though, as I've helped put the university on the map: people who visit here have usually heard about my singing.'

Esko then suggested that we watch Dr Ammondt's new DVD on his big-screen television at the far end of the restaurant. Inspired by the death of Pope John Paul II, *Codex Fluitans* is Dr Ammondt's first self-composed release.

'Codex Fluitans roughly means "The tree branch in the stream", like driftwood,' he told me as Esko placed the disc into the player. 'It's me looking back over my life, at the things that have happened to me. I'm very proud of it.'

He paused for a moment as the screen blinked into life. 'It's very serious,' he said.

The room filled with a slick, rock backing that chugged along, and Dr Ammondt appeared on the telly. He was sitting on a wall by a river, in jeans and a denim shirt with a red jacket slung casually over his shoulder. He looked pained, serious. His free hand gestured in time with the words, which he mostly recited rather than sang. It was a professional production – shots of Dr Ammondt were interspersed with babbling streams, weddings and happy children. The lip-synching may have been suspect in places, but this was Dr Ammondt's life compressed into three minutes of rock 'n' roll in Latin. The final chord died, and we all murmured approval. Dr Ammondt looked genuinely moved.

Tempus fugit, however, and Dr Ammondt and Esko needed to run through some of the songs they were performing in ancient Greek at the conference in France a few days later. Esko took his seat and fired up the clavinova, while Dr Ammondt picked up the microphone. They ran through an ancient Greek version of 'The Sunshine of Your Smile' a couple of times, and then it was time for the rocking academic to return to his day job. He shook my hand warmly, wished me every success, and then was gone, half scampering over the snow to his producer's car, which pulled away from the motel and disappeared around the bend. I watched the car glide over the bridge above the lake with a couple of icebound boats moored by the jetty in front of me. As it disappeared over the bridge, the snowy blanket of silence returned.

Bad Nauheim, Germany

'Move back a little bit,' said Constance as the freezing wind tried to find a way inside my coat. 'Just a little bit more. OK, there.' The camera clicked and whirred, and the four of us all but ran for the relative warmth of the camper van. As I pulled the sliding door closed, blew on my hands to try and get a vague illusion of warmth into them and regarded the last vestiges of snow on the rooftops, I reflected upon how I was now practically stalking Elvis Presley.

I'd recorded a song in the studio where Elvis had recorded and I'd played the guitar in the shop where Elvis bought his first guitar. I'd bought shirts off the man from whom Elvis bought his shirts and looked at the same view of the Pacific as Elvis had. And now, here in the otherwise anonymous freezing backstreets of a small German spa town, I was having my photograph taken in exactly the same spot as Elvis did nearly half a century earlier. For all my doubts about Elvis impersonators, save the ones who actually seemed to put something of themselves into their performances, like Dr Ammondt, Schmelvis and Elvis Priestley, my life looked to be turning into an Elvis tribute act itself. My sprint for the van had commenced at the old city gate of Bad Nauheim in Germany, after I'd just had my photograph taken where Elvis stood in full dress uniform for the shot which became the famous cover of 'A Big Hunk o'Love' –. there's a plaque on the wall to commemorate the event. For all my homages, however, I took comfort from the fact that nobody would get me into a jumpsuit. Not ever. Nohow.

Elvis's two years in the military in Germany are often referred to as his 'missing years'. In career terms that's probably true: he made no records, played no concerts and acted in no films, but his time in Germany was notable for several reasons. First, it came immediately after the loss of his mother Gladys, who died while he was doing his basic training in Texas. Much has been written about Elvis's relationship with his mother, and they certainly were extraordinarily close. Gladys's death at the age of forty-six, related to excessive drinking and a dependency on diet pills, was something from which Elvis never really recovered, and being whisked back to the Army within a couple of weeks and almost immediately shipped off to Europe can't have helped him come to terms with losing the most important person in his life. Many people say that up to that point Elvis's whole career had been dedicated to his mother, and her passing left the rest of his life directionless and creatively lethargic. Certainly he began to lose some of the good, polite Southern boy lustre that had characterised his early years, not to mention how the flame of creativity seemed to gutter, and while he never entirely lost either, his time in Germany can be seen as the turning point for both these changes.

It was also a turning point for a kindly, quietly spoken man from Bad Nauheim, the man driving the van providing warm sanctuary from the icy Swabian blasts outside. I'd encountered people whose lives had been changed by Elvis despite never having met him, but for the man at the wheel they were very real encounters with the former Memphis truck driver that had come to define his life.

For Elvis military service took him away from the relentless glare of publicity for a while. Although he was in the spotlight during his time there, it was nothing like the constant scrutiny he faced at home. Elvis only ever had one number-one hit in Germany, and that would be years later with 'In the Ghetto', and while he was still an undoubted celebrity, the small-town atmosphere of Bad Nauheim and the everyday mundanity of military life were probably a welcome break for the young star, particularly with Gladys's death so fresh in his mind. When off duty in Germany, he was able to move around with a relative degree of freedom, certainly more so than at home. It's also thought that during his spell in the Army Elvis was first introduced to amphetamines by fellow GIs, and perhaps most significantly Germany is where Elvis met the woman who would later become his wife.

He arrived on 1 October 1958 at the North Sea port of Bremerhaven, after a ten-day journey from Brooklyn, where he received an enthusiastic welcome from around 1500 fans, and then travelled by troop train to the barracks at Friedberg, just outside Frankfurt. For most of his time there Elvis was accompanied by his father and grandmother, and also old friends Red West and Lamar Fike. He was given special dispensation to live off base, and made the nearby town of Bad Nauheim his home for the best part of two years.

I arrived in Bad Nauheim by a much less circuitous route than Elvis – who en route had made a two-hour stopover at Prestwick Airport outside Glasgow – taking a plane to Frankfurt where I was met by Constance, a friend of a friend who had kindly offered to ferry me around during my short stay. I'd also arranged to meet Claus-Kurt Ilge, possibly Elvis's biggest fan in Germany and a man who knows more than most about the singer's time there, given that he shared much of it with Elvis himself.

Germany was just coming out of a particularly harsh winter when I arrived. A few weeks earlier the snowfall had become so severe that the roof of an ice rink in Bavaria had collapsed, killing fourteen people. Most of the snow had gone from this part of the country, but there were still a few pockets of white around and, most noticeably, an arctic wind. Constance, a flight attendant by trade who towered over me at more than six feet in height (she'd sent me a text when I arrived at the airport saying, 'You'll have no problem recognising me, no other woman is as tall as me or has as much hair'), drove us through the hilly countryside, dropping extraordinary nuggets of information into the conversation, such as how she is actually by birth an Italian countess, about how she worked with Aids orphans in Malawi as part of a solo overland journey through Africa she undertook at the age of eighteen, and about how she plays a didgeridoo that she carved and decorated herself. Indeed, when we parked in Bad Nauheim she produced the didgeridoo and gave me a quick in-car demonstration, parking the business end of the instrument in the passenger side footwell between my feet, puffing her cheeks and parping away with impressive technique. Given that the sound of the didgeridoo carries a long way in the Australian outback, inside a small hatchback car it produced an eardrum-shuddering, window-rattling sound that turned heads up and down the street.

We left the car and walked to Bad Nauheim's impressively large tourist office, where I'd arranged to meet Claus and his partner Elvira. I'd no sooner pushed open the door when a bespectacled woman with a bob haircut jumped up from behind a desk. 'Mr Connelly?' she asked. Slightly startled, I replied in the affirmative. 'Elvira has just telephoned and asked me to tell you that they're on their way and will be here shortly. Would you like some coffee?'

It was just the kind of hospitality Constance and I needed on a freezing day in a strange town. We sat down at a small table close to a little cable-car carriage, part of a display commemorating the filming of *GI Blues* in the area. The town had also produced a special leaflet about the Elvis sites, handily organised into a short walking tour. I picked up one detailing a little of the history of the place and learned that people had taken the spa waters here since around 500 BC. It took until 1835 for a physician called Friedrich Wilhelm Beneke to open the first bathhouse, and among those to have travelled to Bad Nauheim for its restorative effects were Albert Einstein and Franklin D. Roosevelt. We pored over the leaflets until the door opened and Elvira arrived. A striking-looking woman with a strong resemblance to the actress Kate O'Mara, she bustled over in a flurry of red hair, blue roll-neck sweater and dark fur coat.

'Claus is just finding somewhere to park,' she said. 'He'll be here in a minute.'

She rummaged in her handbag and pulled out some old black and white photographs. 'Look,' she said, 'here is Claus with Elvis.' She fanned out the pictures on the table. All of them featured Elvis, usually in military fatigues with the name 'PRESLEY' stitched over the breast pocket and a peaked forage cap, and a young man in a flying jacket with blond hair swept up into an impressive DA.

'That's Claus,' she said. 'He was sixteen years old then. Ah, look, here he is now.' The door opened, accompanied by an icy blast of air, and Claus entered. Dressed in a black bomber jacket, blue jeans and, I was delighted to see, blue suede Nike trainers, Claus looked barely a day older than in the photographs on the table. The DA was quite the same, only now it was silver in colour where fifty years earlier it was blond, but facially he looked no different. He walked across to us with a big smile, shook our hands and sat down. It really was astonishing how little Claus had changed from the fresh-faced youth in the pictures. Although he could speak a little English, Elvira explained, he wasn't very confident with it so she would do most of the talking.

'Nice jacket,' I said appreciatively, indicating Claus's apparel in the pictures. He and Elvira exchanged glances and chuckled. 'Elvis signed that jacket for Claus,' she said. 'But, can you believe this, his mother tried to scrub it off?'

We all set off into the cold, ready to walk in Elvis's footsteps. Then Claus decided that given the sub-zero temperatures we'd be better off going in his little camper van which, as we'd lost the feeling in our fingers and toes, we all agreed was a really good idea. After a quick chug around the corner we pulled up outside the resplendent frontage of the Hotel Grunewald.

Elvis had spent a few days at the now-demolished Hilberts Park Hotel on his arrival in Bad Nauheim, but had been put off by the presence of a Saudi prince, there to take the waters, complete with entourage and bodyguards. He was also unimpressed by how the press could wander around the hotel, so upped the Presley party and brought them here, to the Hotel Grunewald. It's a beautifully ornate nineteenth-century building on the corner of a quiet street, and in 1958 was a popular choice for elderly visitors in town. The arrival of Elvis, Vernon, Minnie Mae and in particular Elvis's compadres Red and Lamar caused a considerable ruckus and much harrumphing, tutting and stern disapproval among the other guests. Elvis hired four rooms on the top floor and another on the floor below to store his fanmail, while youthful high spirits were indulged with water fights and

chases through the corridors. The owner was forced to remon-
strate with the Memphis party several times and when Elvis
bought a puppy called Cherry, and then left it for long periods
with the owners while he was away on manoeuvres, it soon
became clear that things couldn't continue. The final straw came
at the culmination of a shaving foam fight, when Elvis locked
himself in his room and Red attempted to smoke him out by
setting fire to some paper under the door.

Nearly half a century on, the tour of us stood outside the
hotel, which because of the preservation order looked just as it
did when Elvis was in residence.

'Even the inside looks the same,' said Elvira, 'as the order
applies to the chandeliers and the decoration. When it was built
there were no en suite bathrooms, so now you open what you
think is a closet and there's a tiny bathroom in there.'

Given that ice was beginning to form between my eyelashes,
I asked if we'd be able to look inside the place. The answer
came back negative.

'The poor woman who owns the hotel is quite old now,' said
Elvira. 'She used to open it up to Elvis fans but a valuable figurine was smashed, and she had a very old cookbook on display
that was stolen.'

Elvira pointed out Elvis's room, none the less, an ornate
window at the end of the top floor.

'Inside it's quite old-fashioned,' she said. 'I'm not sure what
Elvis would have made of it, because when you think of the
Jungle Room at Graceland and things like that, it really would-
n't have been to his taste.'

Not able to go inside, there was some small consolation to the
side of the hotel when Claus and Elvira showed us the memorial
erected to commemorate the fortieth anniversary of Elvis's
arrival in the town. A black plinth stood at the end of a little

paved footpath on a patch of grass between the Grunewald's perimeter hedge and the pavement. On it a small inscription gave the dates of Elvis's time in Bad Nauheim beneath a relief representation of the face of, well, Christopher Walken, it seems. It's not a great likeness, but the care the shrubs and paving around it receive helps to demonstrate the pride with which the local Elvis fan club, of which Claus and Elvira are leading lights, hold his time in Bad Nauheim. Elvis's short stay in the hotel that overlooks his monument ended when the little fire set by Red West caused the Grunewald's owner to turf the Presley party out. Now I've never been thrown out of a hotel, at least not at the time of writing, but I hope that if ever I do engage in a bit of chucking of bread rolls in the breakfast room or tweaking of the concierge's nose, within forty years someone will have erected a plinth with my name and Christopher Walken's face on it.

After some cursory photographic posing with the monument we climbed back into the van and headed the short distance across town to Goethestrasse. Once Elvis and his cohorts had been kicked out of the hotel they had to find somewhere new to live as a matter of urgency. Rather than run into similar problems with a hotel, Elvis sent Red and Lamar out into Bad Nauheim to look for a house to rent. Bearing in mind Elvis's stature and the sudden need for accommodation, it was never likely that the party would find a bargain. Indeed, when they did find some-where, in early January 1959, it was a modern, solid-looking house with four bedrooms at 14 Goethestrasse, the only draw-back being that at $800 a month Elvis was paying something like five times the going rate. Not only that, they'd still have to share the place with the owner, a Frau Pieper. The house was not in the best shape and despite the small fortune that the owner was accruing month by month, she didn't spend any of it on making her tenants' stay more pleasant. Moreover, at one point the back garden became so overgrown that Elvis went out and bought a lawnmower. Frau Pieper failed to take the hint, and in the end Red had to mow it himself.

We climbed out of the van and walked across the street to the house. It's a fairly nondescript kind of place, of solid, square postwar design. A retired surgeon lives there now and, according to Elvira, he has little truck with the historical resonance of his residence.

'Oh, the number fourteen's been stolen,' she noted as we reached the gates where Claus used to stand almost daily during Elvis's tenancy. 'Someone was smart enough to take it.'

As Claus looked up at the house with a possibly dreamy expression, Elvira set about describing the scene as it would have been.

'There was another gatepost here,' she said, indicating where the pedestrian gate was once separated from the gate to the driveway. 'He had a white BMW parked inside the gates, and an old Cadillac Fleetwood that he didn't really like so he left it on the street. When it rained the kids waiting outside the house would get in it for shelter. Claus was in there one day and found some cigarillos that Elvis had smoked. He took them home but his mother threw them away.

'Claus knows a lot of stuff,' she said, as he stood with his arms behind his back gazing up at the house, presumably remembering the countless evenings he spent here accruing autographs and priceless memories. 'But I only came here once because my family moved away to another town altogether. A BMW appeared at the end of the street and everyone cried out, "Ohhh, he's coming, he's coming", and he drove by very, very slowly but didn't stop.' She swept a pointing finger along the road to demonstrate exactly where the car had passed. 'We thought he wasn't coming back but he got to the end of the street, turned around and parked right here, in front of us. There was a woman in the car with him, we didn't know who, a blonde with a scarf and a very stuck-up attitude, and we all nudged each other and said, no, she's too old for him.' Elvira let out a throaty laugh.

'She went straight into the house, but he stopped and signed a few autographs before going towards the house himself. I can still see what he wore: a black shirt, black pants, black shoes and a white scarf. It was a hot day and he was sweating. I even remember the ring on his pinkie finger, the one he always wore. I remember everything so clearly, it was a fantastic day.'

It wasn't an older blonde woman who would capture Elvis's heart, however. Some time in August 1959, his friend Currie Grant, the entertainments manager of the Eagle Club, a nearby social and community centre for the military and their families, spotted there one afternoon a beautiful fourteen-year-old named Priscilla Beaulieu. He asked her if she was an Elvis fan, which she was (when her father was posted to Wiesbaden, Priscilla and her friend looked on a map to see just how close it was to Bad Nauheim), and then offered to take her to Goethestrasse to meet him. Her father agreed once it became clear that Currie and his wife would act as chaperone, and one late-summer evening, dressed in a blue and white sailor-style dress with white shoes, she walked nervously through the very gates at which we now stood, went into the house and began arguably the most famous rock 'n' roll romance in history. Around the same time, Elvira was chancing her arm.

'I went up to him and I wanted him to know that my name was Elvira, because it's like the female version of Elvis,' she said. 'but I didn't speak English then and all I could say was "Elvis, I love you". I had a little invoice pad with me and I handed it to him and he signed it. Then I turned it around and handed it back for another signature and he smiled and said, didn't you get enough? And then he reached out and brushed my cheek with his hand like this', she passed the back of her hand over her left cheek, 'and I couldn't believe it. I was standing right here, on this spot.'

Elvira still has her autograph on a piece of that invoice pad. Claus, though, has a few more.

'Claus has so many autographs from Elvis,' said Elvira. 'More than three hundred. Elvis used to ask him if he was selling them because he had so many. Claus helped Elvis in some ways too: he had a paper round and delivered newspapers and magazines, which he would get two days before they were in the stores, so he'd come down here and show them to Elvis before they were published. Elvis would look and see what they were saying about him and then sign the papers for Claus. Sometimes he called Claus 'my paper boy'. Claus had a transistor radio, and Radio Luxembourg had *Elvis Time* in the evenings. He would bring the radio here and Elvis would come out and listen and fool around and sign more autographs. Claus would help carry the groceries as well; he'd take them into the house and put them in the kitchen. He got to know him quite well, and Elvis seemed to like him a lot.'

The couple then took us to the local museum, where the small but influential fan club in the area had succeeded in siting a permanent display dedicated to Elvis's time in Germany. We walked in past exhibitions chronicling the Roman occupation of the area and went upstairs, where Claus and Elvira led the way to the Elvis exhibit. A television was embedded in the wall, playing a looped DVD of a short film about Elvis's life in Germany, or at least it would have done had it been working. Some fantastic framed photographs of Elvis in his military fatigues lined one wall, but the focus of the display was a glass cabinet at the end of the room. At the back of the cabinet was a life-sized blow-up of

a wonderful photograph of Claus and Elvis. Elvis is again in
military overalls and forage cap, and to his right, gripping his
hand in a firm handshake, is a beaming Claus, squinting slightly
in the sunlight, but with a look of sheer thrilled delight on his
face. Claus stood and looked at the picture, and much the same
expression crossed his features. He must have seen this picture
just about every day since, yet in his eyes he was back there on
that sunny afternoon, sixteen again, shaking the hand of the
greatest cultural icon of his and ensuing generations.

He was just an ordinary kid in a flying jacket in a largely
anonymous central German town, but he was a friend of Elvis
Presley, who had landed on his doorstep like a fantastic creature
from outer space. To me Elvis will always be a voice on a CD
and the face in thousands of photographs, but in Claus's mind he
is a tangible, walking, talking, laughing human being. Claus has
memories of Elvis that nobody else has. Right then he wasn't on
the first floor of a small local museum, he was a teenager again,
feeling the sun on his face and Elvis's hand pressed into his. It
was only a brief moment that I happened to catch out of the
corner of my eye, but to me it said more about the influence of
Elvis than all the thousands of miles I'd covered on my journey.
That fleeting moment encapsulated the phenomenon that was
Elvis Presley, and it lived on fifty years after Elvis changed his life
for ever in the striking blue eyes of a quietly spoken man living
in a small town in Germany.

The light was starting to fade now and the temperature was
dropping further. We clambered back into the van and Claus
drove us to Ray Barracks, where Elvis spent most of his time on
duty when he wasn't away on manoeuvres. There's little of Elvis
to see there – the whole of Friedberg's only visible connection to
Elvis is the sign denoting Elvis Presley Platz on a patch of grass
in the centre of the town's main street – but Elvira told us that

there used to be a small museum in the barracks dedicated to Elvis. When his unit left in the early nineties the memorabilia went too. A sign at the entrance announcing that this was where Elvis spent his military service was also taken away.

'Twice a year our fan club has a candlelit march from Bad Nauheim to Elvis Presley Platz in Friedberg,' said Elvira, 'and we also have an annual Elvis festival weekend. It's such a shame when things from the past are forgotten, so we're determined to keep alive the memory of Elvis in Germany.'

We drove around to the rear of the barracks, pulling up in what appeared to be an anonymous yard outside the metal-fenced base perimeter.

'This is the place where Claus first saw Elvis,' said Elvira, pointing out of the van window. It was then I noticed alongside a small, raised concrete platform an old, disused railway line that came to a stop in front of some rusting buffers.

'This is where Elvis first arrived in Friedberg, on the troop train from Bremerhaven,' explained Elvira. 'Everyone expected him to arrive at the station in the town, so a big crowd gathered there, but somehow Claus found out that the train wouldn't go to the town station, it would come straight here to this little siding away from the crowds and the reporters. He told no one except a couple of his friends, so when the train arrived the three of them were the only ones there to greet it. A couple of reporters had gathered at the base ready for Elvis's arrival, but Claus and his friends were the only fans.'

Claus and I walked over to the platform. It was just starting to get dark and it was utterly quiet as we walked along the abandoned, flaky tarmac. Looking at the rusty tracks with long strands of coarse grass growing between the sleepers it was hard to imagine the train pulling in here, the hiss of the engine, and the noise and bustle of the nervous GIs, most of whom were abroad for the first time. What might they be thinking as they disembarked at the place where they'd spend the best part of the next two years, thousands of miles from home? But again it was my companion's eyes that told the tale. I was just standing shivering on an abandoned platform in a less than scenic part of an old army barracks, whereas Claus was seeing Elvis, resplendent in his brand-new uniform, duffel bag over his shoulder, stepping down from the train carriage. He was again feeling the awe, the butterfly-nervous excitement of his first glimpse of the man who at that moment, on that very spot, ensured that Claus-Kurt Ilge's life would never be the same again.

Abu Ghosh, Israel

Shortly after I'd flown low over the Mediterranean into Tel Aviv's Ben Gurion Airport I was barrelling along Highway 1, the main road between Tel Aviv and Jerusalem, in a taxi driven by a grumpy Russian in wraparound sunglasses. The end of this ride would be the final destination of my journey in search of Elvis. In contrast to the freezing temperatures of Germany, the sun shone out of a deep-blue Israeli sky and the driver rested his bare elbow out of the window of his cab as the hot air blew in. Road signs in Hebrew and English flashed past until, after about half an hour, I saw a sign full of symbols. There were the usual ones you'd expect to see on most highways around the world: a petrol pump, a bed, a knife and fork; but in the middle of this one, in huge blue capital letters on a white background, was the word 'ELVIS'. The cab driver indicated and left the motorway, coming down through the gears as we descended to the road below. A couple of minutes later we pulled up at what would be regarded as your run-of-the-mill petrol station, were it not for the two giant statues of Elvis Presley in evidence, and the Elvis Inn attached to it.

I hopped out of the back of the taxi as 'Return to Sender' played over the garage speakers, fished my bag out of the boot and paid the grouchy Russian, who raised his eyes upwards to indicate the music. 'Elvis,' he said, something almost akin to a smile tugging at the corners of his mouth, 'ochen kharasho.' I laughed out loud. Not only had he said that Elvis was very good, he'd used the same Russian word I'd used to bond with my Uzbek friend by a turquoise river months earlier. Still smiling, I walked past a vast golden modernist statue of Elvis up to glass doors decorated with the Elvis logo that had served as the backdrop for the *Comeback Special*. They opened automatically, and I stepped into the most extraordinary Elvis-related establishment I've seen. It was a large American-style diner absolutely smothered in pictures of Elvis. There wasn't a square inch of wall unadorned with a picture of the King, from childhood snaps to pudgy Vegas jumpsuit shots.

I ordered a Coke at the bar and took a seat at a table by the window. Outside was a breathtaking view: desert hills sugared with little green shrubs led off for miles, and I'm sure I could see the sea in the distance. A waiter came over with a menu.

'You don't read Hebrew?' he asked when he registered my alarm at not recognising the symbols in the snazzily coloured booklet. An English menu appeared and I ordered a cheeseburger and fries. As I sipped my Coke, I looked up at the ceiling and saw the most remarkable thing – a fantastic painted mural that depicted Elvis's life from start to finish and ran the length of the room in a distinctly Sistine manner. There was the famous photograph of the young family with Elvis as a toddler in dungarees and hat, Vernon looking handsome and Gladys a strikingly beautiful woman; there was Elvis's high school photograph; then it went through all the famous shots, film stills, the *Comeback Special*, his marriage to Priscilla, the Vegas years until his death, with a representation of an angelic Elvis at the gates of Graceland that was, believe me, much more tasteful than it sounds. It's an awesome piece of work. Even though there are so many pictures available that are allegedly of Elvis but are basically just a bloke with a quiff, every one here was unquestionably him with tremendous detail and accuracy. It was quite the most stupendous piece of Elvisiana I have seen.

My cheeseburger arrived, and it was nearly worth the journey to Israel on its own. As I made short work of sticking it away, I looked out at the view across to the distant Mediterranean and the amazing ceiling mural, and reflected upon how far I'd travelled with Elvis since that central London fry-up opposite Bap months earlier. The sun was preparing to set, just as it had been when I'd looked at it across the frozen fields of Aberdeenshire at the very start of my journey. I'd met some extraordinary people and seen some extraordinary things around the world. My understanding of the King was much better – my stock of Elvis trivia had certainly multiplied too, which would come in handy for pub quizzes – and I could now picture the places with which he'd been associated through memory rather than imagination. I'd gleaned a sense of how much he means to different people from different places, to Muslim, Christian and Jew.

But I'd seen nothing like this – a fully fledged Elvis diner in the heart of the Middle East. A young man in a fitted jumper, with cropped hair and an ear stud came over and asked where I was from. He turned out to be Amir, who was the son of the owner and managed the place. When I told him I'd travelled from London just to be here his eyebrows shot up and he slid into the seat opposite me. I asked how such a thing as an Elvis diner came to be here, on the road between Jerusalem and Tel Aviv. He smiled; it was a question he must be asked on a daily basis.

'My dad bought this place in 1974,' he said. 'He'd had a couple of grocery stores in Jerusalem, but then this place came up. It was nothing like it is now, of course – we've extended the building a couple of times – but he put up an Elvis picture next to the cashier. He used to have it hanging in the house, though when he married my mother and she moved into the house she said either the picture went or she did. He didn't want to throw it away, so he hung it here by the till. It was something that people talked about because there weren't a lot of Elvis pictures in Israel then – this one had come from the States. Anyway a couple of weeks after the picture had been put up he had to take a food mixer to Tel Aviv to be fixed, and he overheard two taxi drivers talking. One of them said, 'I'll meet you at the Elvis place.' My dad was intrigued by the idea of there being an Elvis place here so he went over and asked them where they were talking about. When they described the place they meant, he realised it was here.

'From that moment on he changed the name to the Elvis Inn, started collecting the pictures, and it led to the place we're sitting in now. Half of the pictures here have come from customers. A lot came from US Marines who used to visit, but they're mainly in Iraq now. A lot of celebrities have been here – Michael Jackson, Sting, Joe Cocker, Sylvester Stallone, to name only a few. Michael Jackson just turned up and the place was packed. I knew he was in Israel because he was playing a concert in Tel Aviv, but he suddenly appeared. Everyone screamed and he ran back to the car and a bodyguard had to come in and get him a Coke. Sylvester Stallone was here when he was filming *Rambo* – a lovely guy.'

In that instant I remembered that I had something in my bag to give to Amir. When I'd sat in the camper van with Claus, Elvira and Constance outside Ray Barracks in Friedberg and told them that I'd be coming here, Elvira had pulled out a copy of the picture of Claus with Elvis, the one that was blown up in the museum.

'You must give this to the people in the café,' she said. Taking the lid from a pen, she wrote on the picture, 'To the Elvis fans of Israel, Elvis united people like the politicians never could. From the Elvis fans in Germany', and passed it across the table to me.

I took the photograph from my bag and handed it to Amir, who looked at it and then read the inscription out loud. 'Wow,' he said after a moment's silence, his eyes wide, 'this is amazing!'

Suddenly my search was over. Sitting there, in of all places a diner next to a petrol station in central Israel, I'd found what I was looking for. The significance of my gesture hadn't struck me in the slightest until I saw the look in his eyes. Of course. How could I not have realised? At first I'd thought the inscription was just a token greeting between people with a common interest – in fact I'd almost forgotten to bring the picture with me – but now I realised that it went deeper than that. Given the not too distant, deeply unpalatable history that exists between Germany and Israel, that the people of two countries with such horrifically connected pasts could be united by the music of a former Memphis truck driver signalled the end of my journey in search of Elvis. I realised that a photocopied print of Elvis and Claus with a hastily scrawled but heartfelt message written on it in the back of a freezing camper van thousands of miles away represented the very thing I'd been seeking. I felt the realisation sink in. A sense of relaxed contentment came over me as I watched Amir, looking visibly moved, examine the picture in front of him. For the first time on my travels I felt a sense of accomplishment. Here was Amir, an Israeli in his early twenties who had grown up in an Elvis café that came about after an overheard snatch of conversation between two Tel Aviv cab drivers. Claus and Elvira, meanwhile, were from a different country and a different generation, yet had similarly dedicated themselves to Elvis after he dropped into their lives as if out of the sky, and totally unprompted had given me the picture to pass on to the people of Israel, who they didn't even know, but who they knew shared their passion despite the dreadful events between their peoples in a past that was still raw. It was a gesture of friendship that reached beyond generations, beyond boundaries and beyond histories, one that brought Claus, Elvira and Amir together because of Elvis, and one that I now felt deeply honoured to convey.

'It's amazing,' said Amir finally. 'It's exactly like what the German people wrote on this picture; Elvis united more people than politicians ever could. It doesn't matter if you're black or white or whatever, people are united by Elvis. It's the same here in the restaurant. We have an Arab village called Abu Ghosh nearby so we have many Arabs coming in here and everyone mixes together. In fact we have a lot of Arab employees here. In the morning we have more Arabs coming in than anyone else. We've had good relations now for the thirty-three years we've been here. So again it's Elvis achieving what politicians can't.'

Amir got up to find a frame for Claus's picture and left me sitting alone, surrounded by photographs of Elvis as the opening bars of 'I Just Can't Help Believing' came out of the diner's speakers. I looked out of the window again as the sun set with a brilliant red light behind the Israeli hills. My journey in search of the King had come to an end in, appropriately, a land populated in the main by a people who had been on a long journey themselves, one of thousands of years. It's a land of perennial conflict, admittedly, but here at the Elvis Inn is the story you never see in the world media: a story of Jews and Arabs mixing freely and happily, united in their love for Elvis Presley.

Had I found Elvis himself? Well, although I felt I understood him a little better than when I started out that freezing day in Scotland, he was still elusive, enigmatic, just out of reach. What I'd found, though, was his indomitable spirit and innate goodness, qualities that manifested themselves in the amazing people I'd met on my wanderings. As the sun dropped further towards the horizon I thought about Karen in Tashkent, about Stuart in Aberdeen, Howard at Tupelo Hardware, Dan and Dorian in Canada, Dr Ammondt in Finland and most of all I thought of the extraordinary Anita in Porthcawl. The elusive, hard-to-define thing I'd been looking for was in all of them, all united by the decency inherent in the spirit of Elvis. They'd first been drawn to the music, but then, like millions of others, they'd seen beyond that to the person who produced that sound; the person whose simple but passionate heart and soul reached out across borders and creeds to inspire an overwhelming, quasi-religious devotion in the most unlikely people and places. From a middle-aged Finnish academic to a central Asian pop star; from a Canadian music therapist to a Mississippi hardware store clerk; and, perhaps most significantly, from a sprightly middle-aged German couple to an Israeli restaurant manager, the bonds created by Elvis Presley criss-cross the world. The second I handed the photograph of Claus and Elvis to Amir I knew that my search was over. I had, so to speak, taken care of business.

I finished the beer Amir had given me and turned to watch the sun drop behind the hills.

Acknowledgements

A book like this couldn't happen without the help and assistance of all sorts of different people. So, depending on what you think of it, these people deserve either your thanks or anonymously mailed mutilated woodland creatures.

The following fine folk aided me in innumerable ways, from helping to arrange visas to being wonderful fellow travellers to talking me in from the metaphorical window ledge as another deadline whistled past: Richard Beswick, Iain Hunt, Jenny Fry, Eva Skalla, Brigid Keenan, Steve Morgan, Jo Coombs, Julie Elrick, Heather Walker, Kristel Julian, Wenche Ringstrand, David Prest, Richard Else, Polly Evans, Donna Howlett, Marty Lacker, Mike Rien, Gulnora Khudayberganova, Shakhista Mukhamedova, Sevara Yakubova, Shakhlo Khudayberganova, Eldar, Dorian Baxter, Dan Hartal, Debbie Hartal, Mia Ylönen, Anna Rafferty, Amanda Lyon, Ben Jackson, Mikey Rowe, Amir Yoeli, Constance Ratazzi, Einat Gadasi, Wenche Ringstrand, Debs McCarthy, Eleanor Hoyle, Bap Kennedy, Mum and Dad, JR Daeschner, Kevin Dawson, Mick Collins, Rebecca Gray, Sarah Williams, Esko and Silje Haaivisto, Dr Jukka Ammondt,

Dara Young, Karen Gleed, Marjorie Williams, Claus-Kurt Ilge, Elvira Spohn, Klaus Ritt, Jon Edwards, the Broadstairs Babes, Richard Shaw, Catalina Restrepo, Cecilia Wallach, Stuart West, Mike King and especially Caroline Potter. Special thanks to Donna, for patience and understanding way beyond the call of duty. Thanks also to anyone whom I've inadvertently omitted from the list by being completely disorganised.

Thanks also to the world's greatest agent Lizzy Kremer and the world's greatest editor Sarah Shrubb, both of whom helped to create this silkiest of purses from the manky old sow's ear I came up with in the first place.

Further Reading

There are, in my opinion, four books that no self-respecting Elvis enthusiast should be without. Half of them are by Peter Guralnick, whose two-volume biography will surely never be surpassed. The first instalment, *Last Train to Memphis: The Rise of Elvis Presley*, takes the story up to Elvis in the Army, where the baton is picked up by *Careless Love: The Unmaking of Elvis Presley*. A really startlingly good biography.

Next comes *Elvis and the Memphis Mafia* by Alanna Nash with Billy Smith, Marty Lacker and Lamar Fike, which is an absorbing oral history of Elvis's life by three of the people who knew him best, and is very highly recommended. Paul Simpson's *The Rough Guide to Elvis* is a pocket-sized volume packed with an extraordinary amount of detail about every aspect of Elvis's life and career, and absolutely invaluable.

Other books I found useful on my travels were *The Field Guide to Elvis Shrines* by Bill Yenne, *Memphis Elvis-Style* by Cindy Hazen and Mike Freeman, *Elvis in Canada* by Bill Burk, and Jerry Hopkins's *Elvis in Hawaii*.

Schmelvis's home on the web can be found at

http://www.elvisschmelvis.com, while Dorian Baxter's Elvis Priestley site is at http://www.elvispriestley.com. Karen Gafurdjanov's site is http://www.karen.uz, while more about Bap Kennedy can be found at http://www.bapkennedy.com. For all you need to know about Elvis in Latin, try http://www.drammondt.com/english/index.php, while the official site of the Porthcawl Elvis Festival is at http://www.elvies.co.uk.

Finally, don't forget to drop by http://www.charlieconnelly.com, where you'll find a bonus *In Search of Elvis* chapter only available there, and the recording of my, ah, idiosyncratic take on 'Blue Moon of Kentucky' recorded in Sun Studio. Play your cards right and I'll make you a sandwich too.